Dating Deuteronomy

Dating Deuteronomy

The Wellhausen Fallacy

Josef Schubert

WIPF & STOCK · Eugene, Oregon

DATING DEUTERONOMY
The Wellhausen Fallacy

Copyright © 2018 Josef Schubert. All rights reserved. Except for brief quotations in critical publications or reviews, no part of this book may be reproduced in any manner without prior written permission from the publisher. Write: Permissions, Wipf and Stock Publishers, 199 W. 8th Ave., Suite 3, Eugene, OR 97401.

Wipf & Stock
An Imprint of Wipf and Stock Publishers
199 W. 8th Ave., Suite 3
Eugene, OR 97401

www.wipfandstock.com

PAPERBACK ISBN: 978-1-5326-3872-5
HARDCOVER ISBN: 978-1-5326-3873-2
EBOOK ISBN: 978-1-5326-3874-9

Manufactured in the U.S.A.

For Monica
And in memory of my aunts
Martha Cohn
Mulle (Amalia) Cohn
Elsa Volkmann, née Cohn

Contents

Preface | ix
Achnowledgements | xv
Abbreviations | xvi

Part I: The Problem

1. Basic Assumptions | 3
2. The Wellhausen Fallacy | 18
3. The Origin of Israel: Archaeological Interpretations | 31

Part II: The Law (Torah) of Israel

4. The Composition of the Pentateuch | 65
5. The Religion of the Pentateuch | 88
6. Deuteronomy | 103

Part III: The Ethnogenesis of Israel

7. From Wandering Aramean (ארמי אבד) to a Nation Bound by a Covenant | 121
8. From Conquest to Monarchy | 134
9. The Religion of Israel During the Monarchic Period | 146
10. Prophecy and Reform | 162
11. Worship Without Sacrifice | 172

Glossary | 181
Partial Index of Additional Topics | 185
Bibliography | 187

Preface
How come?

Why does no one find it remarkable that in most world cities today there are Jews but not one single Hittite, even though the Hittites had a great flourishing civilization while the Jews nearby were a weak and obscure people?[1]

How come both the Israelites/Samarians[2] and the Judeans/Jews, though dispersed and persecuted, have adhered to their religious heritage until today? Archaeological research has revealed the existence of many civilizations in the Middle East, each with a rich cultural heritage preserved in writing. But when these people—the Akkadians, the Babylonians, the Assyrians, the Hittites, and the Egyptians, the civilizations of Canaan-Syria—were subjugated, their ethnic identity was lost until we learned to decipher the inscriptions on their ruins. Only two small groups, the Samarian Israelites and the Judean exiles in Babylon, by accepting the Torah, developed a lifestyle which clearly differentiated them from their neighbors. It will be argued in this book that the success of the Judean exiles and the Samarians of maintaining their identity as a "chosen people," as descendants of Abraham, Isaac, and Jacob, whose ancestors had been slaves in Egypt, were liberated by God and had experienced a public theophany, was only possible because these very traditions, or at least the majority of them, had already been formulated in the eighth century BCE or earlier.

1. Percy, *Message*, 6
2. The Samaritans prefer to be called Samarians (inhabitants of the Assyrian Province of Samaria) or Shomrim (Guardians) and consider themselves to be the descendants of the tribes of Manasseh and Ephraim. Cf. chapter 4 of this book, "The Composition of the Pentateuch."

Preface

Biblical scholarship assumes that the Pentateuch was written at the time of Ezra during the fifth century BCE or later. I shall argue in this book that what I call the "Wellhausen fallacy"[3] is based on a misreading of Deuteronomy and the historical books of the Bible. I shall argue that an analysis of existing documents, including the Dead Sea Scrolls and the Samaritan Pentateuch, leads to the conclusion that the Pentateuch in its entirety existed before the divided kingdom of Israel-Judah; i.e., before 930 BCE. This conclusion calls for a reorientation of biblical scholarship.

I do not arrive at these conclusions lightly—I had accepted the Wellhausen fallacy assumptions for the last seventy years. I tried and failed to find grounds to refute my propositions. This book will detail my arguments. Part I discusses the Wellhausen fallacy and its implications. Part II discusses the theology of the Pentateuch. Part III offers an alternative view about the ethnogenesis of Israel.

As our views are significantly determined by our background, I shall include here some relevant biographical data. At the age of fifteen I emigrated from Germany to what was then called Palestine and enrolled in an agricultural school. The curriculum included six hours per week of Bible Studies. Our group (about twenty adolescents) protested vigorously—we all are atheists and not interested in religious studies. The answer was firm: we are not fundamentalists, but study the Bible as a document composed by humans. It informs us about the thoughts and lives of the people in the biblical period. It is also the basis of our ethnic heritage, which cannot be understood without knowledge of its source. These ideas have determined my approach to biblical studies.

Synopsis

Section I

Chapter 1 discusses the basic assumptions underlying various theories of biblical scholarship. The approach of this book is secular. The Bible is a historical document. The writer of the Early Prophets (EP) explains events in terms of interaction between human behavior and divine intervention.[4]

---

3. Wellhausen, *Prolegomena*.

4. I assume that biblical writers were honest reporters; they did not feel free to invent data and present them as divine truth.

The next section of chapter 1 discusses various theoretical options when juxtaposing a biblical report with archaeological data.

Chapter 2 analyzes the Wellhausen fallacy in detail. It is argued that Wellhausen's conclusions rest on two premises:

a. Deuteronomy could not have been written before the time of Josiah (650 BCE).
b. The existence of a group of redactors in the fifth century BCE or later.

The first premise is based on the mistranslation of the biblical text. The second premise is based on an unproven assumption. The absence of references to the religious thought of the Persian period or later in the Pentateuch and EP demonstrates that the editors working during the time of the Second Temple did not feel free to edit old documents or to ascribe their own writings to Mosaic times.

Chapter 3 reviews the archaeological evidence concerning the origin of Israel. It is argued that extrabiblical evidence is compatible with the essential parts of the biblical narrative.

Section II

The first section of the book discussed and rejected the Wellhausen fallacy. The second section offers an alternative view about the composition of the Pentateuch and the origin of Israel.

Chapter 4 discusses the origin of the Pentateuch. The Samarian version of the Pentateuch is virtually identical to the Masoretic text. It strains credulity to assume that the Samarians would accept a fictitious Torah composed by Judean exiles of the Persian period or later as authoritative. The books of the Pentateuch were already recognized as a unit before the separation between the kingdoms of Judah and Israel. The implications of this assertion are discussed.

Chapter 5 discusses the religion of the Pentateuch. The Pentateuch is not a homogenous book. It includes three different law codices, each one embedded in other material. There are contradictions between these sources. Nevertheless, the entire Pentateuch is unequivocal in its major ideas. The monotheism of the Pentateuch constitutes a paradigm shift in religious thinking: it stipulates a deity who is the absolute creator of the entire world, not bound by any laws and not to be represented by any image, with no personal mythology.

Preface

Chapter 6 discusses Deuteronomy 12. The prohibition of sacrifices outside the sanctuary is not concerned with the centralization of the cult, but with the rejection of Canaanite holy places. A sanctuary can only be at a place chosen by YHWH. However, a semi-profane sacrifice may be offered on earth-altars. Deuteronomy explicitly permits sacrifice outside the sanctuary (Deut 12:15). The term "you shall sacrifice" (תזבח) is mistranslated as "you shall slaughter." This mistranslation was deliberately introduced by rabbinical sources in the Aramaic Targum, accepted in the Vulgate and cited in most later translations. Thus the (de Wette) Wellhausen Fallacy is based on a mistranslation which reflects the cultic practices of the Second Temple period.

Summary of section II:

a. The virtual identity of the Samarian and Masoretic Pentateuch shows that the Pentateuch existed before the establishment of the Northern Kingdom.
b. The Pentateuch is monotheistic and includes the major ideas by which Israel was distinguished from other nations.
c. There is no ideological difference between Deuteronomy and the Tetrateuch. The main topic of Deuteronomy is not the centralization of the cult but the renewal of the covenant by Moses and the interdiction of the use of Canaanite cultic places.

Section III

The third section of this book offers an alternative view of the ethnogenesis of Israel, based on biblical sources, scrutinized with respect to their plausibility in the light of extrabiblical evidence.

Chapter 7 discusses the stories of the lives of the patriarchs, the exodus, and the sojourn in the desert.

Chapter 8 deals with the conquest and settlement of Canaan and with the controversy concerning the establishment of the monarchy. The invading Israelites were a tribal nation. Each individual was identified by his tribal membership. The Bible reports that the invasion under Joshua was undertaken by all Israel, but the actual possession of the land was

Preface

accomplished separately by different tribes. The Canaanite population was not annihilated and influenced the Israelite invaders: fetishist cults were practiced (*teraphim*) and sacrifices were offered at Canaanite holy places. Nevertheless, for all the practice of Canaanite rituals, the God of Israel was YHWH. The chapter then discusses the controversy surrounding the establishment of the monarchy. The monarchy, as an institution, was consolidated by the establishment of Jerusalem as a royal city.

Chapter 9 discusses the religion of Israel during the monarchic period. The biblical report on the practice of religion is as follows: YHWH was worshipped at three official sanctuaries as well as on the *bamoth* (and probably at private shrines and at home). At the same time, Canaanite rituals were practiced, specifically to Baal, Asherah, and the "host of heaven." These cults were occasionally officially encouraged, leading to the erection of formal cult places but mainly practiced at unofficial sites and in private homes. It is argued that a careful analysis of the technical terminology of worship shows a clear distinction between the formal worship (*avodah*) offered at an official sanctuary and unofficial ceremonies.

Chapter 10 discusses the impact of the Latter Prophets (LP, נביאים אחרונים) and the reforms of Hezekiah and Josiah. The Latter Prophets emphasized the following ideas which, though present in the Pentateuch, are not stressed in the books of the EP.

a. God, the creator of the universe, is concerned about all the nations of the world. In the future all the world will recognize God's sovereignty.

b. God manifests himself and can be approached, all over the world, not merely in the promised land.

c. The prime command of the Covenant is the establishment of a just society. Israel's major sin is social injustice, the flouting of the moral commandments of the Covenant.

d. God needs no sacrifices.

This prophetic message enabled the Babylonian exiles to maintain their ethnic identity. It had not yet been absorbed by the Samarian exiles.

The chapter then discusses the reforms of Hezekiah/Josiah. These reforms did not take root in Judah. The cults on the bamoth were restored after the deaths of Hezekiah and Josiah. The destruction of the high places must have appeared to be sacrilegious in the eyes of many.

Preface

Chapter 11 discusses the events leading to the destruction of the temple and the establishment of the Babylonian exile. At this time, Jeremiah and Ezekiel introduced two new ideas: a) the Diaspora will be a reality, and b) the generation of exiles is not to be punished for the sins of their forefathers, but judged on its own merit.

The destruction of the temple was interpreted not as a victory of Marduk, but rather as demonstrating the power of YHWH: Israel was punished for its sins. The exiles of Judah decided to follow strictly the provisions of the Pentateuch. This required a codification of the law. The achievement of the Babylonian community of exiles (*Golah*) was the acceptance of the idea that YHWH might be worshipped at any place on earth. This led to the introduction of alternative rituals of worship without a holy sanctuary and without sacrifices.

In order to substantiate my hypotheses, it was necessary to include detailed technical discussions which will appear in a different format. These passages are addressed to experts and may be skipped by the general leader. Hebrew terms and technical terms will be explained in the glossary. Biblical quotations will be based mainly on NRSV with alternative expressions in brackets. Each translation is checked by me; occasionally I suggest alternative translations. Instead of "the Lord," the tetragrammaton YHWH will be used, and whenever "God" is used as a personal name it will be transcribed as ELOHIM. Some Hebrew terms will be quoted in transcriptions and explained in the text as well as in the glossary.

Acknowledgments

MANY THANKS TO RABBI Jeremy Parnes, who read together with me all the sections of the book and helped me to clarify my thoughts, and to Dr. Steve Wolfson, who helped me in my struggle with the computer, produced a readable manuscript, and (most importantly) gave useful editorial advice when my writing was incomprehensible. I also want to express my thanks to the library staff of the University of Regina. And finally, thanks to Matt Wimer, Caleb Shupe, Calvin Jaffarian and Joe Delahanty of Wipf and Stock for their patience in dealing with my naïve questions. I could not have written this book without the help and encouragement of my wife Monica, who suggested the title of the book and wrestled with my German/English style.

Abbreviations

BBR	*Bulletin of Biblical Research*
BH	Biblical History
CBQ	*Catholic Biblical Quarterly*
DH	Deuteronomistic History
DSS	Dead Sea Scrolls
EP	Early Prophets
HEP	Historian(s) writing the Early Prophets
IH	Israelite History
JANER	*Journal of Ancient Near Eastern Religions*
JBL	*Journal of Biblical Literature*
JE	The JE (Jahvist/Elohist) stratum of the Pentateuch, comprises Genesis and the narrative sections of Exodus and Numbers.
JEOTS	*Journal for the Evangelical Study of the Old Testament*
JQR	*Jewish Quarterly Review*
JSOTS	*Journal for the Study of the Old Testament Supplement Series*
LP	Latter Prophets
LXX	Septuagint: Greek bible translation from the third century BCE
MT	Masoretic Text, the traditional text of the Hebrew Bible.
P	The second stratum of the Pentateuch is the so-called Priestly code, found at the end of Exodus, Leviticus, and parts of Numbers.

ABBREVIATIONS

Time Periods

MB II	Middle Bronze Age II 1750–1650 BCE
MB III	Middle Bronze Age III 1650–1550 BCE
LB I	Late Bronze Age I 1550–1400 BCE
LB IIa	Late Bronze Age II A 1400–1300 BCE
LB IIb	Late Bronze Age II B 1300–200 BCE
IA Ia	Iron Age I A 1200–1150 BCE
IA Ib	Iron Age I B 1150–1000 BCE
IA IIa	Iron Age II A 1000–900 BCE
IA IIb	Iron Age II B 900–700 BCE
IA IIc	Iron Age II C 700–586 BCE

I

The Problem

1

Basic Assumptions

Ploni and Almoni argue before their Rabbi. Ploni explains his interpretation and the Rabbi says: "you are right." Almoni fervently denies Ploni's interpretation. Says the Rabbi: "You are right." Both cry out: "But we can't be both be right!" Says the Rabbi: "You are right."

CONTROVERSY AMONG SCHOLARS OF Israelite history (IH) has escalated during the last forty years. Wenham, reviewing the "search for a new paradigm" in biblical studies, concluded that:

> In the present situation of scholarly polarization, sometimes the polemic is becoming so strident that the different sides in the debate are in danger of neglecting valid criticism of their own positions.[1]

Controversy is not restricted to biblical scholarship. Bateson points out:

> The study of behavioural development has attracted some of the most bitter and protracted controversies in the whole field of animal behavior . . . The difficulty is that people have very different views about what constitutes evidence adequate to enable useful classifications to be made.[2]

Gödel's Theorem, which is paraphrased and discussed in detail by Hofstadter, states: "All consistent axiomatic formulations of number

---

1. Wenham, "Pondering the Pentateuch," 144.
2. Bateson, "Genes, Environment," 52, 55.

I: The Problem

theory include undecidable propositions."³ A mathematical system, such as Euclidean geometry, may be logically consistent in its derivations, but ultimately it rests on axioms which can neither be proven nor disproven. Non-Euclidean geometry is based on different axioms which lead to different theorems. A critical analysis of any theory must therefore consider the basic assumptions on which it is built. The rabbi of our story realizes that each of two incompatible theories may be logically correct, though derived from different basic undecidable premises which cannot be proven.

> I can get somewhere when I challenge the deductions you make from your fundamental assumptions. But I can get nowhere if I think that I am challenging your deductions when in fact I am differing from your assumptions, your presuppositions, your premises, your beliefs.⁴

For example, some scholars maintain that pure monotheism was developed only during the Persian or Hellenistic period and that pre-exilic Israel was not monotheistic; YHWH was not the only deity, and most of the biblical stories, including the story of the conquest of Canaan by Israelites, the exodus, and the Sinaitic covenant, as well as the stories of the patriarchs, are fiction. On the other side stand those who argue that most biblical reports reflect the historical reality of their time (not of the Persian period) and should be accepted unless proven unreliable by external evidence. There is no independent evidence for either position. There are no manuscripts proving that the biblical stories were invented in the Persian epoch. Neither the tablets of the law, or the "book of the law of God" (ספר תורת אלהים; Josh 24:26) have been produced. All "evidence" is indirect and its interpretation must be evaluated on the basis of its credibility. Both theories may be "right," meaning that they are presented in a logical and convincing manner. Both depend on the interpretation of biblical writings, viewed in the light of our general knowledge about the entire area of the ancient Middle East. In the final analysis the difference between the theories reflects differences in basic assumptions.

Every theory is colored by the personal bias of its proponent. "Historians have their personal predilections, their own *idées fixes*, their own curiosities . . . the final colour and shape of a historian's construction is bestowed by his or her own *Weltanschauung*."⁵ Such bias is essential, because

---

3. Hofstadter, *Gödel*, 17.
4. Long, "Historiography," 168n83, quoting Greenstein, "Role of Theory," 167.
5. Stanford, *Nature of Historical Knowledge*, 96.

it leads to the asking of new questions and directs the search for new evidence. It also may make the researcher impervious to valid criticism. A common offense is the ignoring of contrary evidence or theories. Scholars cite each other, but their bibliographies ignore most of the work of their opponents. The identification of the source of the bias—the *ad hominem* argument—is irrelevant to the evaluation of the theory, which should be analyzed on its own terms.[6]

Long emphasizes "the importance of scholars' offering some indication in their writings of their core beliefs about Reality."[7] Hence I will state my personal core beliefs: my approach is absolutely secular. The Bible is a human document. Any reports of divine intervention or of supernatural events are manifestations of human experience. I also accept Kaufmann's definition of monotheism as being "utterly distinct" from paganism,[8] but reject the assumption/prejudice of the Bible and of most biblical scholars that monotheism is the pinnacle of religious insight. Monotheism assumes an unbridgeable rift between the deity and the universe: God is not a part of the universe he has created. Paganism experiences the world as one indivisible unity. Both views are valid experiences of humans faced with the question, "What is the meaning of existence?"

The Bible as a Historical Document

According to Jewish tradition, the Hebrew Bible is divided into three major sections: a) Torah (Pentateuch), the five books of Moses, (b) Nevi'im (Prophets); and (c) Ketuvim (Hagiographa). This leads to the acronym *TeNaKH*. The Nevi'im are subdivided into the "Early Prophets" (EP) and the "Latter Prophets" (LP). The EP includes the "historical books" of Joshua, Judges, Samuel, and Kings.[9]

---

6. To give an example from a different discipline, it has been suggested that the theory of the "Oedipus complex" merely reveals Freud's troubled relationship with his father. This may be so. In that case, Freud's personal bias enabled him to ask new questions about parent/child relationships. This has no bearing on the evaluation of the validity of his observations or his conclusions.

7. Long, "Historiography," 168.

8. Kaufmann, *Religion of Israel*.

9. The Christian editions include the same books in a different order; Ruth, Esther, Ezra/Nehemiah, and Chronicles are included in the section of historical books and Daniel is included among the Prophets.

I: The Problem

Long points out that the term "Historiography of the Old Testament" is ambiguous.

> [It may] ...focus ... on "biblical history, i.e., the history as told in the Bible," or on "Israelite history, i.e., the history of ancient Israel as modern research represents it"... Some scholars regard the two as rather closely tied—"biblical history" being an essentially reliable literary presentation of selected aspects of "Israelite history"—while others view the two as virtually unrelated—"biblical history" being little more than literary fiction with minimal bearing on the reconstruction of ancient Israelite history.[10]

The following section discusses the assumptions underlying various theories of "Israelite history" (IH) as well as the criteria for evaluating the credibility of "biblical history" (BH).

Herodotus is generally called the father of history because he subjected his data (reports on the past) to critical scrutiny. I suggest that history—as contrasted to annals—does not merely report: it attempts to understand. Ancient historiography explains events in terms of interaction between human behavior and divine intervention ("A" did this, and a divine agent rewarded/punished, or a divine agent initiated an event and "A" reacted to it). As stated in the Foreword p. x n4, I assume that biblical writers were honest reporters; they did not feel free to invent data and present them as divine truth. A prophet reporting "thus said YHWH" probably believed in the validity of his experience. The biblical text includes editorial comments, mostly evaluations: "He did evil in the eyes of the Lord," as well as general historical explanations of the fate of Israel (2 Kgs 17). There also are comments like "to this day" (Josh 9, 27).

It is mandatory to distinguish between "events" reported, the embellishment by the storyteller, and the explanation given. E.g., the Midianites invaded Israel, which was an event, and they were sent by God to punish Israel for their sins, which was an explanation. A critical analysis of a biblical story should investigate the reliability of any report and not reject it out of hand. "Editorial comments" or explanations will be considered as factual information describing the beliefs of the writer.

When may a biblical narrative be accepted as reliable, and correspondingly, when can a theory about its origin be accepted as credible?

---

10. Long, "Historiography," 145–46. I might suggest another meaning of the term, namely the "History of Biblical Scholarship in the Last 200 Years." Some future scholar will enjoy tracing the convolutions of theories proposed.

Basic Assumptions

Two points must be considered. a) What independent evidence supports or contradicts the report? b) What is the significance of reports of supernatural events?

The historical books of the Bible are the EP (נביאים ראשונים) as well as Ezra, Nehemiah, and 1–2 Chronicles. They cover the period from about 1300 BCE until the Babylonian exile (586 BCE). The term "Deuteronomistic History" (DH) refers to the book of Deuteronomy together with the EP. This term represents the theory that the historical books were edited by the author(s) of Deuteronomy, which was not written in Mosaic times. Second Kings ends with the story of the liberation of King Jehoiachim. That is the earliest possible date of its final redaction. The logical possibilities are as follows:

a. The EP is an invention, like the *Chronicles of Narnia*.

b. The EP is a historical novel, like *Ivanhoe*, a romance which, though based on some valid knowledge about past events, essentially reflects the views of the author and his time.

c. The EP is an attempt to write "history"; i.e., to record past events and interpret their significance for the writer. The historian (or redactor) may base his reports on written documents or on oral tradition. His selection of events to be reported is an indication of his personal bias.

I have chosen the third approach. I assume that the Bible reports events which were considered to be significant for the comprehension of the world of its authors, tries to explain them and also endeavors to convey a message to the audience. I assume that its authors believed in the veracity of their accounts—including their reports on divine manifestations. A secular approach denies the factuality of reports about miracles. Statements contradicting established scientific findings are rejected. The sun does not revolve around the earth, which was not created about 5765 years ago. Any report of a "supernatural" event is to be interpreted as an old tradition, describing the beliefs of the time in which it originated. The text may report a simple event (a report of a battle or the name of a king's mother, his age, and the duration of his reign). It may be embellished, including speeches or reported supernatural events. One should ask: what natural events may have led to the formation of the narrative?

For example, Joshua 10:8–14 describes in detail Joshua's victorious battle in Gibeon. The city, which had concluded a peace treaty with the invading Israelites, was attacked by a coalition of five Canaanite kings.

I: The Problem

The Gibeonites asked for Joshua's help. The narrative then reports an encouraging speech by YHWH to Joshua. The Israelites left their camp in Gilgal and, after a forced night march, surprised the Canaanites and attained a large victory. The Israelites pursued the Canaanites and YHWH himself intervened: rocks fell from heaven—"there were more who died because of the hailstones than the Israelites killed with the sword" (Josh 10:11). Joshua hoped to kill as many Canaanites as possible. He prayed to God, who created some cosmic upheaval: the sun and moon stood still, prolonging the day.

A critical reading will evaluate the plausibility of each part of the story. was there such a battle? Could such a speech have been made? Could the divine intervention be explained as a natural event? If not, what is the possible source of the story? Is there is any outside evidence that such an event occurred? Is there outside evidence that it could not have occurred? Is the report plausible, considering our general knowledge of the historical background? Is there evidence for later editorial additions? Could the story be an invention of the editor?[11]

People listen to stories about old times. If there was a battle in which the Israelites won a decisive victory, the story would be told at the gates of the city or at religious festivals and would be well-embellished to the delight of the audience. The storyteller, quoting the book of the Jashar, would declaim (Josh 10, 12–13):

> Sun, stand still at Gibeon,
> and Moon, in the Valley of Aijalon.
> And the sun stood still, and the moon stopped,
> until the nation took vengeance on their enemies.

That we don't believe that the sun stood still does not imply that there never was a victorious Joshua, nor does it invalidate the claim that a battle took place in which Joshua was victorious. Kitchen points out that divine intervention is claimed by Egyptian, Hittite, and Assyrian kings:

> The support of deity is repeatedly invoked in what are otherwise straightforward historical accounts, because that is simply how the ancients saw their world . . . This feature does *not* imply nonhistoricity either outside the Hebrew Bible or inside it.[12]

---

11. For a discussion of this battle see Younger, "Rhetorical Structuring," 3–26.
12. Kitchen, *Reliability*, 175.

Basic Assumptions

The writer of the EP is not satisfied with reporting events: he wants to make sense of them. He assumes that the past is not a collection of random events, but can be understood to be a lawful sequence of cause and effect. He does not always give his sources, nor does he attempt to verify them. He omits topics which would interest the contemporary historian. Nevertheless, his search for understanding makes it a true history, perhaps the first of its kind.

The author(s) may report conflicting stories. For example, some passages are pro-royal, others are anti-royal. Some stories about David show him in a favorable light; others paint a rather sad picture. This merely shows that the author (or the reader) liked some of the things David did but disapproved of others. It does not prove that two different sources were combined by a later editor, or that one or both sections are later additions inserted for propaganda purposes. The text depicts the reality of an earlier conflict.

In the seventies, Dever proposed that what was then termed "biblical archaeology" should be labeled more accurately by a properly descriptive term: Syro-Palestinian Archaeology.[13] Dever intended to free archaeology from theological-biblical associations, and to become instead a secular discipline. This suggestion evoked a stormy debate which is well-reviewed by Zevit.[14] What struck me most was the emotional intensity of the discussion. The name is evidently a slogan defending the author's assumptions. After all, Dever as well as his opponents deal with two kinds of data—biblical texts and archaeological records—which should be integrated. Scriptural passages may enrich the interpretation of archaeological data; archaeological data may indicate the likelihood of the historicity of the biblical narrative.

As observed by Avishur and Heltzer, "Archaeology, without strengthening with narrative sources, and inscriptions cannot give us a full historical picture of the society . . . we have to combine the narrative sources of the Old Testament."[15] No scholarly investigation of a biblical narrative can ignore archaeological data. Unfortunately, archaeological and epigraphic evidence, though crucial, is rarely unequivocal. There are frequent disagreements concerning the dating of layers, or the reading of an inscription.[16]

---

13. Dever, "Syro-Palestinian," 263–69
14. Zevit, "Biblical Archaeology," 3–19.
15. Avishur and Heltzer, *Studies*, 10.
16. See Ortiz, "Deconstructing," 121–48.

I: The Problem

The interpretation of archaeological data often depends on the interpretation of the biblical sources. Mazani notes: "It is intriguing to note that different investigators use the same data on the evidence for early Israel but draw contradictory and irreconcilable conclusions."[17]

There are several considerations when juxtaposing a biblical report with archaeological data.

Archaeological Data Confirm a Biblical Report

(1) About 870 BCE, Jehoshaphat, king of Judah, entered an alliance with Ahab, king of Israel, which was sealed by intermarriage: the son and heir of Jehoshaphat, Jehoram, married the daughter of Ahab. The EP historian describes a number of joint military expeditions in Transjordan, aiming to strengthen Israelite dominion in this area. After the death of Ahab (852 BCE) Mesha, king of Moab, rebelled against Israel. These events are described in the Mesha Stele (840 BCE) as well as in 2 Kings 3. Both accounts agree on the basic facts: Mesha acknowledges that Moab was subservient to Israel during the time of Omri and Ahab. He rebelled against Israel at the time of Jehoram. Mesha describes a number of battles. In some Israel was victorious; in others Moab defeated Israel. Ultimately, Moab regained its independence from Israel. Mesha ascribes his rebellion and victory to the intervention of his god Chemosh, who was angry with Israel and promised victory to Mesha. The biblical record acknowledges the successful rebellion of Moab. It gives no specific details about any battles and cities conquered or abandoned. It claims that the coalition of Israel, Judah, and Edom was initially victorious.[18]

> When the king of Moab saw that the battle was going against him, he took with him seven hundred swordsmen to break through, opposite the king of Edom; but they could not. Then he took his firstborn son who was to succeed him, and offered him as a burnt offering on the wall. And great wrath came upon Israel, so they withdrew from him and returned to their own land. (2 Kings 3:26–27)

17. Mazani, "Appearance of Israel," 96.

18. The biblical narrative tells that the coalition forces of Israel, Judah, and Edom lacked water. They applied to the prophet Elisha, who predicted an Israelite victory and divine intervention to help the Israelites. "Next morning at the time when the oblation was being offered, water came from the direction of Edom, and the whole terrain was flooded" (2 Kgs 3:20). This was interpreted as a miraculous event. It was not a supernatural event: flush floods frequently occur in desert areas.

Basic Assumptions

Thus both sources agree on the basic facts—Moab was a vassal state of Israel and Mesha rebelled successfully—but differ in their evaluation. The focus of the biblical report is on the relation between the kings and the prophet and on the description of the miraculous help rendered by YHWH. It describes a military victory but glosses over the final retreat. The Mesha stele stresses the help of Chemosh and boasts of his successes after the successful rebellion. The Mesha stele reports more details about the course of the war but does not mention the sacrifice of Mesha's son. The Bible does not mention the name of Chemosh. There is no *a priori* reason for deciding which account—Mesha or 2 Kings—is more reliable. Both select the facts they wish to be remembered.

(2) After the death of the Assyrian king Sargon II (705 BCE), King Hezekiah rebelled against Assyria. The events following this rebellion are described in detail in the Bible as well as in the Assyrian report of Sennacherib's campaign against Judah (701 BCE) and in the Lachisch inscription from Nineveh. Both reports agree on the basic facts: Hezekiah refused to pay tribute. Sennacherib invaded Judah successfully and destroyed most of its cities, but did not capture Jerusalem.

The reports differ fundamentally in their appraisal of the events. Sennacharib boasts of a great victory. Forty-eight cities were destroyed. The siege of Lachish is described in detail. The number of prisoners is inflated. About Hezekiah, "he himself I locked up in Jerusalem."[19] Hezekiah surrendered and had to pay heavy fines. The Bible, on the other hand, describes Hezekiah's rebellion and surrender in four verses (2 Kgs 18:13–16). The destruction of the cities of Judah is mentioned in one sentence only: "King Sennacherib of Assyria came up against all the fortified cities of Judah and captured them (2 Kgs 18:13b)." The destruction of Lachish is not mentioned at all. The siege of Jerusalem, on the other hand, is described in detail—58 verses (2 Kgs 18:17—19:37, as well in Isa 36–37 and 2 Chr 32:1–23). The failure of the Assyrians to capture Jerusalem is ascribed to divine intervention and seen as a victory of YHWH. It gave rise to the belief that YHWH will never allow the destruction of the Jerusalem sanctuary.

> Therefore thus says YHWH concerning the king of Assyria: He shall not come into this city, shoot an arrow there, come before it with a shield, or cast up a siege ramp against it. By the way that he came, by the same he shall return; he shall not come into this

---

19. The Assyrian documents are cited and discussed in detail in Cogan, *Racing Torrent*, 110–29, especially text #28 and #29.

I: The Problem

city, says YHWH. For I will defend this city to save it, for my own sake and for the sake of my servant David. That very night the angel of YHWH set out and struck down one hundred eighty-five thousand in the camp of the Assyrians; when morning dawned, they were all dead bodies. (2 Kgs 19:32–35)[20]

Altogether the Bible extols Hezekiah's reign in glowing terms.

He trusted in YHWH, the God of Israel; so that there was no one like him among all the kings of Judah after him, or among those who were before him. (2 Kgs 18:5)[21]

The Historicity of a Biblical Report is Refuted by Archaeological Data

Extreme caution is warranted. The refutation of the historicity of a biblical report may be based on an erroneous reading of the biblical text or on mistaken readings of archaeological data. The best known example is the "proof" that Joshua is fictitious. Hess shows that this proof depends on the "assumptions that the long tradition of interpretation, both popular and scholarly, has assigned to these sites."[22] Re-examination of the text by Hess and others indicates that the biblical record is supported by archaeological data.[23]

---

20. A different story is told in 2 Kgs 19:6a–7: "Thus says YHWH . . . I myself will put a spirit in him [king of Assyria], so that he shall hear a rumor and return to his own land; I will cause him to fall by the sword in his own land." The reign of Hezekiah is discussed in chapter 10.

21. Lemche ("Problems," 216–21) uses the same data to prove that the EP narratives are largely fictional. As the reports of different sources contradict each other, their reliability can never be established. In his view, the story of miraculous divine intervention (plague in the Assyrian army, water in the desert) discredits the entire report. "Miracles are certainly out of focus in a historical report . . . It is safe to say—from a historian's point of view—that it never happened" (ibid., 219). Lemche rejects data arbitrarily: "Mesha's story . . . maybe is as much literature as the version in 2 Kings 3" (ibid., 220). The Old Testament "is simply an invented story with only a few referents to things that really happened and existed. From an historian's point of view, ancient Israel is a monstrous creature" (ibid., 233). Lemche's analysis differs from mine because our basic assumptions differ. In my view, different biblical accounts merely reveal the bias of the author.

22. Hess, "Jericho and Ai," 33.

23. For further discussion about the interpretation of Joshua, see chapter 3, "The Origin of Israel: Archaeological Interpretations."

Basic Assumptions

Archaeological Evidence Will Rarely Prove or Disprove a Biblical Report

Rarely will archaeological evidence prove or disprove a biblical report. It may, however, be relevant when evaluating its credibility. The data are equivocal and open to different interpretations. Thus, Egyptian sources reporting the settlement of Semitic nomads ("Asiatics") in the Nile Delta and their work as forced laborers support but do not prove the biblical account of the sojourn in Egypt. The sudden increase of settlements in the highlands of Canaan may indicate a military invasion or a peaceful infiltration. The most one can hope for is an estimate of the likelihood that the biblical narrative is based on fact.

The argument of "absence of evidence" is frequently evoked when the historicity of biblical narratives is discussed. However, "The archaeological axiom remains that absence of evidence . . . is not equivalent to evidence of absence."[24] Evidence about the Israelite History (IH) is not to be expected before the eighth century BCE. Assyrian records are available from the eight century BCE on, and show conclusively that the biblical writers were accurate in their reports of names, dates, and major events, though describing them from a perspective different from ours. The biblical reports corroborate the claims made by Assyrian/Babylonian writers. Why should we assume that later redactors felt free to invent stories from earlier times? I suggest that the proven accuracy of the late chapters in 2 Kings indicates that we should also take earlier historical narratives seriously.

Thus, I agree with Younker: "Take the history of the Bible seriously, but do not place upon archaeology the burden of 'proving' the Bible."[25] This is not "fundamentalism." It does not imply an uncritical acceptance of rhetorical embellishments or explanations offered in the Bible. Every report should be scrutinized separately. I do not believe that a public theophany occurred at Mount Sinai. This opinion is not based on the evaluation of archaeological facts, but is derived from my basic assumption (prejudice) as a secularist. There is no objective evidence forcing its rejection by a religious person, following his/(her) basic assumption (prejudice).

An examination of the structure of the biblical texts shows that most reports of historical events are based on available written historical records—annals, genealogical lists, lists of places—as well as on oral

---

24. Chavalas and Adamthwaite, "Context of Early Israel," 70.
25. Younker, "Integrating Faith," 52.

traditions. Such information was routinely registered in the royal archives all over the near East, and there is no reason to assume that Israel was an exception.[26] Zevit refers to the author(s) of the EP as "the Deuteronomistic historian."[27]

> It is therefore likely that the chronicles utilized by Dtr, the Deuteronomistic historian, were based on information similar to what was available to Mesopotamian chroniclers and to those composing historical types of inscriptions in Northwest Semitic dialects ... There is no *a priori*, or for that matter *a posteriori*, reason to suspect him of fabricating sources or details to bolster his historiosophic hypothesis.[28]

History reports are selective. Biblical historiography was never meant to give a historically accurate picture of events or religious phenomena. The goal of the biblical writers was to express the divine will, as they understood it. They were interested in evaluating kings and nations according to their own concept of Yahwism.[29] The writers of the EP and Chronicles reported selectively, but they did not invent stories. Their reliability must, of course, be investigated independently.

A useful strategy for the understanding of a biblical text is to consider it in isolation: what if "this" (book or passage) were the only document available? Kaufmann raises this question regarding the biblical understanding of paganism.

> The Bible is utterly unaware of the nature and meaning of pagan religion ... What would we know [about paganism] if we had no other source than the Bible? The Bible knows that the pagans worship national gods ... But it is remarkable that not a single biblical passage hints at the natural or mythological qualities of any of these named gods. Had we only the Bible, we should know nothing of the real nature of the "gods of the nations."[30]

Absence of references to pagan mythology does not imply that pagan mythology did not exist when the Bible was written, or that the biblical writers did not know about it.

26. Further discussion of literacy in Israel pp. 32–34.
27. I shall refer to him simply as "the Historian" (HEP): his ideas are not merely "Deuteronomistic," but reflect the theology of the Tetrateuch as well.
28. Zevit, *Religions*, 445.
29. Ahlstrom, "Archaeological and Literary Remains," 140.
30. Kaufmann, *Religion*, 7, 9

Basic Assumptions

Another example is the book of Esther. If this book had been our only source of information about Judaism during the Persian period, we would know that many Jews lived in the Persian Empire and that they followed their own laws. We would not know what these laws were; nor would we know about the existence of the Persian province of Jahud and Jerusalem. This would neither imply that Ezra and Nehemiah did not exist, nor that the author of the book did not know of their existence.

A comparison of 1–2 Kings with 1–2 Chronicles is another example. What would be our knowledge of the relations between the kingdom of Israel and the kingdom of Judah, if only one of these two sources were known? Each book mentions items which are not reported in the other one. This does not mean that an event reported in only one source did not occur. Nor does it imply a lack of knowledge by the authors. They had different agendas. Their selection of material reflects their bias.

The EP recount the history of Israel's disobedience and its consequences. The HEP was not interested in reporting on ritual or liturgy. Any references to living conditions of the time are incidental to the narrative. The evidential value of such reports is significant, because they are not made to prove a point, but to show what was considered self-evident at the time. For example, passages such as "Why go to him today? It is neither new moon nor sabbath" (2 Kgs 4:23); "One-third of you, who go off duty on the sabbath ... two divisions that come on duty in force on the sabbath" (2 Kgs 11:5, 7); or "The covered portal for use on the sabbath" (2 Kgs 16:18) show clearly that the New Moon and the Sabbath were observed in both Judah and Israel. The passage "Such a thing is not done in Israel; do not do anything so vile" (2 Sam 13:12) implies the concept of a society bound by a special moral law.

The EP do not report systematically on social economic conditions, on technological developments, on royal administration, on the judicial system, or on the religious cult. If only the EP were preserved, we would know practically nothing about the worship of YHWH. We would know that the Sabbath, the New Moon, and Passover were celebrated. Nobody tells us how. We would not know about the Festival of Weeks or about Succoth. What would we know about the life in Israel during that time or about its civil or criminal law? We would know that there were judges and that the king is the chief judge. We do not know how judges were appointed, or what laws they followed. There is a report that people demanded the death sentence to be pronounced on a man who killed his brother (2 Sam

I: The Problem

14:6–7).[31] There are reports about Solomon's judgments but they do not mention a specific law (1 Kgs 3:16–28).[32] The story of Naboth's vineyard (1Kgs 21:1–13)[33] shows clearly that the law of inheritance of landed property was well-known and acknowledged by the king and many other references show that the king in Israel was subject to the law of YHWH.

The festival of Sukkoth is not mentioned. Does this mean that it is an invention of the Persian period? Certainly not! It would be ludicrous to assume that the inhabitants of Judah and Israel went through life without celebrating seasonal festivals which were celebrated everywhere else. I think that there is a high likelihood that the winter solstice or the end of winter were celebrated even before they were called Chanukah or Purim. The Water Festival, which was the occasion of strife in Hasmonean times, was an old tradition, surely not invented in the first century BCE.

We must assume that sacrifices were an important aspect of ritual. The fact that these rituals are not described in Deuteronomy does not imply that they were not practiced. Nor may we assume that sacrifices were offered haphazardly. The ritual was probably rigidly fixed. For that reason the P source was necessary. The sections in the Pentateuch which are generally ascribed to P are a manual for priests (in modern language, how to be a good priest; a complete manual of instruction).

The HEP reports, but does not judge. Any moral evaluation is part of the reported event. For example, the story of David and Bathsheba is told without any comment. The intervention by Nathan is a part of the story. This objective reporting of events, with neither condemnation nor attempted justification, which is also found in the Pentateuch, is a remarkable feature. My teacher, Ernst Simon, used to say, "The Bible is not a hagiography, but the story of sinners." No hero, no group is blameless. The

---

31. A woman tells King David that her son killed his brother and is under sentence of death. She asks for clemency.

32. Two prostitutes claim a newborn baby as their own. The king orders that the infant be cut in two, upon which the true mother renounces her claim.

33. Naboth refused to sell his vineyard, an ancestral heritage, to King Ahab (873–852 BCE). Ahab was not an insignificant chieftain. The Assyrian inscription of Salmanaser III mentions Ahab as a member of an anti-Assyrian coalition. He is reported to have contributed two thousand chariots and ten thousand soldiers to the coalition. The numbers are probably exaggerated, but the inscription proves that Ahab was an important king. Nevertheless, he was bound by the law of inheritance and unable to buy the vineyard. His wife Jezebel procured two false witnesses who accused Naboth of "cursing the king." Naboth was convicted, executed, and his property went to the king. Ahab and Jezebel obviously knew the laws of Israel.

behavior of the patriarchs and the matriarchs, the behavior of Moses or David or Solomon, the attempted genocide of the Canaanites, even the behavior of God himself (2 Sam 6:6–7), makes the modern reader shake his head. Most nations talk about their early days with admiration; their heroes are descendants of gods. Only Israel consistently describes its ancestors in negative terms. The stubbornness of the Israelites during the exodus and their wanderings is extraordinary. All this is reported without comment. The question which the biblical scholar should ask himself is this: why would an editor invent such stories?

We may disagree with the HEP's view of history; his selection of reported events is biased. However, he did not doctor his reports; they should be evaluated on their own merit. Are they possible? Are they plausible in view of what is known about the culture of the Middle East in the period of which the event speaks? Is there any outside evidence which makes them unlikely? The Bible is "history" because it does not merely report events but attempts to explain them. The rejection of the writer's explanation does not refute the event reported.

2

The Wellhausen Fallacy

The Problem

THE PENTATEUCH IS NOT a well-edited homogenous book: there are unnecessary repetitions, obvious contradictions and differences in style. Such problems are not only apparent when comparing different books of the Pentateuch, but may occur even within one chapter, even in a single passage. The traditional rabbinical interpretation claims that such repetitions are meaningful. Biblical scholarship asserts that they are proof of the existence of different sources, produced in different times by different groups of authors, revised, and rewritten by later groups of editors/redactors.[1]

The first book of the Pentateuch, Genesis, starts by describing the creation of the universe (Gen 1—2:3). In this chapter, the deity is always called "ELOHIM"—God.[2] But the next chapters give a different account of the creation. Here the deity is called by the personal name of YHWH (traditionally translated as "the Lord"). Some passages in the Pentateuch use only YHWH, other use only ELOHIM, and others use the combination "YHWH/ELOHIM," or "the Lord God." The story of the flood, for example,

---

1. Bible criticism was not invented by Wellhausen or even during the Renaissance. The first critical students of the Hebrew Scriptures were fundamentalists, the Tannaim. They believed that the scriptures had divine authority, but recognized that there were contradictions among various law codes, unnecessary duplications, and inconsistent historical reports. They developed rules of interpretation to account for these contradictions. They also concluded that each of two different interpretations may be valid: "These and those are the words of a living God." As the Rabbi of our story said, "Both of you are right."

2. See pp. 90–91.

has unnecessary repetitions and contradictions. Genesis 6:1–8 and chapter 7 refer to YHWH when narrating the story. Genesis 6:9–22 and 8:1–19; 9:1–17 refer to ELOHIM. Such reiteration points to two authors who are called "the Jahvist" and "the Elohist." Scholars differ in their identification of the source of many passages. However there is now general consensus that these two sources were combined and gave rise to the so-called JE parts of the Pentateuch.³ The JE stratum of the Pentateuch comprises Genesis and the narrative sections of Exodus and Numbers. The second stratum of the Pentateuch is the so-called priestly code, P, found at the end of Exodus, Leviticus and parts of Numbers. The third stratum is Deuteronomy, which cites the final speeches of Moses. Each stratum includes a collection of laws. The JE law code (Exod 20:1—23:19) includes the Decalogue (the ten commandments). The P legislation includes the so-called "holiness code" (Lev 17–26), and the bulk of Deuteronomistic laws is found in Deuteronomy 12–27. This short review is an oversimplification. Scholars have suggested subdivisions, called J1, J2, P1, P2, etc. Scholars often disagree about the identification of a biblical passage. Some theorists may find several sources combined in a short passage, assuming that some phrases are added to an earlier source. There appears, however, to be a general consensus identifying three basic strata: JE, P, and Dt.

The JE text assumes that, after the conquest of Canaan, sacrifices will be offered in many places:

> You need make for me only an altar of earth and sacrifice on it your burnt offerings and your offerings of well-being [שלמים, *shelamim*, peace offerings], your sheep and your oxen; in every place where I cause my name to be remembered I will come to you and bless you. (Exod 20:24)⁴

On the other hand, Deuteronomy demands:

> Take care that you do not offer your burnt offerings at any place you happen to see. But only at the place that YHWH will choose in

---

3. There are notable exceptions; cf. Cassuto, *Documentary Hypothesis*, and Segal, "Book of Deuteronomy," [x-ref].

4. The NRSV adds: "for me *only*." *Shelamim* is generally translated as "peace offering." NRSV translates this as "offerings of well-being"; REB translates it as "shared-offerings"; and JB translates this as "communion sacrifices"; it is a technical term (see chapter 6 of this book, "Deuteronomy"). A part of *shelamim* may be eaten; "burnt offerings" are totally burnt (*olah*). "Flock" refers to sheep and goats, distinguished from cattle.

I: THE PROBLEM

one of your tribes—there you shall offer your burnt offerings and there you shall do everything I command you. (Deut 12:13–14)

This passage is interpreted as demanding a single sanctuary.[5] The historical books (the EP and Chronicles) report that sacrifices were offered at many places, notably on the "High Places" (*bamoth*). This observation led to the conclusion that cult centralization was not known in Israel until the seventh century BCE. This is the theoretical basis for the Wellhausen fallacy.

The Theory

For the last 150 years, the bulk of biblical scholarship follows Wellhausen,[6] though his theories were modified. Wellhausen's ideas were not original. The main points were already made by de Wette,[7] as he acknowledged freely.[8] However, his *Prolegomena* popularized the so-called "documentary hypothesis." Wellhausen is an excellent writer; it is a pleasure to read his book, and his arguments are persuasive. His theories, as well as the modifications made by later scholars, have been well-described in many publications.[9]

Wellhausen accepts the identification of "The three strata of the Pentateuch: Deuteronomy, Priestly Code, Jehovist."[10] Wellhausen's main argument is that only Deuteronomy commands the centralization of the sacrificial cult. The rest of the Pentateuch, as well as the pre-exilic prophets, take it for granted that YHWH may be legitimately worshiped at other places, by laypeople as well as by priests. He suggests that the book of the Law "found" at the time of King Josiah was Deuteronomy. It is is a pseudepigraphy attributed to Moses and was written in the seventh century BCE.[11]

5. See chapter 6, "Deuteronomy."

6. Wellhausen, *Prolegomena*.

7. de Wette, *Dissertatio Critica Exegetica qua Deuteronomium a Prioribus Pentateuchi Libris Diversum* [A Critical Exegetical Discussion Which Shows That Deuteronomy Is a Work that Differs from the First Books of the Pentateuch]. De Wette's theories are discussed in detail by Merrill, "Deuteronomy and de Wette," 25–42.

8. Wellhausen, *Prolegomena*, 3–4.

9. For a summary and discussion of the documentary hypothesis, see the excellent reviews by Wenham, "Pondering the Pentateuch," 116–44; Long, "Historiography of the Old Testament," 145–75; Knight, "Pentateuch," 263–96. For a critique, cf. Cassuto, *Documentary Hypothesis*, and Segal, "Book of Deuteronomy."

10. Wellhausen, *Prolegomena*, xi.

11. King Josiah ordered the renovation of the temple. The high priest found what he

About the origin of Deuteronomy there is still less dispute; in all circles where appreciation of scientific results can be looked for at all, it is recognised that it was composed in the same age as that it in which it was discovered, and that it was made the rule of Josiah's reformation.[12]

The topic of part I of the prolegomena is "the question is as to the Priestly Code and its historical position."[13] According to Leviticus, the priestly ritual is of Mosaic origin; according to Wellhausen, the ritual described in Leviticus was only developed in post-exilic times.

Chapter II of Wellhausen's work discusses the difference between the "Jehovist" cult and the priestly cult. Wellhausen argues that the old "primitive" concept of sacrifice, as expressed in JE (as well as in the EP), differs fundamentally from that of the priestly code (called "RQ" by Wellhausen). "In RQ the point is How, according to JE and D To Whom, it is offered."[14]

Before the destruction of the temple, the emphasis is always on serving YHWH only. Leviticus is mainly preoccupied with ritual, how sacrifices are to be offered.

> At all times, then, the sacrificial worship of Israel existed, and had great importance attached to it, but in the earlier period it rested upon custom, inherited from the fathers, in the post-exilian on the law of Jehovah, given through Moses. At first it was naive ... afterwards it became legal.[15]
>
> According to the universal opinion of the pre-exilic period, the cult is indeed of very old and (to the people) very sacred usage, but not a Mosaic institution; the ritual is not the main thing in it, and it is in no sense the subject with which the Torah deals.[16]

Neither the historical books nor the pre-exilic prophets know of the ritualistic cult described in P. Wellhausen concluded that the tabernacle could not have existed in Mosaic times.

---

called "the book of the Torah of Moses." De Wette, and most biblical scholars after him, assume that this book was a pseudepigraphy, written during the seventh century BCE and falsely attributed to Moses. For a detailed discussion see pp. 169–71.

12. Wellhausen, *Prolegomena*, 9.

13. Ibid., xi. The Table of Contents (xi–xvi) highlights the main points to be made in the book.

14. Ibid., xi.

15. Ibid., 61.

16. Ibid., 59.

> For the truth is, that the tabernacle is the copy, not the prototype, of the temple at Jerusalem.... Very strange is the contrast between this splendid structure ... and the soil on which it rises, in the wilderness amongst the native Hebrew nomad tribes, who are represented as having got it ready offhand, and without external help ... It is clear that in Solomon's time neither tabernacle, nor holy vessels, nor brazen altar of Moses had any existence ... there was no tabernacle in the time of the last judges and first kings, as little was it in existence during the whole of the previous period.[17]

Therefore, the priestly code (RQ) must have been composed after Deuteronomy in post-exilic times, taking the centralization of the cult for granted.

To summarize, Wellhausen argues that the early Jehovist Israelite religion is "fresh and natural"; it does not know of the centralization of the cult in one place, nor of the exclusive control of the cult by priests. The Jehovist texts are the earliest part of the Pentateuch. The Josianic reform demanded the centralization of the cult and led to the formation of the book of Deuteronomy. The priestly code—mainly Leviticus—was composed at the time of Ezra (fifth century BCE) or later. Wellhausen's arguments are well-documented by biblical quotations. One might therefore say, "you are right."

Wellhausen's method is exegetical. He accepts the historicity of the lives of the patriarchs, of the exodus, of the Sinai revelation, conquest, and history as described in the EP, but reinterprets many passages. His conclusions rest on two premises:

1. Deuteronomy could not have been written before the time of Josiah;
2. The existence of a group of redactors, working at the time of Josiah and later during the exilic and post-exilic periods, who felt free to edit old documents and to ascribe their writings to Mosaic times.

Critique

There is no independent evidence indicating that Deuteronomy was composed during the Josianic period. This theory relies entirely on exegesis, which is always open to revision.[18] Segal points out that Deuteronomy does

---

17. Ibid., 37, 39, 44.
18. Different interpretations are summarized by Craigie, *Book of Deuteronomy*, and Merrill, "Deuteronomy and de Wette," p. 20n9.

not refer to any of topics relevant to the time of Josiah.[19] It does not mention Manasseh, the *bamoth*, any of the sanctuaries, or the divided kingdom.

> On the other hand the author does not tire in his constant descriptions of his hearers as being about to cross the Jordan into Canaan, and of the task facing them in the conquest of promised land and the establishment therein of an obedient and pious and God-fearing society. It is incredible that an author in the age of Josiah or in any other post-Mosaic age would so persistently shut his eyes to his own age and his own generation and identify himself so completely with the remote age of Israel in the land of Moab. What sense was there in an age like Josiah's in the insistent command to destroy utterly the Canaanites and Amalekites (7.2, 16, 24; 20.16–17; 25.19), peoples who had long disappeared; or in the command not to appoint a foreigner as king of Israel (17.15) in a time when the Davidic dynasty had occupied the throne for more than four centuries? . . . These commands and many others like them in our book could only have a meaning to the young contemporaries of Moses prior to their crossing the Jordan, but no meaning whatever to the Israel of the age of Josiah or of any other post-Mosaic age to which critics assign the composition of our book.[20]

In a detailed analysis, Segal demonstrates that Deuteronomy is aware of the content of the Tetrateuch. It applies the old legislation to the new conditions to be expected after crossing the Jordan, but does not introduce contradictory legislation. "In its all-important doctrinal aspects Deuteronomy is the direct logical sequence of the four preceding books."[21] Segal demonstrates:

> The Sinaitic law permits a plurality of sanctuaries duly consecrated by the divine presence, such as existed in patriarchal times . . . The singular number in the expression "the place" in Deuteronomy denotes a single class to which the law applies and not one exclusively single locality . . . The singular denotes not single individuals but single classes of individuals. Therefore the singular "the place" in Deuteronomy does not exclude a plurality of sanctuaries.[22]

Deuteronomy will be discussed in detail below, chapter 6.[23]

19. Segal, "Book of Deuteronomy."
20. Ibid., 317.
21. Ibid., 321.
22. Ibid., 330.
23. Segal's work was virtually ignored by Biblical scholars. Otherwise this book would be redundant.

I: The Problem

Wellhausen's analysis of the Bible rests on his theological assumptions:

> In my early student days I was attracted by the stories of Saul and David, Ahab and Elijah; the discourses of Amos and Isaiah laid strong hold on me, and I read myself well into the prophetic and historical books of the Old Testament ... [but] ... I had no thorough acquaintance with the Law, of which I was accustomed to be told that it was the basis and postulate of the whole literature. At last I took courage and made my way through Exodus, Leviticus, Numbers ... But it was in vain that I looked for the light which was to be shed from this source on the historical and prophetical books. On the contrary, my enjoyment of the latter was marred by the law ... I found it impossible to give a candid decision in favour of the priority of the Law. Dimly I began to perceive that throughout there was between them all the difference that separates two wholly distinct worlds.[24]

Sweeney points out that "Wellhausen ... argued that the Mosaic Torah ... was in fact composed largely in relatively late times by priestly figures who projected a ritualistic and spiritually stagnant form of religion."[25] Wellhausen misunderstood Leviticus. The sacrificial ritual is not a Mosaic invention. It transformed existing Israelite rituals. P was not written to evoke religious inspiration, but to ensure that the ritual is non-pagan. Wellhausen represents the Christian (Pauline) interpretation of Judaism: a spiritually stagnant form of religion, dominated by ritual. The theological bias of Wellhausen is clearly expressed in the conclusion of his article "Israel" in the Encyclopedia Britannica.[26] After quoting Spinoza's opinion that the Jews maintained themselves because of the hatred they incurred by separating themselves from others, he concludes his article as follows:

> The consistency of the race may of course prove a harder thing to overcome than Spinoza has supposed; but nevertheless he will be found to have spoken truly in declaring that the so-called emancipation of the Jews must inevitably lead to the extinction of Judaism ... *For the accomplishment of this* centuries may be required [my emphasis].[27]

---

24 Wellhausen, *Prolegomena*, 3.
25. Sweeney, "Latter Prophets," 71.
26. Wellhausen, *Prolegomena*, 427–548.
27. Ibid., 548.

The Wellhausen Fallacy

It follows from Wellhausen's basic premise that the final text of any passage, book, or group of books in the Bible is the result of redactions, based on selective choices of previous sources, and reflects the times and ideology of the editor. However, there is no evidence—biblical or external—for the existence of redactors/editors who felt free to add new texts to old manuscripts. The Dead Sea Scrolls (DSS) show conclusively that the text of the Pentateuch was not codified by the second century BCE. However, changes made by copyists were either linguistic or editorial comments, quotations from other passages. For example, the Decalogue appears twice in the Pentateuch, in Exodus 20:2–17 and in Deuteronomy 5:6–21. The fourth commandment, "Remember the Sabbath Day" (Exod 20:8), explains the Sabbath law as follows:

> For in six days YHWH made heaven and earth, the sea, and all that is in them, but rested seventh day; therefore YHWH blessed the sabbath day and consecrated it. (Exod 20:11)

The Deuteronomy version gives the following explanation:

> Remember that you were a slave in the land of Egypt, and YHWH your God brought you out from there with a mighty hand and an outstretched arm; therefore YHWH your God commanded you to keep [guard] the sabbath day. (Deut 5:15)

Deuteronomy does not mention the six-day creation. The Decalogue text of the Dead Sea Scroll 4QDeutn adds after Deuteronomy 5:15: "In six days YHWH made heaven and earth." This is a quote from Exodus 20:11, an editorial comment; a modern editor would give it as a footnote. It does not add new material to the Pentateuch. There are numerous instances of such insertions. Some merely clarify the text, others are ideological statements. The important point is that these interpolations do not add new external material to the Pentateuch.[28] All additions are quotes taken from the Pentateuch. There are no quotes taken from the rest of the Bible, the Mishnah, the Apocrypha, or other writings of the Pan Hellenistic area.

When the Babylonian exiles decided to follow the Torah, they found that the Torah was out of date. To make it applicable to their time, they were

---

28. There are a few exceptions; e.g., 4Q365 adds a passage describing the crying of Rebecca—her fear for Jacob, added to Gen 28:6. Gen 30:26 adds "fourteen years" when referring to the time Jacob worked for Laban. 4Q365 shows a fragment of the song of Miriam, added before Exod 15:22. These are elaborations, probably based on older sources. They do not add new ideas and use a vocabulary related to the text.

I: The Problem

forced to rely on oral traditions and interpretations of the text. This oral Torah was considered to be "Law from Sinai." However, the Pentateuch states, "You must observe [guard] everything that I command you; do not add to it or take from it" (Deut 13:1; 12:32; my translation). Rabbinical decisions were orally transmitted from teacher (rabbi) to student.[29] The librarians of the Qumran caves would have been aware of the teachings of the Pharisees, including the injunction against committing the oral Torah to writing. Therefore, we do not find any Mishnah quotations in the Qumran library or in any biblical manuscript.

Significant changes in religious thinking took place during the time of the Second Temple. The belief in reward and punishment in the afterlife became a part of Judaism during the Second Temple period. The Sadducees rejected it; the Pharisees made it a cornerstone of Jewish doctrine. Since the book of Daniel, eschatology has been important in Judaism. So is the folklore about angels (influenced by Persian theology). The book of Enoch includes mystical visions. Literary activity was prolific: Ben Sirach, the Apocrypha, and the books of the Dead Sea sects. Any redactor of biblical writings from the Persian period on would have been aware of these developments. None of these new ideas appear in the Pentateuch—there are no references to resurrection and rewards in the world to come (עולם הבא) in a speech by Moses, in any of the legal codes, or in the stories about the Patriarchs. The *Aggadah* (non-legalistic exegetical texts), however, is full of such references. The Qumran library contains copies of a vast extra-biblical literature. Some of it refers to biblical times; e.g., the book of Enoch. Others are specific to the practices of the Qumran sect. No DSS Pentateuch insertion shows additions reflecting the ideas of the Dead Sea community. The injunction against writing down the oral Torah proves that there existed a written Torah. Contemporary biblical scholarship wrongly assumes that, during the Persian-Hellenistic periods, every scribe did what was right in his eyes (only modern scholars can do this).

Lemche suggests that "The society reflected by the biblical historiographers is not a society of the past, but the Jewish society of the writers' own time transported into earlier times."[30] If so, we should expect these ideas to appear in the Pentateuch. I suggest that the absence of references to resur-

---

29. About 200 CE, Rabbi Judah the Prince decided that this oral Torah must be committed in writing. It is called the Mishnah and is discussed in the Gemara and together comprise the Talmud.

30. Lemche, "Good and Bad," 131–32.

rection in the Pentateuch and the EP demonstrates that the editors working during the time of the Second Temple did not feel free to insert their own opinions into texts they considered to be sacred.

Von Rad calls the specific laws of Deuteronomy "*Sondergut*," meaning "of special value."[31] He argues that these laws reflect the conditions of life after the Israelite settlement in Canaan suitable for an agricultural society. In the desert there was no need for laws regulating loans; there were no non-Israelite slaves, rebellious fortified cities, kings or prophets. Therefore, Deuteronomy could not have been written before the time of the monarchy.[32] But the author of Deuteronomy (I'll call him "Moses" for the sake of brevity) explicitly legislated for the future. He considered hypothetical events. His list of contingencies does not reflect the actual historical conditions of the post-Mosaic period. Moses knew about agricultural societies, ruled by kings and maintaining prophets. Thus his *Sondergut* is relevant for an agricultural society. But not all his hypothetical contingencies actually happened. There were no rebellious cities or prophets. True, he makes one correct prediction: if you don't succeed with the planned genocide, you will intermarry with the Canaanites and accept their customs. Yet he omitted legislating for another critical contingency: he did not foresee the divided kingdom. If the Deuteronomistic legislation had been written during or after the divided kingdom, it surely would have provided some rules of how to cope with such a situation.[33]

There is a basic flaw in Wellhausen's approach, a flaw which prevents the development of a coherent theory: once it is accepted that the final text of the Pentateuch is the result of later editing, the field for theoretical speculation is wide open. There are always alternative logical interpretations of the text.[34] Wellhausen suggests that the JE predates Deuteronomy. Van Seters maintains that Deuteronomy predates the JE. Some theorists

---

31. Rad, *Das fünfte Buch Mose*, 9–10.

32. Similar arguments have been advanced concerning the dating of Leviticus. The sacrificial ritual described is supposed to reflect practices of the Second Temple ritual. Some of these assertions have been clearly refuted. For example, it has been argued that the anointing of the high priest is a post-exilic custom. Meanwhile, it was shown that such anointing, as well as other Levitical rituals, was known in the ancient Middle East even before the time of the exodus. On the other hand, Kaufmann shows that the biblical provisions for the Levites do not fit the conditions of Judah during the Persian epoch.

33. See chapter 6 of this book, "Deuteronomy."

34. See Excursus on creative writing in chapter 3 of this book, "The Origin of Israel: Archaeological Interpretations," pp. 56–59.

I: The Problem

found two "Deuteronomists," others found three. Correspondingly, some scholars identify several different sources in Leviticus. The possibilities are endless. Each one is "right" according to its own reasoning. They all assume hypothetical later redactors; therefore anything goes. This has been recognized by a number of scholars.[35] "It is all the more disconcerting to observe that uncertainties and disputes at very fundamental points are prevalent in current Pentateuchal studies. Not long ago it seemed that real clarity had been achieved, but the state of affairs has now turned."[36] These controversies—and animosities—have escalated in the last thirty years. The dominant theories are all based on the premise that the ideas expressed in the Pentateuch could not have existed as early as the Bible claims. Therefore, the text must be late, reflecting the thinking of the Assyrian, Persian, Hellenistic periods. "The first problem with the documentary hypothesis concerns the lack of empirical evidence. There is no biblical text discovered in any manuscript that preserves the kind of distinctions that appear in the sources proposed in this theory."[37] Theories are well-argued and documented by biblical quotations, but ultimately they rest upon unproven assumptions and can only be maintained by ignoring other biblical passages (or ascribing them to later editors).

> Setting aside the biblical text has done little to resolve the crisis in biblical scholarship... It has merely freed scholars from the constraints of the biblical story line[sic] to write monographs and textbooks that tell stories of their own construction.[38]
>
> Among those writing most prolifically about the Pentateuch today there is thus no consensus. "Every man does what is right in his own eyes."[39]

A good example is Garbini.[40] Garbini posits a late (second century BCE) author within a priestly milieu who, imitating the Hellenistic genre

---

35. For a summary and discussion of the documentary hypothesis see the excellent reviews by Wenham, "Pondering"; Long, "Historiography"; Knight, "Pentateuch"; Auld, "Former Prophets," 58–63; Hess, *Israelite Religions*. They report a profusion of theories with little consensus. The documentary hypothesis is rejected in toto by Cassuto, *Documentary Hypothesis*.
36. Knight, "Pentateuch," 264.
37. Hess, *Israelite Religions*, 49.
38. Long, "Historiography," 160.
39. Wenham "Pondering," 119.
40. Garbini, *Myth and History*.

of historiography, was responsible for altering the texts at his disposal to create a grand narrative cast within a distinctive ideological frame. A postexilic hierocratic group in Jerusalem projected a set of mythical origins for Israel. Hoffmeier comments on Garbini:

> It defies logic to believe that Joshua and Judges originated in the very period when the Qumran scribes were already copying the same documents because they were deemed to be canonical. And it must be recalled that the Septuagint was already translated a century before the Hasmonean period. It seems, rather, that Garbini's observations reflect his own ideology, not an accurate portrayal of Hebrew historiographic ideology.[41]

Such assumptions are not always clearly spelled out; e.g., "The Yahwistic version of the tradition dates to the exilic period. The priestly version . . . must be later and post-exilic in date."[42] These are two assumptions, based on the interpretation of the written text. There can be no independent proof of the dating of either the priestly or of the Yahwistic tradition.

> It is ironic, is it not, that the soundest historical critical scholar, who will find talk of themes and structures "subjective" in the extreme, will have no hesitation in expounding the significance of a (sometimes conjectural) document, from a conjectural period for a hypothetical audience of which he has, even if he has defined he period correctly, only the most meager knowledge, without any control over the all-important questions of how representative of and how acceptable to the community the given document was.[43]

> Not the least embarrassment for historical scholarship is the lack of agreement, after so long an investigation, on the basic thematic thrust of the supposed Deuteronomistic editing.[44]

Whybray, commenting on Noth, concludes that "Much of Noth's detailed reconstruction of the Pentateuchal traditions was obtained by *piling one speculation upon another* . . . an undue propensity to pile hypothesis upon hypothesis and so to construct a whole 'tradition-history' out of the flimsiest of 'clues.'"[45]

---

41. Hoffmeier, *Israel in Egypt*, 12.
42. Van Seters, *Yahwist*, 310.
43. Clines, *Theme*, 14; quoted in Wenham, "Pondering," 140.
44. Polzin, *Moses*, 15.
45. Whybray, *Making of the Pentateuch*, 194, 196; quoted in Wenham, "Pondering," 131.

I: The Problem

In spite of such criticism, the Wellhausen fallacy has not been abandoned. Van Seters asserts, "The Yahwist history was a product of the exilic period ... The challenge of the larger world of the Diaspora ... called for a transformation from a national religion of the land of Israel to a world religion in which the chosen people of the Promised Land continued to have a destiny beyond the crisis of the state's demise."[46] Newer textbooks also accept the Wellhausen fallacy. Gottwald's textbook concludes that "It is likely that the bulk of DH was composed as a propaganda work for Josiah's reformation."[47] Collins, in his *Introduction to the Hebrew Bible*, asserts the following:

> The parallels with the Assyrian vassal treaties constitute a powerful argument that the book of Deuteronomy was not formulated in the time of Moses but in the seventh century BCE... One of the great turning points in the history of the religion of Israel was the Deuteronomic reform of king Josiah in 621 BCE, which forbade sacrifice outside the one place that the Lord has chosen (Jerusalem).[48]

Contemporary scholars, attempting to boost Wellhausen's theories, rely on extrabiblical epigraphic or archeological evidence. These scholars argue that external evidence proves that the biblical narratives of the exodus, the sojourn in the desert, and the conquest of Canaan under Joshua are historical fiction—there was no conquest under Joshua. These theories are discussed in the next chapter.

---

46. Van Seters, *Prologue to History*, 332.
47. Gottwald, *Hebrew Bible*, 300.
48. Collins, *Introduction*, 162, 164.

3

The Origin of Israel
Archaeological Interpretations

CONTEMPORARY BIBLICAL SCHOLARS GO beyond exegesis; they also invoke non-biblical, archaeological evidence, purporting to show that Deuteronomy could not have been written during the time of Moses. Some go far beyond Wellhausen by denying the historicity of the exodus and Joshua. Their main arguments are as follows:

a. Writing skills were not available to a group of nomadic desert dwellers.

b. The Deuteronomy description of the covenant, especially of the curses for breaking it, copies the language of Assyrian treaties.

c. The account of the conquest in Joshua is fictitious. Archaeological surveys of the central hill country in Canaan prove that the increase of population in the area was the result of a gradual peaceful infiltration, and that there was no invasion by a large ethnic group. According to this view, archaeological evidence shows that Israel as a nation only developed in the tenth century BCE or later.

d. There is no independent evidence for the exodus of a large nomadic population, as described in the Pentateuch.

This led to the conclusion that most of the biblical historical reports are fiction:

I: The Problem

> Biblical Israel [is] mainly a literary, ideological construct, dating to post-exilic times.[1]

> The development of the tradition reflects the historically significant formative process by which "Israel," through its use of tradition, was created out of the political and historical disasters of the Assyrian and neo-Babylonian periods. The formation of biblical narrative—this ideologically motivated, originating process that makes Israel—begins at the earliest during the course of Assyria's domination of Palestine. At the latest, the Israel we know from the tradition comes to be during the pre-Hellenistic postexilic period.[2]

The following section will challenge these assumptions.

Literacy Was Well-Developed in the Middle East at the Time of the Exodus

Recent archaeological findings revealed a rich literary culture in many centers in Syria and Anatolia. Extensive archives in Alakh, Ebla, Emar, Hamath, and Ugarith give evidence of intense literary activity.[3]

> Epigraphic material from Syro-Mesopotamia, although not always having a direct bearing on the Bible, continues to give evidence of a massive literary tradition in the ancient Near Eastern world to which the Israelite writers belonged.[4]

These inscriptions have been preserved on clay tablets. In addition to annals, they include descriptions of rituals, of prophetic announcements, of stories and myths. Parchment scrolls were also known. A nomadic population which maintained a dismountable tabernacle and a complicated sacrificial cult must have used parchment (except, perhaps, one set of stone tablets).

There is now clear epigraphic evidence of literacy in Judah-Israel during the time of the monarchy. An alphabetic script was known and used in commerce and royal administration. The *mazkir* (recorder, secretary) and the *sofer* (scribe) were important officials. Avishur and Heltzer published

---

1. Finkelstein, "Rise of Early Israel," 7.
2. Thompson, "Text, Context," 66–67.
3. Chavalas and Hostetter, "Epigraphic Light"; Also Pitard, "Before Israel."
4. Chavalas and Hostettler, "Epigraphic Light," 44.

and reviewed epigraphic sources of ancient Israel.[5] These are relatively short messages, written on small *ostraca* or *bullae*. Many seals show the names of royal officials. There is evidence for the maintenance of royal archives in Israel. Sixty-three ostraca were found in the Western part of the acropolis of Samaria—a large building from the time of Ahab.[6] These were records of oil and wine deliveries. The petition by a worker for the return of a cloak which had been impounded was probably written by a scribe, not by the applicant himself[7] which indicates that there existed a substantial number of officials, merchants, scribes who were familiar with alphabetic script.

> This forces us to reject categorically the insistments that in the tenth century B.C. there was in the Land of Israel only a primitive chiefdom.[8]

These writings come from the monarchic period. There would be law codices and genealogical records. The book of the deeds of the days of the kings of Israel/Judah" (e.g. 1 Kgs 14:19; 29, translated as "the Chronicles") covered the entire monarchic period. It is improbable that such widespread use of written documents appeared suddenly; it points to the existence of an older literary tradition. It is unlikely that such a society lacked historical records. These documents would have been written on parchment. The EP and Pentateuch quote "the book of (the) Jashar" (Josh 10:13; 2 Sam 1:18) and "the book of the wars of YHWH" (Num 21:14). These refer to collections of songs and stories.

The Israelites had been settled in Egypt for a long time. Though subjected to corvée (to forced labor owed to an overlord), they were never a bunch of unorganized slaves. In the desert they organized a complicated sacrificial cult, with a dismountable tabernacle. Their priests would have been literate. There is nothing implausible about the following statement: "And Moses wrote down all the words of YHWH . . . then he took the book of the covenant, and read [קרא, called out, my translation] it in the hearing of the people" (Exod 24:4, 7). Niditch stated:

> Our position throughout this study is not that ancient Israelites knew little of writing, but rather that Israelite literacy . . . has to be understood in the context of an oral-traditional culture . . .

---

5. Avishur and Heltzer, *Studies*.
6. Mazar, *Archaeology*, 418; 518–29. .
7. See p. 165.
8. Avishur and Heltzer, *Studies*, 10.

I: The Problem

The oral and the literate interact throughout Israel's literary history, as is true also of the ancient Near Eastern cultures of Mesopotamia and Egypt.[9]

The Bible was not written in order to be "read"; it was designed to be declaimed, "called out" (קרא). People did not go to libraries to borrow a book. Whether it was an official document, "called out" by a scribe, or an admonition called by a prophet, or a story told at the gates of the city—the cultural tradition was transmitted orally. The author who wrote the saga of Joseph did not write for a reading public. He would have imagined the audience to whom the story will be told. Moses did not have a ready script for his oration: "Hear Israel" (Deut 6:4–9).[10] Once a speech/story was committed to writing, it was venerated.

> Writing is respected ... validating religious practice and belief ... [this] points to an attitude toward writing that regards it on some level as extraordinary and sacred.[11]

Conclusion: There is evidence for a massive literary tradition in the ancient Near Eastern world to which the Israelite writers belonged. Even at the time of the sojourn in Egypt Israel was an organized society. During the sojourn in the desert they developed an elaborate sacrificial ritual and it is reasonable to assume that Moses and the priests/Levites were literate. Living in the desert they wrote on parchment, which was widely used at that time. While there is no archaeological evidence demonstrating that the basic events described in the Pentateuch and EP actually occurred, these reports are credible in view of our knowledge about the civilizations of the Ancient Middle East, taking into account the archaeological and epigraphic evidence from the first and second millennium BCE.

> It is therefore likely that the chronicles utilized by Dtr, the Deuteronomistic historian, were based on information similar to what was available to Mesopotamian chroniclers and to those composing historical types of inscriptions in Northwest Semitic dialects ... There is no *a priori*, or for that matter *a posteriori*, reason to suspect him of fabricating sources or details to bolster his historiosophic hypothesis.[12]

---

9. Niditch, *Oral World*, 99, 134.
10. In order to savor the Bible, it should not be read in silence, but declaimed.
11. Ibid., 107.
12. Zevit, *Religions*, 445.

The Deuteronomy Description of the Covenant Displays the Style of Hittite Treaties

The language of Assyrian vassal treaties shows many striking similarities with the language of Deuteronomy. For example, in the loyalty oaths of Esarhaddon, quoted by Römer, we find,

> You shall love Assurbanipal ... king of Assyria, your lord, as yourself.
>
> You shall hearken to whatever he says and do whatever he commands, and you shall not seek any other king or other lord against him. This treaty ... you shall speak to your sons and grandsons, your seed and your seed's seed which shall be born in the future.[13]

The parallels with Deuteronomy 6:4–7 are obvious. Similarly,

> If you hear any evil, improper, ugly word which is not seemly or good to Assurbanipal ... from the mouth of your brothers, your sons, your daughters, or from the mouth of a prophet, an ecstatic, an inquirer of oracles, or from the mouth of any human being at all, you shall not conceal it, but come and report it to Assurbanipal ... If you are able to seize them and put them to death, then you shall destroy their name and their seed from the land.[14]

The same language is used in Deuteronomy 13. Finally, the curses of Deuteronomy 28:24, 26–28 are found in the vassal treaty of Esarhaddon.[15]

On the basis of such similarities, scholars have concluded that Deuteronomy was composed in the seventh century BCE, either during the time of Hezekiah (eighth century, minority opinion) or during the time of Josiah (the prevalent assumption).[16] The authors of Deuteronomy had access to copies of Assyrian treaties (for example, a copy of the treaty between Assyria and Judah under Manasseh). The report of the finding of the Torah of Moses was a "pious lie," based on similar stories from other countries: "The Neo-Assyrian period (more specifically the seventh century BCE) should be regarded as the starting point for the Deuteronomistic literary production."[17] Kitchen demonstrated that the form of

---

13. Parpola and Watanabe, *Neo-Assyrian Treaties*, quoted by Römer, *So-Called*, 75.
14. Ibid., 76.
15. Ibid., 77.
16. The reforms of Hezekiah and Josiah are discussed further on [x-ref].
17. Römer, *So-Called*, 43.

I: The Problem

the Pentateuch covenants (Exodus/Leviticus as well as Deuteronomy) follows the style of Hittite vassal treaties (1400–1200 BCE) in the Near East.[18] The elements of these treaties are as follows: the treaty starts with the title (generally the name of the suzerain king), followed by a historical introduction. Then follow the main stipulations of the treaty (including the injunction against serving another overlord). Then comes the report of the deposition of the treaty (generally in the temple), of public reading, of the naming of witnesses, and finally a list of blessings and curses. This framework is also found in the Pentateuch descriptions of the covenant. It opens with a title, which is followed by a historical prologue: "Then God spoke all these words: I am YHWH your God, who brought you out of the land of Egypt, out of the house of slavery" (Exod 20:1–2); "These are the words that Moses spoke to all Israel ... to expound this law as follows" (Deut 1:1, 5). Then follow the basic stipulations of the covenant—e.g., the Decalogue (Exod 20:1–17; Deut 5:6–21, as well as the law codices). This is followed by a report on depositing the document in the Ark, by the official reading (calling out aloud) of the treaty's provision and by the naming of witnesses, blessings, and curses.

Assyrian treaties, on the other hand, only include the title, witnesses, stipulations, and curses. There is no historical prologue, no public reading of the treaty stipulations, and there are no blessings. This poses no problem for Römer:

> Since treaties occur already under the Hittite emperors (second half of the second millennium BCE), some scholars have used this analogy to claim a second-millennium date for Deuteronomy. This apologetic view is impossible: there is no social location during the second part of the second millennium BCE for editing such a document in Judah or Israel (which do not even exist at the time).[19]

Römer is clearly aware of the Hittite treaties. His basic, unproven assumption is that Judah or Israel did not even exist at this time. This premise permits him to ignore the evidence. Römer does not cite the work of Kitchen, who is a noted Egyptologist and documents his statements by citing his sources.[20]

The Deuteronomy list of curses is comprehensive. No other Middle Eastern treaty lists all of them. Let us assume for a moment that the

---

18. Kitchen, *Reliability*, 283-294.
19. Römer, *So-Called*, 74-75.
20. Kitchen, *Reliability*, 562n104.

Deuteronomy treaty was composed during the reign of Josiah. How was this done? It must have been composed by an extraordinarily gifted author (or authors) who knew Assyrian treaties (presumably a copy of the treaty between Esarhaddon and Manasseh).[21] They copied the seven curses from that treaty, assuming that these curses were standard formulas; then added eighteen more curses which appear in Hittite documents. It would be an extraordinary coincidence if all these old curses were independently invented by those presumed authors. Do we claim that there existed copies of treaties of defunct Hittite civilizations in the royal archives in Jerusalem? This would enable the scribes to copy the fashionable style of the middle and late twelfth century BCE, write historical introductions, describe the ritual of deposing the book in the ark, and also invent some blessings. Such a scenario is, of course, absurd. It is more plausible to assume that the Deuteronomy covenant was established during the sojourn of the desert and that it stresses the solemnity of the occasion by citing all the curses known at that time. The very fact that the covenant versions of the Pentateuch adopt the style of the Hittite treaties and do not use the style of Assyrian treaties proves that they were not written in the seventh century BCE, but during the late second millennium BCE. Of course, this does not imply that the Assyrians copied their treaties from Deuteronomy. Both used a generally known style.

The Account of the Conquest in Joshua is Compatible with Archaeological Findings

Archaeological Surveys

Comprehensive surface surveys were carried out in the highlands of Canaan, as well as in the Transjordanian plateau and in Galilee.[22] They show a cyclical rise and fall of population in Canaan and Transjordan, from the Chalcolithic period until the Second Iron Age. Between the LB (Late Bronze) and the IA I (First Iron Age, about 1250–1000 BCE), there was a substantial increase of population in the Highlands of Canaan. Finkelstein reports twenty-nine sites with forty-seven hectares of built-up area in the LB (1500–1200 BCE), increasing to 254 sites with 219 hectares of built up

---

21. Cogan, *Racing Torrent*, 136.

22. Finkelstein, "Southern Samarian Hills," *NEAEHL* 1313–14; Zertal, "Mount Manasseh," *NEAEHL* 1311–12.

area during IA I (ca. 1200–1000 BCE).[23] The Ephraim-Samaria Survey registered nine sites for LB I–II, increasing to 131 sites in IA I. Similarly, the Manasseh Survey registered thirty-nine sites for the LB, increasing to over two hundred in IA I. It should be noted that these settlements were not large villages or walled cities. They are hamlets or family homesteads, at most small villages inhabited by a few families. Most settlements were new, occupying sites which had not been inhabited previously. In contrast, new settlements in the Lowlands of Canaan reoccupied previously abandoned sites. This dramatic increase of the population is undisputed.

Dever summarizes the survey data, concluding the following:

> In the heartland of ancient Israel about 300 small agricultural villages were founded *de novo* in the late 13th–12th centuries... None are found on the ruins of a destroyed Late Bronze Age site... Population estimates, based on well-developed ethnographic parallels and site size, indicate a central hill-country population of only about 12 thousand at the end of the Late Bronze Age (13th century), which then grew rapidly to about 55 thousand by the 12th century, then to about 75 thousand by the 11th century. *Such a dramatic "population explosion" simply cannot be accounted for by natural increase alone, much less by positing small groups of pastoral nomads settling down. Large numbers of people migrated here from somewhere else* [my emphasis].[24]

Who were these people and where did they come from? The biblical narrative describes a military invasion by an organized army, the so-called "conquest model." Alternatively, "infiltration" theories try to account for the increase of the highland population by referring to social economic conditions. As Finkelstein states,

> The rise of Early Israel was not a unique event in the history of Palestine. Rather, it was one phase in long-term cyclic socio-economic and demographic processes that started in the 4th millennium BCE. The wave of settlement that took place in the highlands in the late second millennium BCE was no more than a chapter in alternating shifts along the typical Near Eastern socio-economic continuum, between sedentary and pastoral modes of subsistence.[25]

---

23. Finkelstein, "Rise," 20–24.
24. Dever, *Biblical Writers*, 110.
25. Finkelstein, "Rise," 8.

Finkelstein neglects to consider the difference between the small size of the population shifts in the earlier periods and the large population increase in the thirteenth/twelfth century BCE.

According to various peaceful infiltration models, the population growth in the highlands of Canaan between the Late Bronze Age and Iron Age I was a slow process of migration, either from inside Canaan itself or through the immigration of pastoral groups from Transjordan. These theories differ in the description of the population settling in the highlands. Most assume that it included a small group of runaway slaves from Egypt. The major theories about the origin of the highland population are reviewed by Finkelstein, Klingbeil, Faust, Kitchen, Younger, Mazani, and Ray.[26] Most theories are based on the assumption that there was no invasion of Israelites under the leadership of Joshua. Faust, after reviewing various theories about the origins of the highland population, concluded that the military conquest theory

> is not supported by evidence and consequently by practically no archaeologist or historian (see, e.g., Weinstein 1997: 87–88). There is no need therefore to discuss it here . . . Today, the main debate can be divided into two questions: (1) whether the first Israelites were semi-nomads or a sedentary group, and (2) whether they came from outside Cisjordan or not . . . those who claim that they were semi-nomads are divided into those who believe they came from the outside or were local.[27]

Surface surveys found the following: (1) Total absence of pig bones in these settlements. Pig bones are found in the Middle Bronze age and in the coastal (Philistine) areas.[28] (2) The prevalence of the four-room house. The main area of these rectangular houses consists of a central hall, with two rows of columns separating the side areas (which then may be subdivided into smaller rooms). At the narrow end, one room is separated, probably

---

26. For a discussion of these models see Finkelstein, "Rise"; Klingbeil, "Between North and South"; Faust, *Israel's Ethnogenesis*, 170-87; Kitchen, *Reliability*, 225-28; Younger, "Early Israel"; Mazani, "Appearance"; Ray, "Classical Models."

27. Faust, *Israel's Ethnogenesis*, 176. Faust ignores the work of Kitchen, Hoffmeier, Hess, and Hasel, who certainly are respected scholars. The papers published in Hess, *Critical Issues*, show a different picture. Faust may not accept the conclusions of the supporters of the conquest theory, but he should have reviewed it, as he has reviewed other theories which he rejected.

28. Finkelstein, "Rise," 19-20; Faust, *Israel's Ethnogenesis*, 35-40.

I: The Problem

for storage. Illustrations of these houses are found in many publications.[29] (3) The pottery is simple, with little or no decoration. The prevalent type is the collared rim jar.[30] (4) The introduction of new techniques, viz. hillside terracing and plastered cistern cut in to rocks.[31]

The interpretation of these data is vigorously disputed.[32] The controversy is about the identification of these new inhabitants: who were they and where did they come from? There are no unequivocal signs identifying the ethnic background of this population. Finkelstein claims that "Pottery and architectural forms in Iron I sites on both sides of the Jordan reflect environmental, social and economic traits of the settlers. They tell us nothing about ethnicity."[33] It is generally agreed that these settlers are the direct ancestors of the population of the later kingdoms of Judah and Israel. The controversy is about their ethnic identity. Did they constitute an "ethnos"; meaning, could they be described as a population who shared a distinctive culture and identity? Archaeological data do not answer these questions. The conquest model gives a clear answer: these are the Israelites settling in the land of Canaan. The prevalent opinion of dominant biblical scholarship, assuming that there was no invasion of Canaan under Joshua, proposes that this population was a heterogeneous mixture of various nomadic or semi-nomadic groups, not different from the rest of the Bronze Age population in Canaan and Transjordan; their ethnic identity as "Israel" only developed during the political struggles which led to the establishment of the monarchy or even later. For example, Finkelstein asserts the following:

> Therefore, the genuinely exceptional event in the highlands of Palestine in the late-second–early-first millennium BCE was not the "Israelite Settlement," but the emergence of territorial states in

29. See Faust, *Israel's Ethnogenesis*, 71–84; Dever, *Recent Archaeological*, 109–12.
30. Ibid., 49–70; 191–220.
31. Dever, *Biblical Writers*, 112–13.
32. The Bible reports that the Israelites first settled in a part of Transjordan and invaded Canaan, crossing the Jordan River from the plains of Moab. Archeological surveys do show a sudden increase of the population in Transjordan. Zertal ("Mount Manasseh") surveyed the area of Manasseh and interpreted his data as showing a population movement from east to west. However, his interpretation was challenged by Dever, who called Zertal a "secular fundamentalist whose ideas are 'dangerous.'" Hawkins ("Survey of Manasseh," 176–77) reviews the controversy and wonders if the conclusions are dangerous because they support the biblical account. This quarrelsome disputation demonstrates that archaeological data are open to different interpretation; it also shows that scholars lose their calm discussing them.
33. Finkelstein, "Rise," 18.

the 9–8th centuries BCE ... The depiction of the Israelite Settlement as a singular event in the annals of the country turned up centuries after the Iron Age I. It was shaped by the history of the Judean state in late-Iron II, by its destruction and by the history of Judah in post-exilic times. The Biblical description of the rise of Early Israel was cast by the Deuteronomistic historians, to serve their ideology.[34]

This statement ends Finkelstein's presentation on the rise of early Israel. It is presented as a valid conclusion. However, the only evidence cited merely shows that there were settlement oscillations during the Bronze Age, culminating in a remarkable increase of population in the twelfth century BCE. His interpretation of these data is based on the assumption that this increase cannot indicate a military invasion.

Both Dever and Faust view the early hillside settlers as an ethnically distinguishable group. Dever concludes that

> The overall "assemblage" [of archaeological data] is sufficiently homogenous and distinctive to warrant *some* label ... We could of course call them "the early Iron Age hill-country settlers." Then there is Thompson's term, "the Iron Age population of Syria's marginal southern fringe" (evidently the very term "Israel" is an embarrassment to him). But even minimalist designations presume a chronological, cultural-evolutionary, and functionalist distinction; and these too are "ethnic markers" ... I have suggested that we go further, adopting the term "Proto-Israelite" to designate this 12th–11th century complex.[35]

Faust reviewed archaeological data from the highlands, from Late Bronze to Iron Age II,[36] of central Canaan and the Galilee. His conclusions are:

a. *Pottery*: Local pottery in the Israeli highlands was not decorated. This is not due to a low standard of living during the Iron I period—it continued during the eighth century. Imported pottery was rare in Israelite settlements, even in places which show non-ceramic trade, while in nearby Canaanite places imported pottery was abundant. Furthermore, there is a limited repertoire of pottery forms in Israelite settlements. The avoidance of decorated pottery and its simplicity "must

---

34. Ibid., 34.
35. Dever, *Biblical Writers*, 118.
36. I.e., including the kingdoms of Judah and Israel until 586 BCE.

I: The Problem

therefore be seen as ethnically meaningful... The limited repertoire of the Iron I pottery reflects an ethos of simplicity and egalitarianism."[37]

b. *The four-room house:* A review of the archaeological records shows that the four-room house is typical for Israelite settlements. It rarely occurs in other places, and a site without this feature should not be considered Israelite. Faust points out two features of this architecture: it encourages direct communication between inhabitants of different rooms, in contrast to the typical Canaanite-Phoenician dwelling, which is hierarchical.[38] It also encourages privacy: one's room is not a passageway for others.

c. *The Israelite Egalitarian Ethos*: The following features are specific to Israelite settlements:

i) Israelite burials are simple inhumations.

> The lack of any observable burials [during Iron Age I] is a clear reflection of an egalitarian ideology, and exhibits a sharp contrast to Late Bronze Age.[39]

ii) Most Late Bronze sites had temples, although temples are absent from most Israelite sites:

> The difference is very obvious in the Iron Age II, when any site that can be safely labeled as Israelite shows no signs of an organized or public cult.[40]

iii) There are no Israelite royal inscriptions, while monumental royal inscriptions were found in Philistia, Moab, Ammon, and Aram.

> Whatever the origin of this population, an issue of heated debate, there is no doubt that as far as settlement patterns and socioeconomic structure are concerned, the discussed population was very much different from everything else in existence during the Late Bronze Age... Israelite society had a strong egalitarian/democratic ethos... It is even likely that in Israel, more than in many other similar societies, the ethos had some impact on social reality.[41]

---

37. Faust, *Israel's Ethnogenesis*, 64, 70.
38. Ibid., 79.
39. Ibid., 93.
40. Ibid., 94. The only Iron Age temple was found in Arad. Zevit (*Religions*), using a different definition, counts more temples; see later discussion of Israelite cults [x-ref].
41. Ibid., 111, 106–7.

In spite of these observations Faust concludes that the ethnogenesis of Israel was a protracted process, and that Israel's "self–identification" developed slowly, mainly through interaction with the Philistines.[42] "It is likely that the inhabitants of twelfth-century villages were not all members of a single group, but had more than one identity ... It is clear that one of the highland groups was called 'Israel.'"[43] It should be noted that this statement is not derived from his data, but from his commitment to the infiltration theory: if there was no Joshua, then the new settlers must be a collection of various groups.

The Merenptah Stela poses a problem for the peaceful infiltration theories. In this stela, Merenptah boasts about his victories in Canaan. After mentioning several places which were destroyed, he refers to "Israel," which is described as a "population," not as a place. These data have been attacked on several grounds. It was suggested that there was a scribal error; that the term "Israel" was misread, or referred to a different place. However, the original reading was confirmed by a number of leading Egyptologists and is now generally accepted. Faust and Dever suggest that "Israel" may refer to one of the small nomadic groups that settled in the highland and the inscription makes a generalization about the entire population. These arguments are well-reviewed by Hasel.[44] Hess points out that Israel is not mentioned before Merenptah; therefore,

> It is reasonable to assume that Israel formed a new group on the scene of Western Asia. This, combined with the sudden appearance in the highlands of Palestine of more than three hundred village sites at the beginning of the twelfth century, provides a positive correlation for the identification of Israel with some or most of settlements in highland Canaan, west of the Jordan River.[45]

> In the end, the theories of indigenous origin face two major challenges: (1) some do not connect the archaeological data satisfactorily with Merenptah's Israel, leaving minimalist scholars to discount, reinterpret, or relegate the stela to a literary metaphor; and (2) others stretch the archaeological data and, in doing so, do not address equally significant anthropological questions ... the Merenptah stela, over a century after its discovery, still cuts through current scholarly reconstructions and rhetoric with a

---

42. Ibid., 147–56, 167–69, 227–34.
43. Ibid., 150–51.
44. Hasel, "Merenptah's Reference," 47–59.
45. Hess, *Israelite Religions*, 18.

simple declaration: Israel exists as a socioethnic people already located in the land of Canaan by 1209 B.C.E.[46]

Mazani concludes his review of the theories about the appearance of Israel in Canaan:

> The fact that these theories continue to be modified indicates the unsettled nature of the endeavor ... Unfortunately, recent theoretical models have been rather narrow in their approach to the data. They have tended to be selective in their use of data and have failed to give a satisfactory explanation of the origin of Israel.[47]

Conclusion: Survey data alone cannot show whether the increase of the population was the result of peaceful immigration or of a military conquest. The rejection of the conquest model is based on the interpretation of the book of Joshua.

Joshua

Coogan declares firmly, "The book of Joshua is historico-theological fiction. The primary purpose of its authors was to present a theological construct."[48] Coogan does not cite any evidence for the existence of such group of authors. The book of Joshua is rejected as historical source on the following grounds:

a. Archaeological evidence contradicts the book of Joshua. Archaeological excavations did not find any evidence of a mass destruction of Canaanite cities. In fact, at the time of the supposed invasion there were no major urban centers in Canaan. The ruins of Jericho come from a previous period.

b. The narratives of the book of Judges contradict Joshua; there was no successful invasion and conquest of Canaan.

c. The style of reporting, especially of chapters 1–10, is mythological.

These arguments have been refuted by a number of scholars.[49] They are based on three kinds of errors: (1) misreading of the biblical text, (2)

---

46. Hasel, "Merenptah's Reference," 59.
47. Mazani, "Appearance," 95, 108–9.
48. Coogan, "Archaeology," 27.
49. See Kitchen, *Reliability*, 161–90; see also Younger, "Rhetorical Structuring"; Hess,

lack of understanding of the terminology and rhetoric style of the era, and (3) errors in the interpretation of archaeological data.

The Accurate Reading of Joshua

Joshua is understood to claim miraculous divine intervention, resulting in a sweeping Israelite victory, culminating in the destruction of major Canaanite cities, including the large fortresses of Jericho and of Ai. Following this, Canaan was successfully invaded, and the Canaanite population subjugated. Hess demonstrates that such interpretation of Joshua is incorrect. He suggests "to consider what it actually reports... [and] lay aside assumptions that the long tradition of interpretation, both popular and scholarly, has assigned to these sites."[50]

Accurate reading shows that the text reports that Joshua invaded Canaan from Transjordan and destroyed Jericho and Ai. These cities were burned, but their area was not occupied. After their first victory, the Israelites returned to their base in Gilgal. Joshua then defeated two coalitions of Canaanite kings in open battle. The Canaanites withdrew into their walled cities, and the Israelites did not succeed in displacing them. They settled in parts of the highlands, not in the valleys. Only three cities were destroyed: Jericho, Ai, and Hazor (Josh 6:24; 8:28; 11:11). This scenario is confirmed in Judges and compatible with the findings of archaeological surveys. The Israelite army was not very large. The book of Joshua does not give a census, but the numbers mentioned in the various reports indicate that there were only a few thousand warriors.

Jericho

The biblical text is misread because of a lack of knowledge of the terminology and reporting style of the era. Canaan did not support thirty monarchies. These kings were not the sovereigns of large cities with a stratified population, surrounded by villages paying taxes, bureaucracy, and army. They ruled small villages.[51] Hess shows that the term "king" (*m-l-k*) de-

---

"Jericho and Ai"; Wood, "Search"; Mazani, "Appearance."

50. Hess, "Jericho and Ai," 33.

51. Lemche ("Problems," 212) points out that that the Egyptians referred to the Canaanite kings as *hazanu*, i.e., "mayors."

notes a wide range of meanings.⁵² It could be an absolute ruler or a local leader recognizing the sovereignty of an overlord. At Ugarit, the verbal root carries the sense of "rule" or "hold," similar to the general Hebrew sense of the term. However, it is used not only of sovereigns, but of anyone holding influence over others.

> This root may have appeared as a verb in West Semitic during the 13th and 14th centuries, with the sense of a ruler or administrator, though not necessarily the sole king who answers to no one . . . A noun from the root *mlk* carries the sense of a commissioner responsible to his overlord for the military security of a region. This is identical to the *melek* of Jericho, who was responsible for the security of the region but was also answerable to his superiors in the hill country.⁵³

The term "city" ('ir—עִיר) does not refer to a metropolis, but to small settlements. Deuteronomy 3:4 and Joshua 13:30 refer to sixty "cities" in Transjordan. Surely, there were no sixty metropolitan centers in the kingdom of Bashan. The term generally refers to an enclosed place (unless specified as "open cities"). These were not monumental fortifications. They may have had mud-brick walls or earthen enclosures, which were effective defenses against Israelite attacks. "The evidence suggests that 'ir can at times designate what is primarily a fort."⁵⁴

The analysis of the text shows that Jericho was actually "a small and militarized center." It could be circumvented by foot seven times within one day. It was possibly surrounded by mud brick walls.⁵⁵ Though a small city, it held an important strategic position. "Jericho is situated at the beginning of several of the main roads that run from the Jordan Valley into the central hill country . . . Thus, it may be concluded that the 'ir of Jericho was not a metropolitan center but more likely primarily a fort."⁵⁶ Kitchen concludes that "The town was always small, an appendage to its spring and Oasis, and its value (for eastern newcomers) largely symbolic as an eastern gateway into Canaan."⁵⁷ Hess refers to the Amarna correspondence, mentioning

---

52. Hess, "Jericho and Ai," 39–41.
53. Ibid., 40, 41.
54. Ibid., 35.
55. Such walls would not leave archaeological evidence: they would be eroded during the long time when Jericho remained in ruin.
56. Ibid., 36.
57. Kitchen, *Reliability*, 188.

Canaanite kings asking for armed support from the Pharaoh. These letters generally only mention small contingents of soldiers. He concluded that "These cities were probably protected by forces of a few hundred, quite possibly even fewer. Given that Jericho was smaller than any of the cities named and that it was likely a fort . . . It would not seem preposterous if the number of men defending Jericho was about 100 or fewer."[58]

The siege of Jericho was an awe-inspiring ceremony demonstrating YHWH's power. The Israelites do not attack the city, nor do they shout threats and curses. They walk around the city in ominous silence. The sacred number of seven dominates the procession. Seven priests blow seven trumpets, followed by the holy ark and the rear guard of the army. On the seventh day the city is encircled seven times: "The defenders of Jericho understood the ominous implications of the events of those seven days. There was nothing silly about the ceremony, and there is no suggestion that the army of Jericho mocked the Israelites. The whole matter was much too serious."[59] Joshua's victory over Jericho was important because it was his first decisive victory; it consolidated his standing as the successor of Moses who can rely on the support of YHWH. "Success in a first battle played a key role in establishing leadership. A victory of this sort secured respect for Joshua, not only among the Israelites but also among the Canaanites."[60]

Ai

Stager, discussing the Conquest Hypothesis in *The Oxford History of the Biblical World*, states that the Bible claims the following:

> When Joshua and his troops moved farther west, up the wadi to Ai (Josh 7.2—8.29), they ultimately scored a great victory over the king of Ai and the inhabitants of the city. But here again archaeology demonstrates that a tall tale is being told. Ai, whose name means the "ruin," had not been occupied during the second millennium. Its "ruins" dated from the latter part of the third millennium, among which an Iron Age I village was planted in the twelfth century.[61]

---

58. Hess, "Jericho and Ai," 42.
59. Ibid., 43.
60. Ibid., 44.
61. Stager, "Forging an Identity," 129.

I: The Problem

This is the standard argument claiming that archaeology proves that the account of Joshua is fictitious. Callaway, reporting on his excavations of et-Tell, asserts that "Ai is simply an embarrassment to every view of the conquest that takes the biblical and archaeological evidence seriously."[62] This statement illustrates the problems inherent in archaeological interpretations. The inference is correct, but the data are wrong. Et-Tell (the "ruin") has been traditionally identified as the site of Ai. The logical error is evident: the traditional thinking is that et-Tell contradicts Joshua; ergo, Joshua is fiction. The alternative is that the location, topology, and archaeological of et-Tell data prove that it could not be Ai; ergo, the error lies in the identification of the site.

A detailed description of the conquest of Ai is given in Joshua 7–8. The biblical narrative gives the following data: Ai is a small city (smaller than Gibeon) located east of Bethel. Joshua sent only a small contingent, which was defeated in battle. In a second attack, Joshua sent an ambush under cover of night.[63] This ambush hid in a deep valley east of the town which was not visible either from Ai or from Bethel. The same night Joshua went with the rest of his forces and set up a command post on a high hill North of Ai. In the morning, Joshua descended into the shallow valley north of Ai. The men of Ai attacked the Israelites, and Joshua pretended to flee. When the city of Ai was open, the ambush from the west occupied it and set it on fire. The men of Ai panicked and The Israelite victory was decisive. The inhabitants were killed; the king was hanged on a tree, and later buried in a heap of stones adjacent to the cities gate. The city was left in ruins and not resettled "until this day" (Josh 8:28–29).

Wood conducted excavations at the site of Khirbet el-Maqatir. After a painstaking review of the archaeological evidence and topological features of the area, he concluded,

> et-Tell does not meet the biblical requirements for Joshua's Ai, and Beitin does not meet the biblical or extrabiblical requirements for Bethel. Based on present evidence, the only combination that meets the complex matrix of biblical and extrabiblical requirements for the three sites is to locate Bethel at el-Bira, Beth Aven

---

62. Callaway, "New Evidence," 312, quoted by Wood, "Search," 205.

63. Josh 8:3 mentions thirty thousand men, but 8:12 mentions only five thousand. Both numbers are probably grossly exaggerated.

at Beitin, and Joshua's Ai at the newly excavated site of Khirbet el-Maqatir.[64]

Khirbet el-Maqatir meets the requirements for Joshua's Ai—(1) Location: adjacent to Beth Aven/Beitin and East of Bethel/el-Bira there is an ambush site at Wadi Gayeh and a militarily significant hill north of Ai, Jebel Abu Ammar; (2) Archaeological data: the site was occupied and fortified at the time of the conquest—a small fortress with a north gate, with walls four centimeters thick, dating to the Late Bronze I period, and destroyed by fire at the time of the conquest and left in ruins after 1400 BCE.[65] Thus the archaeological data concerning Ai, far from being an embarrassment, turn out to buttress the credibility of the biblical narrative.

The Books of Judges and Joshua Complement Each Other

It is asserted that Joshua appears to claim a total victory and occupation of Canaan, while Judges shows that the occupation of the land was a slow process. However, a careful reading of Joshua shows that no such claim was made in this book.

Joshua reports two decisive victories in open battle. Many "cities" were taken, but not destroyed. The set phrase is that Joshua "caught/captured (*l-k-d*—לכד) the city and put it to the sword with every living person in it." The Hebrew term originally means to catch an animal in a trap. A few times, the phrase "put it under the ban" is added.[66] However, after each major victory, the army returned to its camp in Gilgal. None of these captured cities were occupied. Only three places were totally destroyed: Jericho, Ai and Hazor. The text explicitly declares, "But Israel burned none of the towns that stood on mounds except Hazor, which Joshua did burn" (Josh 11:13). Both Joshua and Judges agree that Canaanites continued to occupy most of the cities. Israelites settled in the region of Judah, and the hillside country, and later in the hills of Galilee. Nevertheless the book of Joshua claims a victory: The land was subjugated ("taken"—לקח), even if Israel had not yet "taken possession" (הוריש).

---

64. Wood, "Search," 205.

65. Ibid., 230–31.

66. Josh 10–12. The phrase "put under ban" (*heḥerim*—החרים) refers to the *ḥerem*, demanding utter destruction. NRSV translates it as "utterly destroying them."

I: The Problem

> So Joshua took the whole land, according to all that YHWH had spoken to Moses; and Joshua gave it for an inheritance [נחלה] to Israel according to their tribal allotments. (Josh 11:23)

> How long will you be slack about going in and taking possession of the land which YHWH, the God of your ancestors, has given you? (Josh 18:3)

The book of Judges does not contradict Joshua, but summarizes the situation: "The Canaanites continued to live [ישב] in that land. When Israel grew strong, they put the Canaanites to forced labor [מס], but did not in fact drive them out [הוריש]" (Jud 1:27a; 28). The historical claim of Joshua/Judges is valid: The victory of Israel was permanent. The invaders retained possession. Though they were influenced by Canaanite customs, their cultural heritage prevailed in the end. Henceforth the land was known as the land of Israel, bound by a covenant to YHWH. There was one military invasion, followed by a slow process of settlement, mainly in formerly uninhabited areas, as shown by archaeological surveys.

The Style of Reporting (Especially of Chapters 1–10) is Mythological

Joshua employs the rhetoric style of the age. There are unnecessary repetitions, followed by backtracking; there are contradictions: all the enemies are killed in battle and the rest retreated to their walled cities (Josh 10). These features do not invalidate the narrative (see earlier discussion pp. 7–8). Younger offers a detailed analysis of the rhetorical structures used in Joshua and demonstrates that these devices *"heighten the sophistication of the narrative."*[67] Quoting Sargon's "letter to the God" he concludes, "Thus, on the basis of the evidence from the ancient Near East, it appears that the narrative of the miracle of the hailstones is a notable ingredient of the transmission code for conquest accounts."[68] Kitchen reviewed the archaeological records of twenty-four locations mentioned in Joshua, concluding that they "show very clearly that Joshua and his raiders moved among (and against) towns that existed and which in several cases exhibit destructions at this period, even though there is no absolute proof of Israelite involvement—short of victory inscriptions, there could hardly be any!"[69]

---

67. Younger, "Rhetorical Structuring," 3; my emphasis.
68. Ibid., 12.
69. Kitchen, *Reliability*, 189.

Nevertheless, mainstream biblical scholarship continues rejecting the conquest model. Thus Dever, though a fierce opponent of "minimalists" could state: "Today ... all archaeologists and virtually all biblical scholars have abandoned the older conquest model ... for 'indigenous origins' and/or 'symbiosis' models in attempting to explain the emergence of early Israel in Canaan."[70] No wonder—the index of names in Dever's book does not include Kitchen or Hoffmeier, who are well-known Egyptologists/biblical scholars (Hoffmeier appears once, in a footnote, as coauthor in a reference).

There are no archaeological data to discredit the conquest model, nor are there archaeological data to discredit various slow infiltration theories. The conquest theory only makes sense if Joshua was the head of a well-organized society. This implies the acceptance of the essential historicity of the narrative about the exodus and sojourn of the desert (not necessarily all the details). The rejection of the narrative of the exodus and sojourn in the desert requires the rejection of Joshua.

Exodus

In *The Oxford History of the Biblical World*, Redmount concludes her review of "Israel In and Out of Egypt" as follows:

> To some, the lack of a secure historical grounding for the biblical Exodus narrative merely reflects its nonhistorical nature. According to this view, there was no historical exodus ... To others, still in the majority among scholars, the ultimate historicity of the Exodus narrative is indisputable ... a historical core is mandated by that major tenet of faith that permeates the Bible: God acts in history.[71]

The last passage cannot be accepted as proof by secular biblical scholars. The monumental volume, *Israel's Exodus in Transdiciplinary Perspective*, offers a comprehensive review of research of about the exodus (forty-three contributions). The importance of the exodus is acknowledged: "The grand narrative about Israel's exodus from Egypt ... holds momentous significance for ancient Israel, Jewish identity, Christianity, Islam and Western thought."[72] Yet most contributions, while acknowledging the importance of

---

70. Dever, *Biblical Writers*, 41.
71. Redmount, "Bitter Lives," 119.
72. Levy, *Israel's Exodus*, v.

I: The Problem

the exodus story, relegate it to the status of a myth. Various papers explore possible historical conditions which led to the development of this myth, but the general conclusion is this:

> The Exodus-Conquest story overall is fiction—the stuff of legend. Whoever the early Israelites were, they were not invaders from Egypt, the Sinai, or Transjordan. They were indigenous peoples, displaced Canaanites, though possibly some had been slaves in Egypt, passing on genuine historical memories.[73]

The "evidence" repudiating the historicity of the exodus is well summarized by Weinstein:

(a) "There is no archaeological evidence for an exodus such as is described in the Bible in any period within the second millennium B.C."[74]

(b) "There is no evidence for the influx of a large population from Egypt into Canaan at the transition from the Middle Bronze Age to the Late Bronze Age."[75]

(c) "The material culture of the early Iron Age settlements in the central highlands and closely adjoining areas (the regions where early Israelite society appears to have developed most intensely) reveals few signs of contact with Egypt—certainly nothing that would lead one to suppose that the inhabitants of these places had any Egyptian heritage."[76]

These are flawed arguments: (a) Pharaohs were not accustomed to memorialize defeats on the walls of their temple. The escape of a group of conscripted workers or the loss of chariots in the Sinai peninsula might possibly have been recorded in some annals, but these would have disappeared together with the rest of the mud-brick temples of the East Nile Delta. The Bible reports that the Israelites built Pithom and Ra'amses with bricks made of clay and straw. This area has no rocks. Stone monuments had to be imported. When the large area of Pi-Ra'amses—thousands of acres—was abandoned (at the end of the twelfth century BCE) the mud bricks disintegrated: "And in the mud, 99 percent of discarded papyri have perished forever . . . A tiny fraction of reports from the East Delta occur in papyri recovered from the desert near Memphis. Otherwise, the entirety of Egypt's administrative records at all periods in the Delta is lost."[77] There-

---

73. Dever, "Exodus and the Bible," 406.
74. Weinstein, "Exodus," 97.
75. Ibid., 95.
76. Ibid., 88.
77. Kitchen, *Reliability*, 246.

The Origin of Israel

fore, one should not expect archaeological evidence about the exodus or Egyptian annals referring to an Egyptian defeat. "The archaeological axiom remains *that absence of evidence* (in this case the inscriptional variety) *is not equivalent to evidence of absence*" [my emphasis].[78]

(b) The Bible does not report a direct "influx of population" from Egypt to Canaan. It talks about a period of nomadic existence in the desert, migration to the Transjordan, and an invasion of Canaan from the east. One should not expect archaeological evidence of the sojourn of a nomadic population in the desert.

(c) Weinstein feels free to ignore biblical evidence indicating ancient Egyptian contact: unless we assume that the later editors of the Bible invented Egyptian names for the early priests, these names—as well as Egyptian terms in Exodus—point towards a historical connection between Israel and Egypt. There also exists some archaeological evidence in support of such a connection. Weinstein may not have been aware of the following data reported by Dever,[79] who discusses the use of Egyptian hieratic numerals in Israel in the eighth and seventh centuries, both in inscriptions and on shekel-weights. At that time, these signs were no longer used by Israelite neighbors, and rarely in Egypt itself. They must have been adopted in Israel in the tenth century at the latest. These findings show a close relationship between Israel and Egypt at the time of the exodus: in the eight and seventh century BCE, both Israel and Judah used an archaic Egyptian numerical notation, which was no longer in use in Syria or in Egypt by the ninth and eighth century BCE. I think that this is a crucial finding proving the historical connection between Egypt and Israel going back to the late second millennium, when this notation was used in Egypt. Dever, who supports the infiltration theory, suggests that this notation may have been introduced in Israel as far back as the tenth century BCE. However, there are no data—biblical or archaeological—indicating close commercial contact with Egypt at that time. This system of notation must have been used by Israelites in the twelfth century, becoming "holy" and retained even when obsolete.

Thus, though there is no evidence about the Israelite presence in Egypt about the exodus or the sojourn in the desert, the biblical narratives are compatible with Egyptian data:[80] Hoffmeier and Kitchen conclude this:

---

78. Cf. Chavalas and Adamthwaite, "Archaeological Light," 70.
79. Dever, *What Did Biblical Writers Know*, 213.
80. This will be discussed in detail in chapter 7, "Origins," pp. 122–124

I: The Problem

> The picture portrayed in Genesis 39 through Exodus 15 [is] compatible with what is known from Egyptian history ... To reject [the Genesis and Exodus narratives] out of hand would be pure obscurantism.[81]

> The exodus and Sinai events are not hereby proven to have happened, or the tabernacle and covenant, etc., to have been made then. But their correspondence not just with attested realities ... but with known usage of the late second millennium B.C. and earlier *does* [author's emphasis] favor acceptance of their having had a definite historical basis.[82]

Propp dismisses the biblical account:

> According to the Hebrew Bible, the Exodus is the departure, in a single night ... of 600,000 adult Hebrew males and their families, embarking upon a trek from slavery in Egypt to freedom in Canaan. It is hard to imagine how that would work spatially, but that is what the text says.[83]

Propp is facetious. No serious scholar takes these numbers at face value. He misses the point: accepting the historicity of the exodus does not imply the acceptance of stories of miracles. Thucydides may have been the first secular historian; for the Bible, the ultimate cause of event is divine intervention. Nevertheless, as I pointed out in chapter one, the biblical author is a historian, because he tries to understand the events he describes. Propp demonstrates how a mythical account of a natural event (the battle of Mons) may receive credence, even in the twentieth century CE.[84] Concerning this event,

> We have precise reference points to support historical analysis. *From my perspective* [my emphasis], the Exodus is *not historical* [author's emphasis] by definition, because it simply is not susceptible to the historical method. There is no paper trail of evidence, what literary sources survive are of uncertain date, and the story lacks a clear anchor in time ... The historian must avoid the Exodus.[85]

---

81. Hoffmeier, *Israel*, 223–24.
82. Kitchen, *Reliability*, 312.
83. Propp, "Exodus and History," 429.
84. Ibid., 433–36.
85. Ibid., 435–36.

From my perspective, if the battle of Mons had been known to me as a biblical manuscript, without any external evidence, I would have disregarded the reports of miraculous events, but concluded that such a battle may have happened. It is one thing to say, "we cannot prove the historicity of the Exodus by external evidence." It is a different thing to declare, "The Exodus did not occur." The question is not whether the exodus was a miraculous event, but whether there existed an organized group, with an ethnic identity, which had been in Egypt for generations and left together. The problem is clearly stated by Dever: "The *fact* [my emphasis] that there was no 'Conquest' means that there was no 'Exodus.'"[86]

If there was no conquest there was no exodus. On the other hand, an organized invasion as described in Joshua indicates that there was an organized society during the sojourn in the desert with well-defined religious rituals and traditions.

Most scholars apparently accept the peaceful infiltration theory in which Israel is relegated to a "small group of fugitive slaves from Egypt." But this designation is a myth of biblical scholarship. The population of *B'ney Yisrael* was a small, but well-organized, society with elders and representatives at the pharaonic court. They had lived and prospered in Egypt for generations; though they kept their language, they were assimilated. The existence of such groups in Egypt has been documented.[87] Finkelstein claims that "There is no single piece of evidence to support a Late Bronze Age origin of the tradition that cannot be understood against the background of other, later periods (e.g., Na'aman 2011:56–60)."[88]

Alternatively, I assert that there exists no evidence supporting the Wellhausen fallacy, which cannot be understood against the background of other (biblical and extra-biblical) data. There is no evidence for the myth of the existence of redactors in the Persian era attributing their own writings to the time of the Pentateuch. The only fact is the archaeological record of a sudden increase of the population in the central highlands of Canaan. The correspondence of the data reported in Assyrian and Babylonian inscription with the data found in 2 Kings prove that the author did not invent his facts, but relied on valid information. There is no reason to assume that reports of earlier events were invented by a post-exilic author. The narratives of the EP and the Pentateuch include later editorial comments and exaggerated rhetorical

---

86. Dever, "Exodus," 406.
87. Hoffmeier, *Israel in Egypt*, 52–76.
88. Finkelstein, "Wilderness," 39.

I: The Problem

language. But every report of an actual event must be taken seriously; it may only be rejected if disproved by other evidence.

Mainstream biblical scholarship rests on the assumption that the Pentateuch was composed during the post-exilic era. Once it is taken for granted that significant portions of the Pentateuch were written after the settlement of Israel in Canaan, the question becomes, when was what written, and why? After all, the Pentateuch exists. One needs a theory explaining how the Pentateuch was constructed. As one is not bound by the canonical text, anything is possible.

This opens the door to an unlimited number of interpretations. It leads towards what I call the "Creative Writing Class Syndrome."

Excursus: A Class of Creative Writing

Imagine a class on creative writing. The class assignment is to first take any passage or group of passages from the Pentateuch. You may combine passages from different sections. You may also assume the existence of passages which have been lost. You may ascribe each passage to any period, beginning in the second century BCE and ending in the Hellenistic area. You will call this "redaction criticism." Your task is to imagine a plausible history of Israel supported by archaeological data. The topic is as follows: write an imaginary history of ancient Israel, based on the biblical books. Your story must be logical and coherent, but you are allowed to assume that any biblical statement is a late editorial insertion. Grades will be assigned for creativity and coherence of exposition. We shall, of course, end up with many theories, each one internally consistent and logical; each one may be challenged by a rival conjecture on the grounds that it does not account for all the features of the text.

Na'aman's theory,[89] cited by Finkelstein in support of his statement, is a good example of this. Na'aman accepts the peaceful infiltration model: there was no conquest under Joshua. Israel originated as a group of Canaanites and nomads coming from Transjordan. At most a small group of fugitive slaves from Egypt migrated to Canaan and joined the pastoral groups which settled in the highlands. However, Na'aman doubts that

> an event that was originally connected to a small isolated group became the basis for the central claim of origin and establishment of the people of Israel. Indeed, the supposition that such early and deeply entrenched common Israelite religious consciousness could have grown from the experience of a small group does not make sense. We should look for another explanation for this central historical-religious perception.[90]

89. Na'aman, "Exodus Story"; see also Na'aman, "Out of Egypt."
90. Ibid., 43.

The Origin of Israel

This explanation is based on Na'aman's analysis of the history of Egypt's domination of Canaan during the New Kingdom (Dynasties 18–20, ca. 1550–1490 BCE). He stresses the increased burden of forced labor and the transportation of thousands of people into slavery.

> The most remarkable element in this society's experience is the severe damage made to its internal structure by the Egyptians under the Pharaoh's leadership. The deportation to Egypt, the trade of slaves and the long subjugation severely harmed many groups from among the future settlers in the hill country. In light of the experience of bondage and suffering, Pharaoh was remembered as symbol of the subjugating king and Egypt as the house of bondage.[91]

Na'aman points out that biblical sources do not mention the Egyptian dominance of Canaan. He concludes that the Canaanite population, which later became Israel, must have suppressed the memory of the Egyptian yoke and transferred it to the memory of the Egyptian bondage of Israel.

> Through a long process, the painful memory of the bondage to Egypt and the miracle that took place causing the Egyptians to withdraw was severed from Canaan and attached to Egypt. The two rival sides of the historical memory—the Israelites and the Egyptians—remained at the center of the plot, but the arena was reversed, so that the retreat from Canaan to Egypt was replaced by a migration from Egypt to Canaan.[92]

> The memory of the long Egyptian occupation of Canaan disappeared from the Israelite historical consciousness and did not reach the late biblical authors. In this light, I suggest that the major event underlying the Exodus tradition is the dramatic Egyptian withdrawal from Canaan after the Egyptian bondage reached its peak during the Twentieth Dynasty.[93]

Na'aman' theory is concisely summarized by Bietak: "According to Na'aman, the oppression of Egyptian rule in Canaan found its way into the Hebrews' collective memory in an altered form, with Canaan and Egypt interchanged, and it is in this 'reversed' route that it made it into the Biblical text."[94] This is an exciting theory, well-argued and logically consistent, once you accept the basic premise: the Israelites descended from displaced Canaanites, there was no conquest under Joshua, and we are allowed to ignore the rest of the narrative. However, the story of the exodus is more than a complaint about hard labor. The major point of the biblical story is the establishment of YHWH's superiority

---

91. Na'aman, "Exodus Story," 61.
92. Ibid., 67.
93. Ibid., 65.
94. Bietak, "Historicity of the Exodus," 18.

I: The Problem

over Pharaoh and the establishment of the covenant between YHWH and Israel. How did these ideas originate? Surely long before the exilic period.

The absence of biblical references to Egyptian dominance in Canaan is a pseudo-problem. The Bible does not mention it because this was not the Israelite experience. The Patriarchs lived before Egypt dominated Canaan and Joshua entered Canaan after the collapse of the Egyptian rule. There is no reason why the history of Canaan during the new kingdom should be considered in the biblical historical books. The Israelites were not prisoners of war or imported slaves. They had lived in Egypt a long time and were conscripted for hard labor under a new dynasty. Na'aman neglects to address that the Bible only reports the Egyptian technique of making bricks out of straw, but does not mention Canaanite stone construction.

Na'aman acknowledges, however, that "My explanation for the drastic change in the historical memory is a hypothesis that cannot be verified." He discusses the Egyptian domination of Canaan. This has little to do with the Exodus narrative. The problem exists only if one assumes that the Israelites of the ninth century BCE descended from the Canaanite population. The only "facts" supporting the theory are: a) Canaan was subjugated by Egypt during the twelfth and eleventh century BCE, (which is not mentioned in the Bible); b) The Bible reports that the Israelites were enslaved by the Egyptians, but succeeded leaving with miraculous divine help. Na'aman neglects to consider the abundance of positive Israelite memories of Egypt. I call this "creative writing," based on an archaeologically established fact, combined with a hypothetical process for which there is no evidence (suppressed memories, selective citation of biblical passage), while ignoring other relevant biblical reports.

The problem of creative writing is also illustrated by Schneider's summary of redaction criticism of Exodus 12.[95] This chapter is structured as follows:

1. Exodus 12:1–6: Establishment of a family Passover Sacrifice on the full moon of the first month of the year.

2. Exodus 12:7–10: The blood of the sacrifice shall be sprinkled on the doorposts and lintels of the houses; the meat is to be eaten roasted with *matzoth* (unleavened bread) and bitter herbs, and any leftovers are to be burnt.

3. Exodus 12:11–14: Explanation of the reason for the rite—YHWH will kill all firstborn in Egypt, but pass over the houses of the Israelites. This sacrifice is to serve as a memorial for this event and is binding for all future generations.

---

95. Schneider, "Modern Scholarship," 539–43.

4. Exodus 12:15–20: Establishment of a seven-day festival during which only *matzoth* will be eaten, and all leavened bread is strictly forbidden. The festival is a memorial of the exodus and is binding on all future generations.
5. Exodus 12:21–28: Repeat of the institution of the Passover sacrifice. It is to be celebrated after the conquest of Canaan.

This chapter obviously combines several passages. The Passover sacrifice and the eating of *matzoth* are seen as separate festivals. Schneider reviewed the redaction history of Exodus 12: "Commentators on Exod 12 perceive it as an amalgamation of rituals from different original contexts that were secondarily reinterpreted and combined with the plague and Exodus narrative."[96]

The review demonstrates the "complex and often inconclusive debate about the layers of the received text and their date, about the origin and context of the rituals and regulations they contain, and about the people and interests responsible for their genesis and perpetuation. The multiplicity of options for every single of these hermeneutic steps has so far prevented scholars from reaching a unanimous conclusion."[97]

It appears that these scholars agree only on one point: "There is today unanimity as to the fact that (layers and dates of the narratives) grew significantly over time, and that some of its most iconic and distinctive parts are late additions and not part of the oldest tradition."[98] This is the crux of the problem. The Wellhausen fallacy, which insists that the Pentateuch was redacted during the Persian period or later, allows scholars to let their imagination run freely. To look for the origin of these rituals is a pseudo-problem. The three rites described in Exodus 12 surely are of great antiquity, being observed all over the Ancient Middle East. Schneider's review of Egyptian apotropaic rites in relation to the tenth plague is instructive. Chapter 12 gives a new meaning to these rites: they commemorate the exodus, which manifested the power of YHWH, and also remind Israel of its future obligations under the covenant: "This day shall be a memorial to you; you shall celebrate it as a festival for YHWH through all generations; you shall celebrate it, an eternal decree" (Exod 12:14; my translation).[99] Sacrifices are neither offered to feed or pacify deities, nor necessary to ensure fertility or to protect the individual or community from evil spirits. They have become acts of devotion.

Let us indulge a hypothetical thought experiment. Imagine the following situation: the Bible is totally unknown, but the facts of the Hillside

---

96. Ibid., 549b.
97. Ibid., 538b.
98. Ibid., 538a.
99. I shall argue in chapter 5, "The Religion of the Pentateuch," that the P legislation does not invent new rituals, but renders a monotheistic view of old pagan traditions.

I: The Problem

Surveys have been established. How would objective scholars evaluate them? They would hardly agree with Finkelstein that the population explosion between Late Bronze and Iron Age I–II was merely one phase in a long-term cycle of development. If there were waves of settlement in the third and second millennium BCE, the latest phase was a tidal wave. Our hypothetical scholars might consider "slow infiltration" theories, but would probably opt for the "military invasion model": it is improbable that the local lowland population would have tolerated such mass immigration without military resistance. Once the invasion theory is seriously considered, scholars will ask themselves, who were these people, and where did they come from? Let us proceed with our thought experiment: the Pentateuch, Joshua, and Judges are discovered (in a cave in the Judean desert of course). Experts in Egyptian and Near East history (not biblical scholars) would now evaluate the biblical accounts in light of the independent data. They would probably concur with Hoffmeier and Kitchen.

Summary

There are two possible scenarios.

(1): The narratives of the exodus, the sojourn in the desert, and the military conquest are fictitious. There was no organized nation called "Israel" and no organized religious cult in the desert. The settlement of the central hillside was the result of peaceful gradual infiltration by diverse groups, one of which may have been called Israel. These groups had a common identity which was strengthened by the confrontation with the Philistines and resulted in the formation of an ethnic egalitarian consciousness. The biblical accounts of the conquest were composed after the destruction of the temple in 586/587 BCE.

(2) The conquest theory assumes a successful military invasion by an ethnically distinct Israel. The Canaanite population retreated to its semi-fortified villages, while the Israelites settled (gradually) in the central hills.

Both theories account for the substantial population growth in the highlands. There is no scientific proof of the peaceful infiltration theory, nor is there any scientific proof of the conquest theory. Both are supported by archaeological data. Scholarly integrity requires that both theories should be discussed. The final choice depends on the plausibility of the theory. It appears to me that the sudden and large settlement of the hills is indicative of a military conquest rather than peaceful infiltration. The next chapters will discuss this scenario in detail.

II

The Law (Torah) of Israel

4

The Composition of the Pentateuch

IT IS GENERALLY AGREED that the biblical texts underwent a process of redaction and revision in the interval between the destruction of the first temple in Jerusalem (587 BCE) and the Hasmonean revolt (167 BCE). This time covers three periods, named after the empire ruling the land: 1) the Babylonian exile (597–547 BCE), when the region was ruled by Babylon; 2) the Persian (or Achaemenid) era, from the ascent of Cyrus (547 BCE) to the conquest of the area by Alexander (332 BCE); 3) the Hellenistic epoch, until the revolt of the Maccabean (165 BCE). It is widely agreed that major revisions/editions of the Pentateuch were written during the periods of the Babylonian, Persian, and Hellenistic era. This chapter discusses the relationship between Samaria and Jerusalem during this period, followed by a comparison of the Masoretic Text (MT) and the Samaritan Pentateuch (SP).

The Samaritans, who prefer to be called Samarians (inhabitants of the Assyrian Province of Samaria) or Shomrim (Guardians), consider themselves to be Israelites, descendants of the tribes Manasseh and Ephraim.[1]

> In the ninth year of Hoshea the king of Assyria captured Samaria; and he carried the Israelites away to Assyria (17:6) ... So Israel was exiled from their own land to Assyria until this day. The king

---

1. They flourished and settled throughout the Roman Empire (estimated population of 2,500,000) and maintained their identity in spite of persecutions by Christians and Muslims. They almost disappeared at the end of the nineteenth century, but now constitute a larger community, living at Nablus and Holon in Israel. The Samaritan Passover sacrifice on Mount Gerizim is the only sacrifice to YHWH offered at present.

II: The Law (Torah) of Israel

of Assyria brought people from Babylon . . . they took possession of Samaria, and settled in its cities. (2 Kgs 17:23b–24)

These events are well-documented by Assyrian sources. However, the number of exiles deported as well as the size of the imported population was probably exaggerated.[2] Archaeological excavations show heavy destruction in Galilee and Bashan, but Samaria became the provincial capital and was soon resettled. The Samarians did not rebel against the Babylonians, and in the middle of the sixth century BCE, Samaria was a flourishing city. A temple for YHWH was built on Mount Gerizim. Cogan concluded,

> Within three to four generations of their arrival in Samaria the foreign settlers were on their way of being absorbed by those Israelites who had escaped deportation and still lived in the land. Assimilating Israelite customs, the foreigners became virtually indistinguishable from the autochthonous population.[3]

Samaria became a province within the empire of Assyria, and later it became a province of Babylon, of Persia, and of the Greek ruler (Egypt or Syria) during the Hellenistic era. It was more important than Jerusalem. The inhabitants of Samaria called themselves Israelites of the tribes of Ephraim and Manasseh.[4] They maintained a sanctuary (*Miqdash*) on Mount Gerizim, dedicated to YHWH. The service was led by a high priest of the Aaronite lineage.

Israelite (i.e., Samarian) communities existed within the Hellenistic world. Knoppers quotes two descriptions from the early third and first century BCE, found in the Aegean island of Delos, referring to "Israelites who make offerings for the temple of (holy) Mount Gerizim."[5] Thus Samarians as well as Judeans recognized each other as Israelites. Both groups were led by Aaronite priests of the family of Phinehas and cooperated with each

---

2. See Cogan ("Into Exile," 340–42) and Grabbe (*Yehud*) for a detailed review of the problem.

3. Cogan, "Into Exile," 342.

4. Shen et al. ("Reconstruction," 248) conducted a genetic analysis of Samarians (twenty-seven men, twenty women), compared with individuals (158 men) from eight other Israeli populations. "Principal component analysis suggests a common ancestry of Samaritan and Jewish patrilineages. Most of the former can be traced back to a common ancestor in the paternally inherited Jewish high priesthood (Cohanim) at the time of the Assyrian conquest of the kingdom of Israel."

5. Knoppers, *Jews and Samaritans*, 171.

other.[6] The rift between the Judeans and the Israelites from the province of Samaria started about 450 BCE at the time of Ezra, who ruled that sacrifices to YHWH may only be offered at the Jerusalem sanctuary. However, there was strong resistance in Jerusalem against Ezra and Nehemiah. "The sharp divisions in the Jerusalem community, and the priesthood in particular, with which we are familiar from the times of Ezra and Nehemiah, were not restricted to the fifth century BC, but continued much longer."[7]

Until the Hasmonean period, the inhabitants of the province of Samaria were "Israelites." Contemporary nomenclature reflects the bias of rabbinical thinking. The term "Samaritans" was coined only during the first century BCE, referring to those Israelites who refused to acknowledge the supremacy of Jerusalem and insisted that Mount Gerizim is the only legitimate location for a sanctuary for YHWH. The term appears in the Talmud and in the New Testament, but not in the Hebrew Bible.

The designation "Second Temple Period" too is biased and misleading. It implies that there were only two legitimate temples in Israel. Neither the first temple at the time of the monarchy nor the second temple, erected during the Persian period, was the only sanctuary serving YHWH at their time. Jerusalem became the sole temple of YHWH only after the destruction of the Israelite temple on Mount Gerizim by the Judean Hasmonean king John Hyrcanus.

The Masoretic Text (MT) and the Samaritan Pentateuch (SP)

The DSS show that the text of the Pentateuch was not fixed by the second century BCE. However, the differences between the Masoretic Text (MT), the Samarian Pentateuch (SP), Septuagint (LXX) and various DSS manuscripts are mainly in spelling and in the placement of verses.[8] A comparison of the MT, SP, LXX, and various DSS shows that the SP sometimes agrees with the MT, sometimes with the LXX, and sometimes with the DSS.[9] An-

---

6. According to the Pentateuch, the priesthood was assigned to the family of Phinehas (Num 25:11–13). The Samarian tradition claims that Eli ben Jafni, from the family of Phinehas's younger brother of Ithamar, usurped the priesthood and transferred the holy Ark to Shilo. See chapter 8, "From Conquest to Monarchy."

7. Williamson, *Studies in Persian Period History*, 89.

8. See chapter 2, "Wellhausen Fallacy."

9. A detailed discussion of the differences between various readings of the Pentateuch

II: The Law (Torah) of Israel

derson and Giles concluded that "the SP is actually closer to the MT in its reading than it is to the LXX."[10]

The Samarian version of the Pentateuch is virtually identical with the Masoretic text. The order of presentation of the material is identical in both versions. Both start with an account of the creation and continue with the emergence of human civilization, ending with the story of the death of Moses.[11] In both versions, the story about Abraham and Isaac (Gen 21–22) is interrupted by the insertion of the encounter between Abraham and Abimelech (Gen 21:22–34). Similarly, the narrative of Joseph (starting Genesis 37, continued Genesis 39) is interrupted by the story of Judah and Tamar (Genesis 38). Another example is the report about the war between Israel and the Midianites in Numbers 25. The chapter ends in the middle of the sentence,[12] followed by five chapters dealing with other topics. The report on the Midianites is then taken up at chapter 31, which completes the last sentence of chapter 25. These textual intrusions are identical in the MT and SP. The content and order of presentations of various items is the same in both books. The Pentateuch is traditionally divided into fifty-five sections, 177 chapters. The order of the sections and chapters is identical in both texts. Altogether there are 5,845 verses in the same order in both the SP and the MT, with a few exceptions where the order of some verses is changed. The consistent correspondence of the order of presentation throughout the five books of the Pentateuch shows that the SP and MT are two editions of the same book, which I call the first edition of the Pentateuch (PT).

Thousands of differences between the MT and the SP have been noted[13]—the estimates vary—but most of them do not affect the meaning of the text. Some are scribal errors.[14] Sometimes words are inserted to clarify

---

is found in Tov (*Textual Criticism*, 17–46) and Knoppers (*Jews and Samaritans*, 178–212).

10. Anderson and Giles, *Tradition Kept*, 17.

11. See chapter 6 of this book, "Deuteronomy," for a detailed discussion of the Pentateuch.

12. The MT concludes that "it was after the plague" (Num 25:19), interrupting the sentence with a division footnote—*pisqah bʼemtza pasuk*. The NRSV and other translation omit verse 19, and start chapter 26 with "after the plague" (26:1a).

13. Knoppers, *Jews and Samaritans*, 179.

14. Scribal errors occur even today, when proofreading is careful. I found the following error in a scroll: the name YHWH was written twice (it occurred also later in the same verse). It is noteworthy that this scroll had been in use for several years before the error was discovered. Such error is rare, but not unheard of. The scroll was sent for repair; there are precise rabbinical instructions for dealing with such a problem.

the meaning of a sentence. For example, Genesis 14:2 mentions Shemeber, king of Zeboiim; the SP reads the name Shemebed. The Hebrew letters *resh* and *dalet* are similar and easily interchanged. Obviously, there is no way to decide which reading should be preferred. The technical term "corruption" for any reading differing from the MT arbitrarily assumes that the MT gives the correct reading.

Many differences are linguistic. The letters of the Hebrew alphabet originally designated consonants only. Vowels were inferred. Later on some letters (*matres lectiones*—a, h, v, and y) also designated vowels. The MT generally uses defective (*ḥaser*) spelling, which only gives the root consonants, but omits *matres lectiones*. The SP prefers the *plene* (*malē*) spelling, which notates some vowels with letters.

For example, twenty-four differences are found in Exodus 1. Among others, the SP introduces the letters *y* (פיתון),[15] *v* (למילדות), and *h* (ותחיינה) in verses 11, 17, 18, 19, and 20, using the *plene* spelling. However, in verse 11 the defective (older) spelling appears in the SP, while the MT uses the plene spelling; for example, וישימו in the MT but not in the SP.

Sometimes the SP adds some words: in verses 2 and 3 the letter "v," denoting "and," is added four times (before the names of Simeon, Levi, Issachar, and Zebulon).

Occasionally we find harmonizing changes which clarify the text.[16] For example, Noah is commanded to put seven pairs of clean animals into the ark: the MT (Gen 7:2) writes: "man and his wife" (איש ואשתו); the SP and the LXX write "male and female" (זכר ונקבה).[17] The NRSV and NAB translate "the male and its mate"; the REB and JB translate "male and female." In these examples, the MT and SP say the same thing, while translations follow the Samarian version, which is clearer.

Numbers 35:9–34 discusses the law for manslaughter (רצח מכה נפש בשגגה). The slayer is put on trial, and if the verdict is manslaughter, "the assembly shall protect the murderer [הרצח] from the blood avenger" (Num 35:25, my translation). SP[lxx, tr] corrects "murderer" to "the slayer [המכה]."

Sometimes unusual spellings or grammatical constructions of the MT are changed in the SP:

---

15. MT: "פתם."
16. Tov, *Textual Criticism*, 85–89.
17. The superscript marks "q," "s," "o," "lxx," and "tr" indicate whether the Samarian reading is acknowledged in the MT (*qere, sebirin*), the Onkelos, the LXX, or modern translations.

II: The Law (Torah) of Israel

Table 4.1

	MT	SP	translation
Gen 1:24	וחיתו־ארץ	וחית הארץ	"beasts of the earth"
Gen 9:21; 12:8; 13:3	אהלה	אהלו	"his tent"
Gen 35:21	אהלה	אהלה (no change)	
Gen 42:11	נחנו	אנחנו	"we"

In some variations, the SP introduces a word or a short phrase. Some of these changes may reflect scribal errors. For example, in Genesis 47:21 the MT reads: "*He transferred them* (the people) to the cities" (העביר אתו לערים). SP reads "he enslaved them to servitude" (העביד אתו לעבדים). The difference between the two versions is in one letter: the "r" of the MT is replaced by "d." The SP version makes more sense, and is reflected in the LXX and modern translations. MT is probably a scribal error.

The following examples are commentaries on the Masoretic text found in SP:

Exodus 3:8 gives a list of Canaanite nations. SPlxx adds "the Girgashi."

Exodus 1:22, MT: "every son that is born you shall cast into the river." SP[o, lxx, tr] adds: "born to *the Hebrews*."[18] This addition clarifies the text.

Deuteronomy 25:11 describes a fight between men; a woman interferes and grasps one man's genitals (במבשיו, MT); the SP, modestly, substitutes "his flesh" (בבשרו).

Genesis 2:2, MT: "and on the *seventh* day God finished his work." SP[lxx] reads: "And on the *sixth* day." The rabbis realized that the text should read "the sixth day." A midrash suggests that the concept of "rest" was introduced on the seventh day.

Sometimes a word in the MT is omitted in the SP:

Exodus 3:18, MT: "*and now* let us go a three days' journey." SPlxx omits "and now" (ועתה).

Sometimes an entire phrase is added:

MT: "Each *woman* shall ask her *neighbor* [מִשְׁכֶנְתָּהּ], and woman living in the neighbor's house" (Exod 3:22). The SP reads: "[each] *man* shall ask of his *neighbor/associate* [רעהו] and [each] woman from her neighbor/associate [רעותה] and of her who sojourns in her house." Note that the MT uses the term *shakhen* (שכן), meaning a

---

18. The SP addition is included in most translations, but not in the Vulgate, nor in a Masoretic translation of the Jewish Publications Society of America.

person who dwells near you. The SP addition introduces the term (רע—*amicus, socius*) which is also generally translated as "neighbor."[19]

The SP introduces editorial comments in the form of quotations. These are additions to the MT, quoting what has been written elsewhere in the Pentateuch without adding new words.[20]

For example, Genesis 30:28–36 tells about the negotiations between Laban and Jacob concerning his future wages. The text is identical in both versions. The SP then introduces Jacob's dream about the striped, spotted, and mottled sheep (Gen 31:11–13), ending the sentence with a citation from Genesis 32:13a.

In Deuteronomy 9, Moses talks about the wrath of YHWH, who threatens to destroy Israel because of the worship of the golden calf. Moses prays for forgiveness: "YHWH was so angry with Aaron that he was ready to destroy him, but I interceded also on behalf of Aaron also at that same time" (Deut 9:20). This passage is identical in both the MS and the SP. It is cited in the SP after Exodus 32:10.[21]

In Exodus 6, Moses promises the people of Israel that God will deliver them from bondage. "But they would not listen to Moses, because of their broken spirit and their hard labor" [Exod 6:9b, my translation; the NRSV translates "cruel slavery"]. The SP inserts the following quotation, taken from Exodus 14:12a: "Is this not the very thing we told you in Egypt, 'Let us alone and let us serve the Egyptians'?"

The brief account of the reaction of the people to the theophany at Sinai (Exod 20:18–19a) is expanded in the SP and the DSS 4Q158 and 4Q175, quoting the Deuteronomistic account of the reaction of the people (Deut 5:25b–26). Then the SP returns to Exodus 20:18–19, followed by the discussion of prophecy (Deut 18:18–22), and then returns to the account of the aftermath of the Decalogue (Deut 5:27–30). Such expansions are not new interpretations of the text. In Deuteronomy, Moses gives a more detailed account of the events at Mount Sinai. The redactor reminds the reader (or listener) of Exodus of these details. A modern editor would introduce them as a footnote: "Description of the aftermath to the Decalogue is found in Deuteronomy 5:28."[22]

Genesis 10:19a declares, "And this is the boundary of Canaan." The territory assigned to Canaan in the MT is in Cisjordan. This area was later called the promised land. Moses looked at it from the fields of Moab in Transjordan, but never entered it. The tribes

---

19. See Lev 19:18: "You shall love your neighbor as yourself." The Vulgate translates "neighbor" as *amicus*. See relevant *CONC* entries.

20. Anderson and Giles (*Tradition Kept*) call these variants "interpolations"; Knoppers (*Jews and Samaritans*) calls them "conflation."

21. The SP Exodus text substitutes "and Moses prayed" for "I prayed."

22. Such a comment is especially useful when the scroll only contains one book; the reader is reminded of another scroll.

II: The Law (Torah) of Israel

of Reuben, Gad, and the half-tribe of Manasseh acknowledged that their inheritance is outside Canaan. The SP version starts with Genesis 10:19a, but replaces the original with a quote composed from Genesis 15:18b and Deuteronomy 11:24b, describing a larger, utopian area "from the river of Egypt to the great river, the river Euphrates." This insertion omits the first half of Genesis 15:18 in which these lands are promised to the descendants of Abraham, which includes the progeny of Ishmael, Esau, and of Abraham's concubines, not only the descendents of Jacob.

Each expansion cleverly combines different verses into a coherent passage, but no new words are added to the original text.

The written text of the MT (כתיב = *ketib*) may not be changed. However, the MT may indicate textual variants in footnotes or by dots above letters:

a) *qere*: (קרי = read). This footnote indicates the correct reading. The original *ketib* is not changed, but the suggested reading is used in cantillation and exegesis. Many of the variant readings of the SP are acknowledged in these footnotes.

Table 4.2

	ketib	*qere* and SP	translation
Exod 4:2	מזה	מה זה	"what is"
Exod 22:4	בעירה	בעירו	"his beast"
Exod 22:26	כסותה	כסותו	"his covering"

Note that in these instances the *qere* is correct, while the *ketib* is an unusual form. In Genesis 24 and in Deuteronomy the *ketib* gives the defective spelling for "girl" (נער—which also means "boy"). The *qere* gives the *plene* spelling.

b) *sebirin*: (סבירין = "this should be understood as"). This footnote suggests alternative readings which may be used in exegesis.

Here are a few examples where the SP renders the alternative variant:

	ketib	*sebirin* and the SP
Gen 19:8, 25	האל (these)	האלה (these)
Gen 19:33	בלילה הוא (in that night)	בלילה ההוא (in that night)
Exod 4:19	מצרים (Egypt)	מצרימה (to Egypt)
Exod 21:30	ככל (as all)	בכל (whatever)

	ketib	*sebirin* and the SP
Exod 22:29	ביום (on the eighth day)	וביום (and on the eight day)
Deut 31:12, 13	אלהיכם (your God)	אלהיהם (their God)

c) *Niqud*: (נקוד = the dotted letter should [probably] be erased

Table 4.3

	niqud	SP
Num 3:39	וְאַהֲרֹן (and Aaron)	omitted
Num 21:30	אשׁר (which)	אש (fire)

These are some of the examples in which the SP agrees with the corrected variant of marginal notes of the MT, but in the majority of instances the SP agrees with the MT and ignores the footnotes.

An interesting example of this is found in the report of the naming of Moses' son Gershom: "She [Zipporah] bore a son, and he named him Gershom; for he said, 'I have been an alien residing in a foreign land'" (Exodus 2:22). Both the MT and the PT read "*He* called his name [ויקרא]." The *qere* of the MT corrects to ותקרא (*she* shall call). This *qere* is read during cantillation of the Torah in the synagogue. The text clearly indicates that "he" is the correct version. The correction was presumably introduced because traditionally a child was named by the mother. In this instance the SP and the translations ignore the *qere*.

I have only quoted some of the variants found in the SP, and should like to stress four points.

1. The SP introduces either stylistic-grammatical changes or exegetic comments.
2. There are no interpolations taken from outside the Pentateuch.
3. The MT and the SP generally agree with each other, both in content and in the organization of the presentation.
4. Various readings are ideologically/theologically neutral.

II: The Law (Torah) of Israel

Samarian sectarian variants

Knoppers observes that "The Samarian and Judean communities could (and did) interpret the ambiguities of the Deuteronomistic centralization legislation to the advantage of their own cultic centers."[23]

There are three important variants in the SP:

1. The description of the ceremony of blessings and curses to be carried out at Mount Gerizim and Mount Ebal (Deut 11:29-30; 27:2-26) is ambiguous. The PT differs from the MT on the following points:
   a. The SP adds "opposite Shechem" to the description of the location of the ceremony (Deut 11:30).
   b. The SP replaces "Mount Ebal" with "Mount Gerizim" (Deut 27:4).
2. The SP quotes the account of the Mount Gerizim ceremony after the tenth commandment of the Decalogue (Exod 20:17; Deut 5:21).
3. Deut 12: the SP replaces "YHWH your God will choose [יבחר]" with "has chosen [בחר]."

Mount Gerizim/Mount Ebal

1) The main topic of Deuteronomy is the account of the renewal of the covenant. The Sinai covenant had been established by the exodus generation. The Deuteronomy covenant was to be re-affirmed by the new generation and should be confirmed after the conquest of Canaan, at a ceremony to be held on Mount Gerizim/Mount Ebal. The report of the renewal of the covenant in the desert is interrupted by the ordinance concerning the ceremony of the Mount Gerizim/Mount Ebal. This became the main text in the later sectarian controversy between Samarians and Jews.

The order of presentation is as follows:

Deuteronomy 11:26-28: introduction to the Deuteronomy covenant

Deuteronomy 11:29-30: interpolation (*inclusio*, bracketing); ordinance of blessing/cursing ceremony with reference to its location on Mount Gerizim/Mount Ebal.

Deuteronomy 11:31-32: rationale of the Mount Gerizim ceremony.

Deuteronomy 12-26: laws of the Deuteronomy covenant.

---

23. Knoppers, *Jews and Samaritans*, 210.

Deuteronomy 27:1–8: second interpolation—location and implements of the Mount Gerizim ceremony.

Deuteronomy 27:9–10: return to the description of the covenant ceremony.

Deuteronomy 27:11–26: third interpolation—the calling of blessings and curses on Mount Gerizim.

Deuteronomy 28: return to Deuteronomy covenant procedure—i.e., blessings if the covenant is adhered to, and curses if it is broken, ending with the concluding statement: "These are the words of the covenant that YHWH commanded Moses to make with the Israelites in the land of Moab, in addition to the covenant that he had made with them at Horeb" (Deut 28:69; 29:1 in NRSV). This presentation is confusing, but it makes sense if you listen to it as a speech which is rendered in what I call the "by the way" style—the technical term is *inclusio* or "bracketing." The general setting is the ceremony of renewing the covenant. Moses starts with a caution:

> See, I am setting before you this day a blessing and a curse: the blessing, if you obey the commandments of YHWH your God that I am commanding you today; and the curse, if you do not obey the commandments of YHWH your God, but turn from the way that I am commanding you today, to follow other gods that you have not known. (Deut 11:26–28).

Then follows an insertion: by the way, you'll need such a ceremony after you cross the Jordan (Deut 11:29–30). The oration then returns to its original topic: These are the laws you must keep (11:31, chapters 12–26). The next insertion (27:1–8) is: by the way, this Torah must be written on stones to be erected. The text then returns to the major theme: "This day you have become the people of YHWH your God" (Deut 27:9), and continues: by the way, thus will the ceremony of the curses be conducted. Chapter 28 returns to the main topic of the speech and specifies the blessings and curses of the Deuteronomy covenant. Because of its importance during the later controversy between both groups, the ceremony is discussed in detail in the following excursus.

II: The Law (Torah) of Israel

Excursus: The Ceremony of Blessings and Curses

The texts of the SP and MT agree[24] except in two places: the SP adds "opposite Shechem" to the description of the locality of the ceremony (Deut 11:30) and substitutes "Mount Gerizim" for "Mount Ebal." These changes accentuate the importance of Mount Gerizim, the site of the Samaritan temple.

Deuteronomy 11:26–28 is the introduction to the renewal of the covenant. This is followed by the first interpolation, which defines the rite of the blessing and the curse, and its location. However, the instructions concerning this ceremony are equivocal[25] with regard to location, implements, and procedure:

> When YHWH your God has brought you into the land that you are entering to occupy, you shall set the blessing on Mount Gerizim and the curse on Mount Ebal. As you know, they are beyond the Jordan, some distance to the west, in the land of the Canaanites who live in the Arabah, opposite Gilgal, beside the oak of Moreh. (Deut 11:29–30)

This instruction is rather vague. Where is Gilgal? The SP adds "opposite Shechem," leaving no doubt about the locality of Ebal/Gerizim. The narrative then reconnects with Deuteronomy 11:28, starting with a general admonition: "When you cross the Jordan to go in to occupy the land which YHWH your God is giving you, and when you occupy it and live in it, you must diligently observe all the statutes and ordinances that I am setting before you today" (11:31–32). This is followed by a description of the conditions of the covenant, emphasizing laws to be kept after the conquest (chapters 22–26). Then follows the second interpolation: chapter 27 returns to the instructions about the ceremony of blessings and curses. "On the day you pass over the Jordan … you shall set up large stones, and cover them with plaster … and you shall write upon them all the words of this law [Torah]" (Deut 27:2–3). This instruction is then repeated: "So when you have crossed over the Jordan, you shall set up these stones, about which I am commanding you today, on *Mount Ebal*, and you shall cover them with plaster [27:4; my emphasis] … You shall write on the stones all the words of this law very clearly" (27:8). Both the MT and SP agree that Mount Gerizim is the place for the blessings and Mount Ebal is the place for the curses. MT assumes that the curses were read from the stones, which must therefore be erected on Mount Ebal. The SP variant reads "Mount Gerizim" instead, thus placing the altar on the mount of blessing. Which was the original reading? Knoppers cites a variety of old textual traditions which indicate that Mount Gerizim is not a Samarian

---

24. Excepting a few insertions or omissions of words.

25. A review of various interpretations is given by Knoppers, *Jews and Samaritans*, 196–212.

sectarian reading.[26] As the stones would be engraved with the words of the Torah, they should not be erected on the mountain of curses. "The MT reading of Mt. Ebal in Deut 27:4 probably represents a later Judean correction."[27]

However, the reference to "all the words of the Torah" is rather vague. It surely did not include a full transcription of chapters 12–26. The cursing Levites probably read the curses from the stone monument which was to be a witness for future generations. Though such a monument may be called "altar"—e.g. Joshua 8—it is not a sacrificial altar. One would not burn a sacrificial animal on it, nor spread blood over its sides. The distinction is clearly expressed in Joshua: "Therefore we said, 'Let us now build an altar, not for burnt offering, nor for sacrifice, but to be a witness between us and you, and between the generations after us, that we do perform the service of YHWH our God" (Josh 22:26–27).

Deuteronomy 27:5–7 orders the erection of a sacrificial altar. On this altar, burnt offerings should be sacrificed, followed by shelamim: "and you shall eat them there and rejoice before YHWH your God."[28] This passage is vague as well. It does not indicate when and where the festive meal will take place. There is no indication that this altar will be a permanent sanctuary. The next verses (11–26) describe the ceremony itself. Six tribes are to stand on Mount Gerizim "to bless the people." Six tribes are to stand on Mount Ebal "for the curse." Then the Levites will call out a list of curses, after which "all the people shall say Amen." The chapter ends with a general curse: "Cursed be anyone who does not uphold the words of this law [Torah] by observing them. All the people shall say, 'Amen!'" (Deut 27:26).

These instructions are also ambiguous and open to different interpretation, even without the Samarian additions. The issue is discussed in detail by Knoppers.[29] The timing of the ceremony is problematic. It was feasible to set up twelve stones at the camp in Gilgal on the day the Jordan was crossed (Josh 4:19–24), to be a witness for later generations. But one must assume that the renewal ceremony, which demanded time for preparation and performance, was to be held later.[30] The reference to Mount Ebal is also problematic. The MT and the SP agree that Gerizim was the mount of blessing. Why should the altar and stone pillar be set up on the place of curses? Knoppers suggests

26. The problem is discussed by Knoppers, *Jews and Samaritans*, 196–203. Knoppers concludes, "The MT reading of Mt. Ebal in Deut 27:4 probably represents a later Judean correction" (203).

27. Ibid., 203.

28. See also Josh 4:8; 22:26–27.

29. Knoppers, *Jews and Samaritans*, 169–217.

30. Rashi cites Talmudic interpretations: there were three monuments, one at the Jordan, one in Gilgal, and one on Mount Ebal.

that the text should read "Mount Gerizim."[31] I do not think this correction is necessary. Surely, the pillar would include the conditions of the covenant only, not the entire collection of laws. The stones were "witnesses" to the renewing of the covenant. The curses to be pronounced by the Levites were possibly read from the writing on the pillar. The monument had to be placed on Mount Ebal to witness this event. The order of presentation of the text is awkward. Deuteronomy 27:2–4 describes the erection of the pillar. This is followed by the description of the altar and the festive meal to be enjoyed (5–7). Then comes the description of the ceremony of curses (11–26). This sequence does not make sense. It is necessary to distinguish clearly between the pillar with the writing of the Torah and the sacrificial altar erected for the celebration. The feast was to be shared by all the people. Did the meal take place on Mount Ebal followed by the trek of six tribes to the other mountain to proclaim their blessings and to listen to the curses? Surely not. The feast probably occurred after the pronouncement of the curses, celebrating the renewal of the covenant. Even if the meal occurred first, as is implied in Joshua 8, it would not have occurred on the place of curses.

What was written on the stones? The text says, "You shall write upon the stones all the words of this Torah." Does this refer to the laws of chapters 12–26 as well as to the blessings and curses of chapter 28? Does it include the Decalogue? One assumes that these words were to be recited during the ceremony. "All the words of the Torah" would be too much for a set of stones, too much to be recited. The text only refers to twelve curses, but does not quote any blessings. The text is also ambiguous in reference to the place from which the blessings and curses were recited. Deuteronomy 11:29b states, "You shall set the blessing on [על] Mount Gerizim and the curse [על] on Mount Ebal." The adverb ʾal (על) does not necessarily denote "upon a place." For example, Isaiah 1:1 speaks of the vision of Isaiah "about Judah and Jerusalem" (על יהודה). Similarly, 11:29 can be understood as a blessing pronounced on Mount Gerizim versus a curse on Mount Ebal.[32]

Rashi,[33] quoting Soṭa 32a, suggests that the Levites stood in the valley between the mountains. They turned their faces towards Gerizim and recited the blessing: "Blessed be the man who does not make (any) graven or molten image etc." Then they turned their faces towards Ebal and called the curses. The people on the mountains affirmed each blessing and curse with "Amen." There are some difficulties with this interpretation: the form of the blessings is awkward. Would the Levites call out: "Blessed be the man who does not lie with any kind of beast"? Furthermore, the stone monument stood on top of Ebal (Gerizim?), and we must assume that the Torah would be read there.

---

31. Knoppers, *Jews and Samaritans*, 196–212.
32. Similarly, David curses the mountains of Gilboa (2 Sam 1:21).
33. Rashi, *Deuteronomy*, 27:12.

The Composition of the Pentateuch

The next chapter returns to the discussion of the Moab covenant. It includes blessings—"If you will only obey the voice of YHWH your God" (Deut 28:1–14)—followed by a very long exhaustive list of curses[34]—If you do not obey the voice of the Lord" (28:15–68). The section then concludes:"These are the words of the covenant that YHWH commanded Moses to make with the people of Israel in the land of Moab, in addition to the covenant that he had made with them at Horeb (Deut 28:69; 29:1 in the NRSV)."

Perhaps the best clue about how the text was understood in biblical times is found in Joshua (Josh 8:30–35):

1. Joshua built an altar of unhewn stones on Mount Ebal.

2. Sacrifices were offered on this altar.

3. On the stones he engraved "a copy of the Torah of Moses," in the presence of the Israelites.

4. The ceremony: priests and Levites were carrying the ark:

> All Israel, alien as well as citizen, with their elders and officers and their judges, stood on opposite sides of the ark in front of the levitical priests who carried the ark of the covenant of YHWH, half of them in front of Mount Gerizim and half of them in front of Mount Ebal, *as Moses, the servant of YHWH, had commanded to bless the people of Israel first.* (Josh 8:33; my translation in italics)[35]

> And afterward he [Joshua] read [recited] all the words of the law [Torah], blessings and curses, all that is written in the book of the law [Torah]. (Josh 8:34)

This description of the ceremony is unclear. It appears that the people and priests stood in the valley between the mountains. In that case, what is the function of the monument on Mount Ebal? What were the "blessings and the curses" read by Joshua? Perhaps he recited Deuteronomy 28? The book of Joshua mentions several occasions when stones were set up as "witness." One monument of twelve stones was mounted at the place of the Israelite headquarters in Gilgal (Josh 4). An additional stone monument was erected by the Transjordan tribes (Josh 22:26–27); then there was the monument on Mount Ebal (Josh 8). Finally, at the end of his life, Joshua renewed the covenant in Shechem:

> Joshua wrote these words in the book of the law [Torah] of God; and he took a large stone, and set it up there under the oak in the sanctuary of YHWH. Joshua

---

34. See discussion of curses in chapter 3, pp. 35–37.

35. My translation follows rabbinical interpretation (see Rashi, Rabbi David Kimchi). It is based on the exact order of words; punctuation marks follow the MT tropes (musical notation). This translation appears in the REV. However, the NRSV translates this verse this way: "as Moses, the servant of YHWH had commanded at the first, that they should bless the people of Israel."

II: The Law (Torah) of Israel

said to all the people, "See, this stone shall be a witness against us; for it has heard all the words of YHWH that he spoke to us; therefore it shall be a witness against you, if you deal falsely with your God. (Josh 24:26–27)[36]

These monuments had a double purpose. They affirmed Israel's obligation under the covenant. They also proclaimed Israel's ownership of the land of Canaan, a gift from YHWH. With these monuments, Israel took official possession of the land of Canaan.[37]

Though the interpretation of the text remains speculative, the basic scenario is clear: prior to the conquest of Canaan, Israel entered into a covenant with YHWH. On that occasion, Israel was commanded to renew the covenant after crossing the Jordan. This ceremony included the pronouncing of blessings and curses. Mount Ebal was to be the mount of curses, and Gerizim the mount of blessings. The text never suggests that Mount Gerizim will become the place of a future sanctuary. The MT agrees with the SP. The only difference is the SP insertion of two quotes which stress the importance of Mount Gerizim: a reference to Mount Gerizim is inserted in the SP after the Decalogue (Exod 20:17; Deut 5:21). This insertion is composed by a combination of quotes from Exodus and Deuteronomy.

> And when YHWH your God brings you into the land of the Canaanite (Exod 13:11a) ... that you are entering to occupy (Deut 11:29b) ... you shall set up large stones, and cover them with plaster (27:2b) ... You shall write on the stones all the words of this Torah very clearly (Deut 27:8) ... So when you have crossed over the Jordan, you shall set up these stones, about which I am commanding you today, on Mount *Gerizim* (27:4a)...And you shall build an altar there to YHWH your God, an altar of stones on which you have used no iron tool. You must build the altar of YHWH your God of unhewn stones. Then offer burnt offerings on it to YHWH your God; and you shall sacrifice shelamim, and shall eat there and you shall rejoice before YHWH your God (27:5–7) ... As you know, [these mountains] are beyond the Jordan, some distance to the west, in the land of the Canaanites who live in the Araba opposite Gilgal, beside the oak of Moreh, *opposite Shechem* (Deut 11:30; my emphasis).

---

36. Examples of such witnesses of events are found in Gen 28:29 (witness to God's promise to Jacob and to his vow to erect a "house for God"), Gen 31:51–53 (witness to the covenant between Jacob and Laban), Exod 24:4 (witness to the confirmation of the Sinai covenant), and Joshua (see further discussion).

37. Invading Europeans similarly claim sovereignty by hoisting the flag of their sovereign over the invaded land.

This passage is clearly a Samarian polemic comment. It is constructed by a careful combination of Pentateuch sources. By combining quotes out of context, the meaning of the original text is distorted: all references to the ceremony of blessings/curses are omitted. The insertion, as it stands, commands that after crossing the Jordan an altar should be erected on Mount Gerizim. It implies—but does not state so explicitly—that the altar on Mount Gerizim will be a permanent sanctuary. As the passage is inserted immediately after the Decalogue, before the verse "When all the people saw the thundering and the lightening" (Exod 20:18), it may be (and was) read as a part of the Decalogue. However, to make it a true commandment, the scribe would have to insert a positive command, as "you shall worship YHWH your God at this place." The text itself does not claim that the sacrificial altar at Mount Gerizim/Mount Ebal would become a sanctuary, or that there should be a central exclusive sanctuary in Israel. This demonstrates that the Samaritan scribes did not feel free to change the original text.

3) The MT reads, "the place which YHWH your God shall choose" (יבחר; Deut 12:5, 11, 14, 26). The SP reads "has chosen" (בחר). It is generally assumed that the SP version is a late Samarian addition. However, Knoppers shows that other interpretations are plausible. "It is no longer self-evident that the consistent appearance of בחר ('He has chosen') in the SP, over against יבחר ('He will chose') in the MT, represents a late sectarian correction."[38] The difference is only important if Deuteronomy 2 ordains the exclusive centralization of sacrificial rites on one place. I shall argue (especially in chapters 6, 8, and 14) that the concept of exclusive centralization was introduced by the Babylonian exiles, promoted by Ezra, and became a dogma only in Maccabean times.[39]

---

38. Knopper, *Jews and Samaritans*, 184–87.

39. The main points I will argue are:

   1) The P source (mainly Leviticus) describes the required sacrificial rites of worship (*avodah*—עבדה)—i.e., when (the sacrificial calendar), what (what kind of animal, how many) and how (by which procedure) sacrifices are to be offered. Such worship may only be performed in a sanctuary (*miqdash*) by an Aaronide priest observing strict rules of ritual purity. A sanctuary is not defined by its locality but by its function.

   2) Leviticus assumes that the tabernacle will serve as sanctuary. Deuteronomy is concerned with the application of the law after the conquest. Deut 12 absolutely prohibits the use of any Canaanite places of worship. The sanctuary must be in a place which is ritually pure.

II: The Law (Torah) of Israel

Conclusion

Both Samarians and Judeans accepted the Pentateuch. They considered themselves to be bound by the covenant between YHWH and Israel to which their ancestors had committed themselves during their sojourn in the desert. They called themselves Israelites, descendants of Jacob. Their tribal membership is irrelevant; the laws of the covenant apply to all Israel, regardless of tribal affiliation.[40] Each group had its own sanctuary dedicated to the service of YHWH. How did Samarians and Judeans differ? The main difference is as follows: the Judeans edited the historical books (the EP and Chronicles) as well as the writings of the LP. The Samarians only accepted the Pentateuch.

I suggest that the Samarians did not possess historical archival documents. The Assyrians, as well as the Babylonians, deported mainly the upper class, including the Levite/scribes. Presumably the Israelite deportees also took archives with them. The Assyrian exiles did not maintain their ethnic identity, and that material was lost (see chapter 10, "Prophecy and Reform"). The Samarians only possessed the Pentateuch, which had been returned to them with the Aaronide priest sent by the Assyrians (2 Kgs 17:28). Their historical books were composed long after the schism between Samarians and Jews had been solidified. The *Samaritan Joshua* (SJ)[41] describes how Eli usurped the office of high priest and the destruction of Shiloh. There is total silence about the history of Israel between Eli and the Persian period. The *Annals of Abu'l Fath*, discussed and quoted by Anderson and Giles,[42] denigrate the prophets of the MT: Samuel is a descendant

---

3) Neither Leviticus nor Deuteronomy anticipate the division of Israel into two states. One sanctuary will meet the requirements of worship. The need for additional sanctuaries is not considered.

4) Sacrifices outside the sanctuary are explicitly allowed (Deut 12:15), provided they are "within your gates." Exclusive centralization of the cult was only introduced by the Babylonian exiles.

40. The inhabitants of the province of Samaria came mainly from the tribes of Ephraim, Manasseh, and Levi; the inhabitants of the province Jehud consisted mainly of Judah, Benjamin, and Levi. Biblical scholarship tends to dismiss the historicity of the tribal divisions. Thus Davies (*Origins*, 176) asserts that *"no text or passage in which Judah belongs to Israel should be dated before the Neo-Babylonian period at the earliest, and perhaps not before the Persian Period"* (emphasis by author).

41. Crane, *Samaritan Chronicle*, discussed by Anderson and Giles, *Tradition Kept*, 49–142. All quotes are based on Crane.

42. Ibid., 71–168.

of Korah "who claimed the gift of prophecy, and they believed him," and Elijah was a false prophet who told lies. The archival material taken by the Judeans to Babylon formed the basis of their historical books—the EP and Chronicles—and were edited during the Persian period. These texts were not accepted by the Samarians. The biblical historical books contain material relevant for the Samarians. Some scholars suggest that much of the material in the book of Kings was originally written in Israel and adopted later by the so-called Deuteronomist Historian. It is not credible that the Samarians would copy the Pentateuch or collaborate with the Judeans in its final redaction, while at the same time dismissing the historical books. The Samarians did not develop the Pentateuch together with the Judeans. It was their own heritage. Anderson and Giles suggest the following:

> Comparison with the LXX, the MT and, more recently, the Qumran materials have demonstrated that the text adopted by the Samaritans was part of a group of texts that existed side by side and, in various ways, related to each other in the centuries before the turn of the eras . . . it is best to consider the SP as a tree branch coexisting with other branches that developed from a common trunk.[43]

Anderson and Giles add a drawing of a trunk with four branches, representing the MT, the PT, the LXX and the DSS. The "trunk" (i.e., the Pentateuch) is the same for the three texts. The "branches" are merely embellishments and do not represent different sources. The only substantial changes are the sectarian interpolations discussed above. As Knoppers concludes,

> Because the additions within a given scroll (e.g., Exodus) do not vary in form or kind from the additions that have been inserted into one book (e.g., Exodus) on the basis of another (e.g., Deuteronomy), it seems clear that the scribes responsible for such additions conceived of the Pentateuch as a single literary whole . . . The scribes responsible for these expansionary plusses did not create new texts ex nihilo but borrowed passages from one text to address perceived lacunae in another . . . The five books in the Pentateuch are but individual parts of a cohesive whole . . . The Pentateuch has to be regarded as a common patrimony from the time before the relations between the Judeans and the Samarians became seriously aggravated in the last two centuries BCE.[44]

---

43. Anderson and Giles, *Tradition Kept*, 4–5.
44. Knoppers, *Jews and Samaritans*, 181, 183, 188.

II: The Law (Torah) of Israel

When was the main stem, the common patrimony, completed? Knoppers suggests that the written Torah is "the result of a prolonged collaboration between the two communities"[45] and that "the Pentateuch was ultimately a compromise document."[46] This conclusion is based on the assumption that Deuteronomy stipulated a single sanctuary. Actually, there was no need for a "compromise document." We have seen that, until the middle of the second century BCE, both sanctuaries were accepted as legitimate, ruled by the Aaronide priesthood. Both groups considered themselves to be Israelites. Samarians in the Aegean Islands called themselves Israelites and sent donations to the temple of Mount Gerizim.[47] The elite of Judea and Samaria intermarried. Ezra and Nehemiah, who represented the views of the Judean Babylonian elite, met strong resistance to their reforms.[48]

> Although some have contended that Ezra–Nehemiah furnishes clear evidence of a major schism between Samaria and Judah in the late 6th or mid-5th century, I shall argue that this is not the case. On the contrary, internal literary evidence from within Ezra-Nehemiah indicates that many contacts continued between the two areas, especially among the elites ... That both Yahwistic groups came to affirm the same collection of scriptures can hardly be accidental ... The proposition that precisely the same changes arose spontaneously and independently in both communities so that both Pentateuchs remained virtually identical over a considerable period of time strains historical credulity. It makes much more sense to view the Pentateuch, at least for a time, as a common literary enterprise.[49]

These conclusions imply that both versions are based on a common source. Biblical scholarship assumes that Deuteronomy did not exist before the time of King Josiah. Therefore, the Pentateuch must have been written at the time of Ezra or later; even if it includes ancient traditions, major parts of it were composed during the Persian, Hellenistic, or even the Hasmonean period, and reflect the religious views of these times. Grabbe suggests that a "recession before 100 BCE cannot be excluded."[50] I sug-

---

45. Ibid., 178.
46. Ibid., 212.
47. Ibid., 171. See earlier discussion of the mounts.
48. Ibid., especially 102–34 and 135–68, reviews the history in detail.
49. Ibid., 138, 190, 192–93.
50. Grabbe, *Yehud*, 471.

gest that it strains historical credulity to assume that the Samarians would accept such a fictitious Torah as authoritative. Why should they do this? During the Babylonian and Persian eras Samaria was more important than Jerusalem. If the Pentateuch did not exist until the time of Ezra—what enabled the Samarians to maintain their Israelite identity after the Assyrian conquest? It has been suggested[51] that a non-sectarian proto-Samaritan Pentateuch was accepted by the Samarians in the late second century BCE. What would be the scenario for "a prolonged collaboration between the two communities?" It implies that representatives of both groups worked together, reviewed older scrolls, and then wrote the Pentateuch as it now stands. This means that they agreed on the order of presentation of each section (see earlier discussion p. 68). Yet in the face of all this cooperation, they maintained differences in spelling and grammar: they could agree where to place the story of Judah and Tamar (Gen 37), but could not agree whether to include "and" before the names of the sons of Jacob in Exodus 1? Such a sequence of events does not make sense. Neither Samarians nor Judeans copied the Pentateuch from each other. The MT, as well as the SP, are different editions of the same document.

The alternative conclusion is this: the books of the Pentateuch were already recognized as a unit before the separation between the kingdoms of Judah and Israel. The PT was deposited safely, possibly in the Ark. The Levites and Cohanim were the traditional scribes in both Israel and Judah, careful guardians of older traditions. There will have been copies of the entire Pentateuch, as well as copies of each of the books and of smaller segments. Each copy will have included scribal errors as well as editorial comments. Once a copy was deposited, it was venerated and not discarded. Subsequent scribes copied a mistake, even if they knew the correct version. The DSS represent, of course, only a small segment of scrolls available at this time. Many copies must have existed when Simeon Ben Shetach founded schools in various cities to teach the Torah (first century BCE). The abundance of Pentateuch variants does not show the existence of different traditions; it merely demonstrates the literacy of the Judean population, at least from the first century BCE on. The rabbinical authorities, and probably the Samarian authorities too, decided to establish an official version. They would scrutinize various manuscripts, deciding which to accept. They did not "construct" new texts. It appears that the rabbinical scribes were guided by the following considerations: they preferred older defective spelling and

---

51. Purvis, *Samaritan Pentateuch*.

II: The Law (Torah) of Israel

archaic diction and generally rejected additions, commentary, or transposition of verses. They often accepted readings which they considered to be a mistake (cf. above, *qere* and *sebirin*, see pp. 65–67). The Samarian generally accepted the *plene* spelling and included many of the conflated passages.

Early dating of the Torah does not challenge the documentary theory per se, but assumes that any redactions of the Pentateuch took place before the divided kingdom era. Nor does it invalidate the analysis of archaeological data from Iron Age I and later. For example, Faust states that

> The question of their origin—whether their ancestors were slaves in Egypt, semi-nomads in Transjordan or in the central highlands, Canaanite peasants, or a combination of some or all of the above, is of lesser importance for the present discussion [i.e., the formation of Israelite ethnicity], as interesting and important as it may be.[52]

Then he acknowledges that "The only exception is if one accepts the view that all Israelites came from Egypt—in which case their ethnogenesis was of course earlier, making the study of their ethnogenesis in the present context, including this monograph, obsolete."[53] I think Faust is too modest. His analysis of the archaeological record is relevant and important even if his theory about the origin of Israel is wrong.

We are now confronted with another big "how come" question. If the Pentateuch was available to Israel since the tenth or eleventh century BCE—how can this be reconciled with the evidence of religious syncretism shown by archeological findings? Did Israel follow this law? Not according to the books of the Earlier Prophets. Israel was always a "stiff-necked" people, rebelling against God even in the time of Moses. Their kings, as well as the common people, followed the customs of the local population of Canaan; they worshiped other gods, and only when things went badly returned to YHWH—for a brief time. Thus, the Bible and biblical scholarship agree: pre-exilic Israel was not a monotheist nation. The difference lies in the interpretation of the situation. The HEP takes it for granted that YHWH is the supreme God of Israel. Israel is bound to serve only God, but sinned. Nevertheless, there is never any doubt in any biblical book that YHWH was worshiped both in Judah and Israel. Other cults were allowed, but they did not replace YHWH. The prophets of YHWH are recognized as authorities, and any oath is made in the name of YHWH. There are no

---

52. Faust, *Israel's Ethnogenesis*, 28.
53. Ibid., 28n15.

mythological stories about YHWH. There is no biblical passage suggesting that the basic principles of Israel's religion were unknown at the time of the monarchy. Biblical scholarship, on the other hand, tends to assert that Israel was not monotheistic because monotheism had not yet been developed, and that the laws of the Torah were not followed, because they did not yet exist. My interpretation assumes that the Israelite invaders under Joshua were an organized ethnic group. The editing of the Pentateuch material started during the sojourn in the desert and was probably completed before the monarchy, certainly at the time of Solomon, even if the impact of the message had not been absorbed.

5

The Religion of the Pentateuch

THE OXFORD DICTIONARY DEFINES religion as "1. The belief in and worship of a God or gods. 2. A particular system of faith and worship." Scholarly research organizes data and classifies religious systems. Monotheism, Syncretism, Monolatry, and Henotheism are useful concepts in philosophy and theology, but may obscure the reality of religious experience.

Monotheism assumes that one deity created the natural as well as the supernatural universe; all other events—including the creation and activities of the "elohim" (gods, godlike beings) which the deity created—are subject to his/her will. Polytheism (paganism), on the other hand, presupposes the existence of many deities, differing in power and function. Monotheism assumes a transcendent deity, not bound by any law, while the deities in Polytheism are part of the cosmos and subject to cosmic laws. Pagan deities generally have specific functions. Thus, in Greek mythology Zeus is the ruler of deities, Neptune rules the sea, and Athena is the goddess of wisdom. Some deities are attached to specific ethnic groups: Dagon to the Philistines; Chemosh to Moab. Monolatry demands the exclusive worship of the "national deity" without denying the existence of other deities. Henotheism too refers to the specific worship of one god, but accepts that other religions may also be derived from valid divine manifestations. Henotheism is the only truly tolerant religious system. Modern religious thought, striving to be "politically correct," tends toward henotheism, calling it ecumenical: there is one God, but s(h)e is legitimately manifested in many (all?) religions. Syncretism refers to the fusion of different religious systems into a new religion.[1]

---

1. The Bible reports syncretistic behavior, e.g., the concurrent conducting of

Such deliberations probably would have been irrelevant in biblical times. Terms like "monotheism" are generalizations which help contemporary scholars to classify their data. I doubt whether a woman offering incense to the "Queen of Heaven" would have thought about the theological implications of the ritual. People in the ancient world took their religious experience for granted.

Biblical scholarship tends to ignore the difference between theological theory (as expressed in a canonical document) and religious practice (as expressed in everyday life). A notable exception is Dever, who distinguishes between "cult" and "theology." "*Theology* will be defined as the intellectual and moral systematization of religious belief . . . *Cult* . . . is the *practice* of religion."[2] Hess distinguishes between (1) the religious beliefs expressed in the Bible, and (2) the religious beliefs and practices of Israel.[3] The theology of Israelite religion cannot be deduced from archaeological findings. It is implicit in the biblical text.

The Pentateuch describes a religious belief system: the attributes of the deity, the relationship between God and humanity and the proper worship of this deity. It is also a statement about the special relationship between God, the patriarchs, and their descendents. Israel is bound to God by a covenant, accepted by the entire people. All the provisions of this covenant—ritual practice, as well as criminal, civil, and constitutional law—have divine authority. Their meaning can only be understood through an analysis of the text as it stands. What Israel actually did is irrelevant to our understanding of the Torah. The finding of Ashera figurines do not imply that monotheism was unknown to the Pentateuch, nor do the pronouncements of the Pentateuch imply the absence of pagan practices in Israel.

The Pentateuch is not a homogenous book. It includes three different law codices, each one embedded in other material. There are contradictions between these sources. Nevertheless, all three sources agree on the basic theological message. The difference is in emphasis. The JE source is mainly concerned with the history of the world and especially with the history of Israel until the conquest. It is what German scholars called the

---

Canaanite and Israelite rituals. It does not report true syncretism after the conquest—namely a religious system which fuses monotheism with paganism. However, the sacrificial ritual—as well as the festivals ordained in the Pentateuch—are based on pagan rituals to which a new meaning was given. See chapter 5.

2. Dever, *Recent Archaeological*, 121–22; emphasis original.

3. Hess, *Israelite Religion*, 15–23.

II: The Law (Torah) of Israel

Heilsgeschichte (history of salvation).[4] The P source is mainly concerned with the holiness of Israel. The D source emphasizes the future, noting the laws to be kept after the occupation of Canaan. Even though different books deal with different topics, and there are three law codes with duplications and contradictions, the entire Pentateuch is unequivocal in its major ideas, which are expressed in all the books of the Torah.

The Hebrew Bible is a monotheistic text.[5] Throughout the entire biblical canon the deity is described as the Supreme Ruler, the Creator of the universe, not subject to any cosmic law, "a supernal God, above every cosmic law, fate, and compulsion; ... An unfettered divine will transcending all being."[6]

The Creation of the World and the Election of Israel

Genesis 1 describes the creation of the universe by the deity (ELOHIM), using the verb *b-r-a* (ברא) to define the act. This verb is used exclusively to describe divine creation—humans do not "create," they merely "form" (*y-ṣ-r*—יצר).[7] ELOHIM does not mold the world out of existing primordial material: "ELOHIM said: 'Let there be light' [*fiat lux*] and there was light" (Gen 1:3). ELOHIM creates "by *fiat*."

The ELOHIM of Genesis 1 is a transcendent deity and does not interact with his creation. ELOHIM blesses animals and humans, that they be fruitful and multiply, but does not talk to them.[8] The Deity described in Genesis 2, YHWH, is immanent: he plants a garden and makes tunics for Adam and his wife. More importantly, he interacts with humans and utters commands which can be disobeyed. He even allows humans to argue with him. Before YHWH destroys Sodom and Gomorrah, he notifies Abraham, who challenges him (Gen 18:17–33): how can you destroy an entire city, killing the innocent with the guilty? "Shall not the Judge of all earth do

---

4. The term originated in Christian theology, referring to the salvation of humanity by Jesus.

5. This includes all the textual variations of the MS, the LXX, the SP, and the various DSS. As far as I know, none include pagan statements.

6. Kaufmann, *Religion*, 121.

7. Other verbs describing God's actions (whether "ELOHIM" or "YHWH") are also used to describe human activities.

8. In later parts of the Pentateuch, ELOHIM is reported to communicate with humans.

what is just?" (Gen 18:25). God is the creator and sole ruler of the entire world, transcending the universe, but he is also immanent: it is possible to enter an "I-Thou" relationship with him.[9] Of course, such anthropomorphic descriptions of YHWH are incompatible with strict monotheism. A transcendent ELOHIM cannot be angry, sad, or regret what he did. The logical development of monotheism leads towards deism, as has been recognized by medieval Jewish philosophers. Jehudah Halevi summarized (and rejected) this position:

> There is no favour or dislike in God, because He is above desire and intention. For an intention intimates a desire in the intending person: by the fulfillment of this desire he becomes complete; as long as it remains unfulfilled, he is incomplete ... God is, in the opinion of the philosophers, above the knowledge of individuals, because they change with the times and there is no change in God's knowledge. He does not know thee ... Everything is reduced to the Prime Cause.[10]

Judah Halevi concluded that philosophy is irrelevant for religion: it does not lead towards religion, does not help to maintain religion, and is not necessary for the manifestation of religious experience. Thus the king of the Khazars exclaims, "Now I understand the difference between GOD and the LORD ... to the LORD we yearn, tasting and viewing Him, to GOD [ELOHIM and YHWH] we draw near through speculation."[11]

Maimonides concluded that the human mind is incapable of grasping the meaning of "God's knowledge" and interpreted all anthropomorphic references to God as allegorical. Nevertheless, whether rational or not, biblical monotheism describes the deity as both transcendent and immanent.

Table 5.1

	Immanence—no	Immanence—yes
Transcendence—yes	deism	monotheism
Transcendence—no	atheism	paganism

9. Buber, *I and Thou*.
10. Halevi, "Kuzari," I.1.
11. Ibid., IV.16.

II: The Law (Torah) of Israel

The Bible is not interested in such deliberations.[12] Zevit puts it beautifully:

> In terms of the idea of deities, it appears to me that for early antiquity, immanence, presence, and availability were supposed to be the normal situation while distance and transcendence created (practical and) theological difficulties; for (many) contemporary theologians, transcendence is the norm while closeness and immanence raise theological issues.[13]

God created humans who are free to choose between good and evil. God may direct, command, reward, or punish, but only rarely does he interfere with human choices.[14] This poses a problem for God. Up to day six, everything created by God was found to be good. Man is the only creation about which was not said "ELOHIM saw it was good," though at the end of the sixth day "ELOHIM saw everything he had made, and indeed, it was very good" (Gen 1:31). But ten generations later,

> YHWH saw that the wickedness of humankind was great in the earth, and that every inclination of the thoughts of their hearts was only evil continually. And YHWH was sorry that he had made humankind on the earth, and it grieved him to his heart. So YHWH said, "I will blot out from the earth the human beings I have created—people together with animals and creeping things and birds of the air, for I am sorry that I have made them." (Gen 6:5–7)

Yet Noah was a just man, and for his sake YHWH decided not to destroy all humanity. Noah built the ark (under God's guidance) and life was not extinguished. After the flood, Noah offered sacrifices: "And when YHWH smelled the pleasing odor, YHWH said in his heart, 'I will never again curse the ground because of humankind, for the inclination of the human heart is evil from youth; nor will I ever destroy every living creature as I have done'" (Gen 8:21). Therefore ELOHIM establishes a covenant with humanity: "And ELOHIM said to Noah and to his sons with him . . . 'I

---

12. The need to define religion arose when Judaism was confronted with Greek philosophy. From the time of Philo onward, Jewish philosophers (Saadyah Gaon, Jehudah Halevi, Maimonides, Spinoza, and contemporary apologists) attempted to prove that monotheism is a rational belief system. They did not write in Hebrew (until modern times)—Greek, Arabic, Latin and contemporary European languages are their mode of expression.

13. Zevit, *Religions*, 81n2.

14. The important exception is the "hardening of the heart" of Pharaoh in Exod 7–14.

establish my covenant with you, that never again shall all flesh be cut off by the waters of a flood, and never again shall there be a flood to destroy the earth'" (Gen 9:8, 11).

Perhaps the most remarkable aspect of this narrative is that the author does not even consider the obvious alternative: God could have changed humanity, instilled more kindness, increased their moral conscience, and strengthened their ability to control their evil inclinations. YHWH allows humanity to go on living as before; he will not interfere with "free will." YHWH anticipates that he might lose his patience. Therefore he establishes a safety device: whenever he starts a new flood, the rainbow will appear as a reminder to God of his promise.

This story does not fit the image of an almighty God as conceived by Greek philosophers. The monotheism of the Pentateuch is not defined by the description of God's activities, but by the following indicators which are evident through all five books: God is the sole creator of the universe.[15] He is non-mythological. There are no stories about God's life; he does not associate with other deities.

> A God ... who does not sacrifice, divine, prophesy or practise sorcery; who does not sin and needs no expiation; a God who does not celebrate festivals of his life.[16]

God will not prevent mankind from being evil. However, he plans to establish a just society to be an example for humanity. God promises Abraham that through him all the nations of the earth will be blessed, because his descendents will be a great nation which will establish a righteous society. The first promise to Abraham is:

> I will make you a great nation, and I will bless you, and make your name great, so that you will be a blessing ... *and through you all the families of the earth will be blessed*. (Gen 12:2, 3; my translation and emphasis)[17]

---

15. See "For the whole world is mine" (Exod 19:5); "For in six days YHWH made heaven and earth, the sea *and all that is in them*" (Exod 20:11a; my emphasis).

16. Kaufmann, *Religion*, 121.

17. The translation of this phrase is disputed. NRSV: "in you ... shall be blessed." REB: "will wish to be blessed as you are blessed." NEB: "will pray to be blessed like you." NAB: "shall find blessing in you." NJB: "bless themselves by you." Biblia: "*serán benedictus en ti*." The grammatical form of the phrase is passive (נברכו בו).

II: The Law (Torah) of Israel

The Hebrew phrase "will be blessed through him" occurs only five times and always refers God's promise to Abraham.[18] The meaning of the phrase is spelled out as follows:

> All the nations of the earth shall be blessed in [through] him. I have chosen [known] him, that he may charge his children [sons] and his household after him to keep the way of YHWH by doing righteousness and justice; so [in order that] YHWH may bring about for Abraham what he has promised him. (Gen 18:18b–19)

The blessing to Abraham is that his descendants will be a blessing to the world, because they pursue righteousness and justice. The same idea is expressed later: "For the whole world is mine. For me you shall be a kingdom of priests, a holy nation" (Exod 19:5–6). It culminates in the prophecy of Isaiah: "Many peoples will come to it and say, 'Come, let us go up to the mountain of YHWH . . . that he may teach us his ways'" (Isa 2:3).

Abraham, Isaac, and Jacob are to be the ancestors of this nation. The Bible never explains why Abraham was chosen for this task. The patriarchs are not role models, but flawed humans. YHWH tells Isaac: "All the nations of the world shall gain blessings through your offspring, because Abraham obeyed my voice and kept my charge, my commandments, my statues, and my laws" (Gen 26:4b–5). This is rather vague. The patriarchs are distinguished by their ability to hear the voice of YHWH and to trust him. The first divine communication to Abraham requires him to leave his country, family, and father's house for an unknown land (Gen 12:1). He trusts God sufficiently to do this. He is old, but without a son. Nevertheless, when YHWH promises him that his descendants will multiply like the stars of heaven, "he trusted [my translation] in YHWH, and YHWH reckoned it to him as righteousness" (Gen 15:6).[19]

The promise to Abraham is contingent upon two conditions: the descendants—later called "Israel"—must be free in their own land, and

---

18. Gen 12:3; 18:18; 28:14 in *niphal*, 22:18; 26:4 in *hitpael*. Three times God speaks to Abraham, once to Isaac, and once to Jacob.

19. This verse is generally mistranslated as "he believed in the Lord" (NRSV), or "He put his faith in the Lord" (e.g. REB). This is the Christian interpretation, which stresses the importance of the correct "belief." The Hebrew word *he'emin* (האמין) is related to the noun *omenet*, which is the nurse to whom the infant is entrusted. The stem *a-m-n* means "to take care" or "to nurse." Thus Moses complains to God: "Did I conceive all this people? Did I give birth to them, that you should say to me, 'carry them in your bosom, as a nurse (omen—אמן) carries a sucking child'?" (Num 11:12). The term "Amen" means—"Trust that this is so." The patriarchs trust that YHWH will fulfill his promise.

they must be taught the meaning of justice. Therefore God promises, "I am YHWH who brought you from Ur of the Chaldeans, to give you this land to possess" (Gen 15:7). This promise is affirmed by a formal covenant. The Hebrew term for concluding a treaty is "cutting a covenant." This describes the traditional Middle East procedure: a sacrificial animal was cut in the middle, the participants of the covenant passed through the cuttings, implying that they would be cut if they break the terms of the treaty. The vision of Abraham (Genesis 15:9–18) displays this rite: Abraham prepared the sacrificial animals, cut them, and arranged them in two heaps. Then he fell into a deep trance: "When the sun had gone down and it was dark, a smoking fire pot and a flaming torch passed between these pieces. On that day YHWH made [cut] a covenant with Abram, saying, to your descendants I give this land" (Gen 15:17–18a). There is no need for Abraham (called Abram at this time) to pass between the pieces: this is an unconditional one-sided grant covenant. Only YHWH commits himself. Of course, the first promise will only be fulfilled when his descendants do "righteousness and justice." What is meant by these terms? God can help Israel by giving instructions (Torah), defining them. The Sinai law is the operational definition of a just society. It gives no formal philosophical definition of what is meant by "justice." Most laws are not "laws," but "examples" illustrating how a just society should function. "If a man shall open a pit . . ."; "If a man's ox hurt another's . . ."; and so forth. All these cases deal with personal responsibility for incidental damage caused by one's action; the formal law is not stated.[20] These examples show what was considered to be "just" at the time of the exodus. At the time of the Second Temple, many provisions of the Torah were out of date. This was recognized by the rabbis of the Second Temple who reinterpreted laws which were not considered to be appropriate in their time.

God liberated Israel from Egypt and entered a covenant with them. YHWH promised them the land of Canaan and a good life. Israel undertook not to worship any other deity and to follow/obey/guard[21] the teaching (Torah—תורה) of YHWH, which instructs them to be a holy nation. All Israel must accept the covenant willingly. Judaism is the only religion, as far as I know, which claims a public theophany, or a manifestation of

---

20. Cf. von Rad, *Deuteronomy*, 17–20.

21. The Hebrew term *sh-m-r* (שמר) is generally translated as "observe," "keep the law." Actually, it means "guard," as the watchman guards a plantation against intruders.

II: The Law (Torah) of Israel

the deity experienced by each member of the community.[22] The covenant was reaffirmed on later occasions; this was always done in the presence of every member of the community, old and young, male and female, rich and poor. Thus the covenant was binding on the leaders as well as on the general population.[23]

The first law of the covenant is this: "You shall have no other gods before me" (Exod 20:3). Monotheism does not deny the existence of divine beings. The Pentateuch acknowledges the existence of other gods, but forbids Israel to worship them. The biblical person does not meditate on the nature of God or other supernatural beings. The Decalogue does not deny their existence. I assume that the people of the biblical world believed in the existence of a supernatural universe which is not subject to the laws of physical nature and interacts with the happenings of the natural world, occasionally benevolently, often maliciously.[24] They believed in the existence of divine beings (*elohim*, referred to in the plural), the whole host of heaven, who will hinder or promote happiness. They also believed that this supernatural world is strictly ruled by universal laws. They believed in the power of amulets. The magician knows these laws and can apply them. Pagan gods too are subject to these laws. YHWH, however, is always described as supreme, other *elohim* being subordinated to him. The Decalogue does not state: "believe in the existence of YHWH," or "don't believe in the existence of spiritual beings—ELOHIM." Such statements would be absurd.

> The statements in the canonical text (poetic or otherwise) inform the reader that, for the biblical writer, Yahweh was an אֱלֹהִים, but no other "אֱלֹהִים" was Yahweh—*and never was nor could be*.[25]

22. This was not a visible manifestation: "You heard the sound of words but saw no form; there was only a voice" (Deut 4:12).

23. In order to establish this society, the nation needs a land, and Abraham (and later Isaac and Jacob) is promised the land of Canaan. This promise is unconditional—it does not depend on the behavior of Israel. However, God never promised that all descendents of Abraham will be included in the blessing. Only those who will follow the law of Sinai will enjoy it. The transgressor will be "cut off" from his people. God's promise will be fulfilled as long there is one "remnant" who will return to God (Deut 30).

24. Not only in biblical times. Nowadays, too, the majority of humans believe in the power of supernatural events: that's why newspapers publish horoscopes, and people want to know under which sign they are born. They also will "touch wood," wear amulets, and avoid having a thirteenth floor in a hotel. While we refer to such notions as superstitions, few people are free of them.

25. Heiser, "Monotheism," 29 (author's emphasis). The quote continues: "This notion

The Israelites were not to construe Yahweh as operating within a community of gods. There was to be no thought of pantheon or consort. He does not function as the head of a pantheon with a divine assembly. In short, he works alone. The significance of this is that the pantheon/divine assembly concept carried with it the idea of distribution of power among many divine beings . . . The first commandment does not insist that the other gods are non-existent, but that they are powerless; it disenfranchises them. It does not simply say that they should not be worshiped; it leaves them with no status worthy of worship.²⁶

Worship of other gods is not *malum* per se. Idolatry is a *malum prohibitum*, but only for Israel. Deuteronomy explicitly permits it to other nations (Deut 4:19). Israel is distinguished by the ban on idolatry. Israel as a nation will prosper, and its members will lead a good life as long as this law is followed. Israel will be punished if the law is breached.

Worship (*avodah*—עבודה) and Holiness

The Decalogue does not require Israel to "worship" God; it forbids idolatry, but neither demands nor describes a sacrificial ritual. However, the people demanded sacrifices. The episode of the golden calf was a regression to old, traditional forms of worship. The Israelites needed formal rituals. Coming from Canaan, they will have had ancient pagan traditions of worship. I suggest that they will have celebrated the seasonal festivals of the time: a spring festival sacrificing a lamb, eating unleavened bread, and summer and autumn harvest festivals, as well as sacrificial rituals when slaughtering animals. The legislator faced a formidable challenge in developing a monotheistic sacrificial ritual (to a Deity who does not need it) based on old traditions. The Pentateuch legislation assimilates old customs, integrating them within the monotheistic system. They became the festivals of thanksgiving to YHWH, celebrating his maintenance of the seasons and the liberation of Israel from Egypt. The sacrificial legislation of Leviticus constitutes religious syncretism. The only new Israelite festival was the Sabbath. All the others are based on old Middle East traditions.

---

allows for the existence of other אֱלֹהִים and is more precise than the terms 'polytheism' and 'henotheism.' It is also more accurate than 'monotheism,' though it preserves the element of that conception that is most important to traditional Judaism and Christianity: Yahweh's solitary 'otherness' with respect to all that is, in heaven and in earth."

26. Walton, "Interpreting the Bible," quoted in Heiser, "Monotheism," 25.

II: The Law (Torah) of Israel

The P document defines the rites of service required ('avodah—עבודה) by YHWH. The Hebrew root 'a-v-d (עבד) originally means "to perform work" (Exod 1:14), especially "to work the land" (Gen 4:2). It also denotes a relationship of servitude (Exod 21:2) of a person to his master, a king to his overlord (2 Kgs 18:7), or of a nation to another nation (Deut 20:11; Isa 19:23). Finally, it means the formal "worship of a deity." This may appear as a general statement—"There you shall serve other gods" (Deut 28:36, 64)—or refer to a formal act of worship—as in "the worship of the chief men of Israel" (Num 7), Absalom fulfilling a vow (2 Sam 15:8), Ahab worshiping Baal (1 Kgs 16:31; 2 Kgs 10:18). "Sacrifice" means to sanctify an offering by dedicating it to a deity. The Pentateuch uses several expressions to designate the act of sacrificing: "raise a burnt offering" (he'elah olah—העלה עולה); "to present an offering" (le'haqriv qorban—להקריב קרבן); "to slaughter before YHWH" (lishḥot lifnei adonai—לשחט לפני יי); and "sacrifice" (zevaḥ—זבח).

The Bible distinguishes between general acts of devotion and formal rites of worship. P describes the *avodah* (service) due to YHWH, which is distinguished by its holiness, and may only be performed in a holy place.[27] The sanctuary meets the necessary conditions for the proper observance of *avodah*, presided over by a priest of Aaronite lineage, with strict observance to rituals of purity. The location of the sanctuary and its appurtenances are holy. The tabernacle is surrounded be a fence and constitutes a *temenos*: only ritually pure people may approach the place or participate in its ceremonies. The officiating priests must be of unblemished lineage and without bodily blemish: "And you shall appoint Aaron and his sons, and they shall attend to their priesthood; but if anyone else comes near he shall be put to death" (Num 3:10, my translation).

When the tent is to be moved, the priest must cover all the appurtenances. The Levites are in charge of the furniture:

> When Aaron and his sons have finished covering the sanctuary and all the furnishings of the sanctuary, as the camp sets out, after that the Kohathites shall come to carry these, but they must not touch the holy things, or they will die. (Num 4:15)

> But they shall not go in and look upon the holy things even for a moment; otherwise they will die. (Num 4:20)

The holiness of the sanctuary does not depend upon its physical location, but is defined by its function. Ultimately, its holiness is ascribed to the

---

27. For a discussion of the various terms for sanctuary see chapter 10, pp. 147–48.

deity. The Tabernacle is a *mishkan* (משכן), a "place of dwelling" of YHWH. Therefore, it is dangerous for an unqualified person to approach it.

The laws of P set out the ritual of *avodah* (עבודה), which is the "service required by YHWH": (1) which sacrifices are required at specific times—daily offerings, Sabbath offering and festival offerings, as well as offerings on special occasions; (2) what is to be offered—animals, birds, agricultural produce, herbs; and (3) detailed procedural rules—how the animal is to be slaughtered, how the blood is disposed of, when incense is to be burned. The obligatory *avodah* is based on the sacral calendar: (a) daily offerings, (b) sabbath offerings, and (c) festival offerings (there are three agricultural pilgrim festivals, as well as the "day of trumpet blasts" and the "day of atonement"[28]). The amounts required are specified; for example,

> On the sabbath day: two male lambs a year old without blemish, and two-tenth of an ephah of choice flour for a grain offering, mixed with oil, and its drink offering—this is the burnt offering for every sabbath, in addition to the regular burnt offering and its drink offering. (Num 28:9–10)

The sacrificial rite is described in minute detail. It encompasses four steps, which are as follows. (1) The donor who offers the sacrifice may either consecrate it verbally or bring it to the sanctuary, where he formally offers (brings near to YHWH—מקריב לי״י) the offering by laying his hands on the sacrificial animal. (2) He then slaughters the animal before YHWH (Lev 1:5–9). (3) Then the priest sprinkles the blood on the altar (in some cases also on the offerer or on himself). (4) Finally, the carcass (or part of it) is burned (מקטיר), "a pleasant odor to YHWH." It should be noted that the first two steps may be taken by a layperson. The last two ceremonies may only performed by a priest.

There are three levels of sacrifice: (1) The "burnt offering" (*olah*—עולה); (2) the "sin offering" (*ḥattat*—חטאת) and "guilt offering" (*asham*—אשם); (3) and various forms of *zevaḥ*—זבח. The olah is totally burnt—it "ascends" to YHWH. The *ḥattat* and *asham* are mostly burnt, but a part must be eaten by the officiating priest. Thus Phinehas and Ithamar are reprimanded when

---

28. They are summarized in Leviticus 23 and Numbers 28–29. Additional instructions about the three agricultural festivals are given in Deteronomy 16:1–17; several passages discuss the Passover ritual; and the Day of Atonement ritual is described in Leviticus 16.

II: The Law (Torah) of Israel

they omit this part of the ritual. The *zevaḥ* may be eaten by laypeople, who must be ritually purified.[29]

Only a priest (*Cohen*) may offer an *olah*. He must be of pure lineage, a descendant of Aaron. He must refrain from an unsuitable marriage (which would compromise the purity of the priestly line) and from attendance at funerals (which would make him unsuitable to serve at the sanctuary). Any physical blemish disqualifies him for service. Furthermore, any person entering the holy precincts must be ritually pure. The Pentateuch devotes much space to describing the circumstances voiding ritual purity, as well as the rituals involved in restoring it. Finally, the *avodah* can only be performed in a consecrated sanctuary. Access to various places within the sanctuary is strictly regulated, and the implements used are "holy" and may not be touched by a layperson.

The religious cult described in Leviticus is definitely monotheistic. Sacrifices are expressions of devotion and thanks. They are presented ("brought near") to YHWH, and their odor is pleasing to YHWH.[30] They are never described as necessary for the preservation of cosmic order. They are not offered in order to secure rain, or to increase the fertility of the earth. They are not needed to sustain the deity or to protect people from the envy of a deity. They have no magical functions. Priests control the ritual and supervise the maintenance of purity, but never engage in mantic magical behavior. When a priest diagnoses a malignant skin disease, he isolates the patient but does not engage in healing practices. He does not offer remedies or medicine. Sacrifices are not offered to speed recovery. The priest merely presides over the ceremonies of thanksgiving and purification of the healed person.

In addition to the obligatory primary *avodah* (the sacral calendar), other sacrifices may be offered on special occasions. There are the expiatory offerings: the "sin offering" (*ḥattat*—חטאת) and the "guilt offering" (*asham*—אשם). Here again the ritual is monotheistic. Sacrifices do not

---

29. Leviticus describes the formal rites of *avodah* to be carried out in a sanctuary. It does not discuss the application of these laws after the conquest, when sacrifices were offered on the high places (*bamoth*). The ritual on the *bamoth* had a lower degree of holiness. It could be performed by laypeople and partaken of by a ritually unclean person. In the later rabbinical view, the sacrifices on the *bamoth* were only acceptable before the establishment of the Jerusalem sanctuary.

30. Cassuto (*Documentary Hypothesis*, 35) points out that sacrifices in Israel are always offered to YHWH, never to ELOHIM (excepting the sacrifice of Moses' Midianite father-in-law, who sacrificed to ELOHIM).

obliterate the consequences of former transgressions, nor do they offer compensation to any damaged party. They are not a punishment to expiate sin. They do not affect the harmony of the world. The commission of a sin has defiled the sinner. The purpose of the *hattat* and the *asham* is to purify the offerer. It is required for unintentional sins, after confession, and for criminal or civil offenses after restitution has been made. It is required by a person who has become ritually unclean. A woman after childbirth, a leper after healing, or a person touching a corpse or coming in contact with impure substances—they all require ritual purification by *hattat* or *asham*. The effect of the sacrifice is that the unintentional sin is forgiven and the ritual impurity removed.

These procedures are complicated and described in great detail, involving the sprinkling of blood in a specific order. I do not think that they were invented by Moses. They probably were ancient ceremonies which had become ritualized. Originally they probably had a magical function. The biblical text does not explain their purpose; it merely describes them. The only "benefit" which God derives from sacrifices is "of pleasing odor to YHWH" (Lev 1:17b).[31]

There is a third group of sacrifices (*zevah*) which are offered on special occasions. These sacrifices have a lesser degree of holiness. Part of the meat is eaten by the priest and the rest is consumed by laypeople. They all are expressions of thanksgiving and joy.

Priests are the guardians of Israel's holiness. God is holy, and the ritual approach to God is awesome and dangerous. Israel is to be "holy," which means "dedicated and ritually pure." The "holiness code" (Leviticus 17–26, specifically chapter 19) gives the operational definition of what it means to be holy: ritual purity, sexual purity, sanitary purity, dietary purity, and concern for others.

There is no priestly liturgy. The Torah describes the sacrificial ritual in detail, but does not mention any spoken ritual, magic pronouncements, prayers, or hymns.[32] The only spoken formula is the priestly blessing (Num

---

31. Medieval Jewish philosophers realized that a monotheistic deity does not need sacrifices. Maimonides (*Guide*, III, 32) thought that they were a "ruse," introduced because the Israelites were accustomed to sacrificial rites. Joseph Kaspi goes further: "Most people strive to imitate their forefathers. For this reason Moses in the Torah told us to offer sacrifices, even though *in truth they are an abomination—*דבר נתעב." (Gevia' Kesef, 127a; my emphasis), reprinted by Herring, Joseph Ibn Kaspi, 159.

32. This does not mean that religious ceremonies were silent. Hymns were sung and prayers called out, but they are acts of devotion or supplication; they have no magic

II: The Law (Torah) of Israel

6:24–26). However, while the priest recites the formula, the actual blessing is done by YHWH himself: "They shall put my name over Israel, and *I will bless them*" (Num 6:27; my emphasis).³³

The bulk of P is a manual for Cohanim and Levites—"What do you need to know to be a priest?" It includes detailed instructions about the construction of the sanctuary and its care and the sacrificial cult, as well as the diagnostic criteria for skin disease and blemishes in clothing, vessels, and houses. The priest is responsible for determining what or who is ritually pure, and how to purify. Priests are not given legislative or executive authority. They are charged with maintaining records and teaching the law (Deut 31:9–13). Though the laws of priesthood deal with the responsibilities of Levites and priests, they are addressed to Israel as a nation. The maintenance of the ritual is considered to be a collective responsibility.

In conclusion, the basic principles of the Pentateuch are already spelled out in the Tetrateuch (Genesis–Numbers). The fifth book, Deuteronomy, is represented as a series of speeches by Moses; it is designed to prepare the new generation of Israelites, born in the desert, for life in the land to be conquered.

---

power.

33. Deut 26:1–15 gives examples of ritual pronouncements by laypersons. The occasion is the presentation of the first fruit and of the tithe made at the sanctuary before the priest. They are official acknowledgments of an obligation, combined with expressions of thanks and prayer for future blessings.

6

Deuteronomy

Deuteronomy is a book about a community being prepared for a new life.[1]

DEUTERONOMY MEANS THE SECOND Law or the Repetition of the Law.[2] It describes events which occurred before the invasion of Canaan, in the fortieth year after the exodus. It consists mainly of speeches by Moses, as well as the report of the installation of Joshua as Moses' successor, and of Moses' death. The narrator quotes Moses; Moses relates past events, quoting his own speech, "I said," as well as the speech of others, "you said." In the main passages Moses quotes YHWH.

Deuteronomy does not dwell on the topics of the earlier books. If we had only Deuteronomy, we would not know anything about the stories of Genesis, such as the creation and the flood. We would know of God's covenant with the patriarchs, but nothing about their history. We would not have heard about the tent of meeting, the sacrificial service described in Leviticus, or most of the regulations concerning ritual purity. The three pilgrim festivals are described as agricultural festivals, but the sacrifices for these days are not mentioned (Deut 16). This does not imply that the writer of Deuteronomy was unaware of the stories of Genesis or of the sacrificial rituals—merely that they were not the theme of his discourse.

---

1. Craigie, *Book of Deuteronomy*, 7.

2. The Greek term is actually based on a mistranslation of *mishneh torah* (משנה תורה), which means "a copy of the law" (Deut 17:18).

II: The Law (Torah) of Israel

Deuteronomy is mainly concerned with the application of the law after the conquest of Canaan.

> When YHWH your God has brought you in to the land that you are entering to occupy . . . (Deut 11: 29)

> If there is found among you, in one of your towns . . . (17:2)

> When you go out to war against your enemies . . . (20:1)

> When you have come into the land that YHWH your God is giving you. (26:1)

The central event described in Deuteronomy is the formal renewal of the covenant[3] between Israel and YHWH in the fields of Moab. The ideas of monotheism had not been absorbed by the Israelites. The sojourn in the desert was a time of conflict and rebellion. The renewal of a covenant was routine in the world of the Levant; it was mandatory if the covenant had been broken, as it was in the affair of Baal Pe'or (Num 25).[4]

Moses has a vision of an ideal society, its life based on the covenant with YHWH, guided by the principles of justice and rationality:

> I now teach you statutes and ordinances . . . you must observe them diligently, for this will show your wisdom and discernment to the peoples, who . . . will say, "surely this great nation is a wise and discerning people!" . . . For what other great nation has statutes and ordinances as just as this entire law that I am setting before you today? (Deut 4:5–8)

But the good life promised can only be sustained if the people adhere to the provisions of the covenant. How are the laws of the covenant to be applied after the conquest? The author of Deuteronomy (let us call him Moses) talks to people who were raised in the desert. Their knowledge of an agricultural society is based on traditions of life in Egypt, and earlier in Canaan, a life that the children born in the desert never had known. They lived close to each other near their sanctuary. They had not seen houses or villages. What problems will they face after the conquest? Moses is confronted with a problem which later on preoccupied the teachers of the Mishnah: the Torah was out of date. The laws of the Tetrateuch do not

---

3. See pp. 35–37. For a detailed review of covenants in the Middle East, cf. Kitchen, *Reliability*, 283–310.

4. Midianite women seduced Israelite men, who started worshiping the Midianite deity Baal Pe'or.

consider the problems of a developed agricultural society with cities and international commerce. Some of the old laws may be obsolete. New laws may be needed.

Von Rad points out that the ordinances of the Pentateuch appear in three forms.[5] The foundation of the codex is the *apodictic law*. These are definite laws, expressed as divine command, such as "honor your father and your mother" or "you shall not kill." Most laws are expressed as *casuistic law*, case law considering a hypothetical situation: "If you buy a Hebrew slave . . ." In addition, there is the *Paränese*, the hortatory sermon: the congregation is admonished to observe the law, which is stated repeatedly. He appeals to their conscience.[6] It should be noted that the apodictic law of the Tetrateuch is confirmed in Deuteronomy: the Decalogue is quoted. The old law stands. The differences in law between Deuteronomy and the covenant code are found in the casuistic law. Moses considers hypothetical contingencies based on the consideration of new situations. Thus Deuteronomy discusses institutions of government after the conquest: monotheism delimits the role and power of public functionaries.

(1) Judges have no legislative power. They are appointed by the people (the procedure is not specified) and are bound by the law of the Torah (Deut 16:18-20). In case of doubt, the priests will interpret the law (17:8-11).

(2) The people may install a king, but his appointment must be ratified by God (through a prophet or through the priestly oracle). They are neither divine nor of divine descent. The king's power is limited; he too is bound by the law (Deut 17:14-20). Deuteronomy does not specify the responsibilities of the king. Von Rad notes that the law mainly attempts to limit the power and function of the king. It does not describe the role of the king, but shows what the king should not do.[7] That is not quite correct. The guiding principle is clearly spelled out: "He shall have a copy of this law written for him . . . It shall remain with him and he shall read it all the days of his life, so that he may learn to fear YHWH his God, by diligently observing all the words of this law and these statues" (Deut 17:18b-19).

---

5. Von Rad, *Das fünfte Buch Mose*. All direct quotes come from von Rad, *Deuteronomy*.

6. Von Rad (*Deuteronomy*, 23) talks of "the pressing, sometimes even imploring, way of speaking, and the endeavour to grip the hearers personally in order to bind the divine commands on their conscience."

7. "For the law endeavours above all to restrict the power and function of the king. It does not draw any positive picture of the kingly office in Israel, only a picture of a king as he ought not to be" (ibid., 16).

II: The Law (Torah) of Israel

(3) *Prophets* were not diviners, predicting the future through their mantic powers. They are spiritual leaders, messengers of YHWH. "I will raise up for them a prophet like you from amongst their own people; and I will put my words into his mouth [my translation], who will tell them everything that I command" (Deut 18:18). The true prophet is not considered to speak for himself: The spirit of YHWH takes possession of him. There is no Hebrew verb "to prophecy." The Hebrew verb (*n-v-'a*—נבא) appears only in the passive (*niphal*) or reflexive (*hitpael*) stem. A correct translation would be "He was *prophesized*," or "he became *prophesized*," or "he *prophesized* himself" (the latter use often applied to false prophets).[8]

Utopias tend to clash with reality. Deuteronomy does not give an accurate picture of life in Israel after the conquest. It considers situations which did not occur, e.g., "the rebellious city." It does not foresee the divided kingdom. Moses knows that the idea of monotheism has not been absorbed by Israel. He foresees that the Canaanites will not be annihilated and will live with the Israelites. The major concern of both Leviticus and Deuteronomy is to safeguard the acceptance of the basic demands of the Decalogue: (1) I am YHWH your God, and (2) do not make idols and do not serve them. The preservation of monotheism is jeopardized by the potential influence of Canaanite rituals. The prohibition of sacrifices outside the sanctuary is not concerned with the centralization of the cult, but with the rejection of Canaanite holy places.

Centralization

Biblical scholarship talks about the "centralization of worship," ordained in Deuteronomy 12. The term "centralization" does not appear in the Hebrew Bible. Boman showed that Hebrew thought differs profoundly from Greek Hellenistic thought.[9] The imagery of Greek thinking is predominantly spatial. Hebrew thought is dynamic.[10] The difference is manifest in the ranking of the significance of important events. Western scholarship follows the

---

8. The noun *navi* is a title, following the qatal form *qatil*—קָטִיל. Other examples include *nasi'*, *qatsin*, and *paqid*—all officials. See Fleming, "Etymological Origins," quoted in Hess, *Israelite Religions*, 89.

9. Boman, *Hebrew Thought*.

10. For example, the Greek term *logos* is derived from a verb meaning "to gather" or "to arrange." The corresponding Hebrew term *davar* is derived from the verb meaning "to prod cattle." *Logos* means "word, reason"; *davar* means "word, deed."

Greek mode of thinking. Important events are at the center of our vision; less important events are located in the periphery. The Bible has no word for "center."[11] For both Leviticus and Deuteronomy, the importance of the sanctuary is determined by its function, not by its locality. It is defined by the rites conducted there, not by its place. The site of the tabernacle is central because it is "most holy" (*qodesh qodashim*) wherever it is erected. It meets the necessary conditions for the proper observance of *avodah*, under the rule of a priest of Aaronite lineage, with strict observance of purity rituals. The sacrificial rites are centralized because wherever they are performed they are subject to the ritual regulations of the Pentateuch, interpreted by the priest. Biblical centralization is also exclusive. The Pentateuch restricts the conditions under which a sacrifice may be offered, as well as the kind of activities which are permitted where "the name of YHWH dwells."

Traditional Judaism—as well as biblical scholarship—assumes that Deuteronomy envisages the total centralization of the cult; sacrifices are only to be offered at one central sanctuary: "Take care that you do not offer your burnt offerings at every place that you see. But only at the place that YHWH will choose in one of your tribes—there you shall offer your burnt offerings, and there you shall do everything I command you" (Deut 12:13–14). This interpretation has been challenged. The singular number in the expression "the place" in Deuteronomy denotes a single class to which the law applies, not one exclusive single locality. Thus the Hebrew text in Deuteronomy 16:11 refers to "you, and your son and your daughter, and your servant and maidservant, and the Levite within your gates, and the stranger and the orphan and the widow who [live] in your midst at *the place which YHWH your God will chose* to have his name dwell there" (my translation and emphasis). All nouns in this verse are distributive: they do refer not to individuals but to groups. The NAB and NJB translate the terms in singular. The NRSV and REB render a distributive translation (your sons) but do not extend this correct understanding to the reference of the sanctuary, translating "the place" in singular.[12]

Zevit argues that Leviticus 17 refers to "a" tent/dwelling place, not to "the" tent/dwelling place.[13] A syntactic analysis shows that the phrase "in one

---

11. Contemporary Hebrew uses the term *merkaz* for "center," based on the root *r-k-s* (רכז). This verb appears neither in the *CONC* nor in *HCAT*. It appears first in medieval rabbinical commentaries (*MGK* on Prov 8:27, and Levi ben Gershom on Job 26:7) and is cited in *DTTY*.

12. See Segal, *Book of Deuteronomy*, 329–31.

13. Zevit, *Religions*, 286–88.

of your tribes" means "in any of your tribes." A change in one vowel mark would amend "the place" to "a place." Therefore a better translation of 12:14 would read; "in a place which YHWH will choose in any of your tribes." Any place which has been properly sanctified may become a sanctuary:

> The Sinaitic law expressly limits sacrifices to a place sanctified by the divine presence. The statement: 'An altar of earth shalt thou make unto Me and thou shalt sacrifice thereon . . .' is qualified and defined by the immediate declaration: 'In every place where I cause My name to be remembered I will come unto thee and bless thee' (Ex. 20.24). The declaration implies that sacrifices will be acceptable and bring a blessing to the worshipper only if they are offered at a place divinely appointed for the remembrance of God's name. But the Sinaitic law also implies that God may appoint more than one place for His name to be remembered there.[14]

> The concept of a legitimate shrine was determined, at least in part, by the pedigree of officiants rather than by its singularity . . . Accordingly, the original core legislation of both Deuteronomy 12 and Leviticus 17, in social and literary contextualizations prior to their extant ones, presupposed the existence of many cult places and recognized the legitimacy of many cult places with their attendant appurtenances.[15]

Kaufmann argues:

> Anciently, there was but one tent in which YHWH reveals himself to Israel, hence it was the only legitimate cult place. There is no intention, however, to exclude the legitimacy of many temple sites in the land after the conquest. This is why P is silent about the sin of the high places (bamoth); it recognizes no such sin.[16]

The major concern of Deuteronomy 12 is to protect the exclusive holiness of the tabernacle. It explicitly commands the total destruction of all Canaanite cultic places, enumerating them:

> You must demolish completely all the places where the nations whom you are about to dispossess served their gods, on the mountain heights, on the hills, and under every leafy tree. Break down their altars, smash their pillars, burn their sacred poles with fire, and hew down the idols of their gods, and thus blot out their name from

---

14. Segal, *Book of Deuteronomy*, 329–31.
15. Zevit, *Religions*, 286–88.
16. Kaufmann, *Religion*, 182.

their places. You shall not worship YHWH your God in such ways. But you shall seek the place that YHWH your God will choose out of all your tribes as his habitation to put his name there. You shall go there, bringing there your burnt offerings and your sacrifices, your tithes and your donations, your votive gifts, your freewill offerings, and the firstlings of your herds and flocks. (Deut 12:2–6)

Clearly, the prohibition of sacrifices outside the sanctuary is not concerned with the centralization of the cult, but with the rejection of Canaanite holy places. The same concern is expressed in Exodus 23:24–33. The tabernacle must be at a place which is not contaminated by pagan rituals. Neither Deuteronomy nor Leviticus anticipate the future division of Israel into two kingdoms. Therefore, they consider only one sanctuary where the requirements of *avodah* are to be fulfilled. Leviticus deals with the conditions of the sojourn in the desert and assumes that the tabernacle will remain the major sanctuary. The tabernacle is exclusive. There is the ark of the covenant but no other sanctuary (*hekhal*) is equivalent. The requirements of *avodah* are specified in Leviticus 23 and Numbers 28–29: the ritual calendar (the "appointed times"—מועדים) and their required sacrifices (see previous chapter, "The Religion of the Pentateuch"). Deuteronomy assumes that the daily sacrifices, the additional sacrifices during festivals and on the Sabbath, and the additional expiatory sacrifices are to be offered at a major sanctuary.

Moses envisages that, after the conquest,

> When you cross over the Jordan and live in the land that YHWH your God is allotting to you [as your inheritance], and when he gives you rest from your enemies all around so that you shall live in safety, then you shall bring everything that I command you to the place that YHWH your God will choose as a dwelling for his name . . . Take care that you do not offer your burnt offerings at any place you happen to see. But only in the place that YHWH your God will chose in one of your tribes—there you shall offer your burnt offerings and there you shall do everything I command you. (Deut 12:10–14)

The sacrifices described in Exodus and Leviticus may only be offered at a place YHWH will choose. As with the "law of the king," the procedure for determining which place is "chosen" is not defined. The only limitation is that it cannot be a place which had been a Canaanite sanctuary. The injunction is stated repeatedly and forcefully (Deut 12:17–18; 14:22–23; 16:5–6, 11).

II: The Law (Torah) of Israel

Deuteronomy does not expect that the obligatory ritual of *avodah* will be performed in every town in Israel (the economic burden would be staggering). Therefore it explicitly permits a semi-profane sacrifice outside the sanctuary:

> Yet whenever you desire you may *sacrifice* [תזבח] and eat meat, as much as you desire, according to the blessings which YHWH your God has given you *within all your gates*: the unclean and the clean may eat of it, as they would of gazelle or deer. The blood, however, you must not eat; you shall pour it out on the ground like water. (Deut 12:15–16; my translation and emphasis)

The Pentateuch recognized different levels of holiness of sacrifices. The required daily *avodah* as well as the purification sacrifices were offered in the tabernacle. People may also have brought voluntary gifts (*zevah, shlamim*, etc.). But one cannot expect that all slaughtering for meat consumption was to be done at the tabernacle—the place was too small! The thrice repeated injunction "you shall not boil a kid in its mother's milk" (Exod 23:19b; 34:26b; Deut 14:21b) shows that meat was cooked outside the sanctuary. Furthermore, it was permitted to eat animals which were not fit to be sacrificed at the major sanctuary. Their slaughter was also a religious ceremony, but it was semi-profane: it could be performed by laypeople and partaken of by a ritually unclean person.

Leviticus describes the formal rites of *avodah* to be carried out in a sanctuary. It does not mention the ritual on the *bamoth*, which had a lower degree of holiness. In the rabbinical view, sacrifice on the *bamoth* was only acceptable before the establishment of the Jerusalem sanctuary. Rashi (1932:3a) comments that "'*He shall offer it before the Lord and he shall lay [his hand upon the head of the sacrifice].*' This implies that there is no 'laying of hands' upon an animal sacrifice on a private 'high place' at the time when sacrifice was permitted on such (Lev 1:3-4)".[17]

In biblical times, every slaughter was a sacrifice. I shall argue in chapter 11 that the notion of "worship without sacrifice" was only introduced by the Babylonian exiles after they had developed a liturgy which did not require a temple. Totally profane slaughter (שחט without sacrifice) seems to be explicitly forbidden in Leviticus (17:3–4). However, a careful reading of Leviticus 17 shows that the legislation is not concerned with profane slaughtering, but with the eradication of Canaanite rituals. Verses 3–4

---

17. Rashi, *Pentateuch*, Lev 1:3a. The bracketed section of this quote of Leviticus 1:3–4 is an editorial inclusion, and not my notation or emphasis.

forbid the slaughter of an animal without bringing it to the tent of meeting as a sacrifice. Why? The text states explicitly:

> This is in order that the people of Israel may bring their sacrifices that they offer in the open field, that they may bring them to YHWH, to the priest at the entrance of the tent of meeting, and offer them as sacrifices of well-being [*zevah, shelamim*] to YHWH (17:5) . . . so that they may no longer offer their sacrifices for goat-demons, to whom they prostitute themselves. (Lev 17:7)

The text refers to well-established (pagan) rituals. Shepherds in the desert did not practice "profane slaughter": traditionally, the animal was dedicated to local deities such as satyrs.

Leviticus does not forbid profane slaughter; Deuteronomy does not permit it. Totally profane slaughter was inconceivable in biblical times. The spilling of blood—whether human or animal—is considered murder, because blood is life. Genesis 9:2–5 gives a special dispensation for the killing of animals for food. However, the spilling of blood must be expiated by a religious ritual. There are two legitimate ways of killing an animal: sacrifice or hunt. The first requires an altar onto which the blood is sprinkled, the second requires the formal spilling of the blood on the ground and covering it with soil. Both are religious ceremonies.[18]

> For the life of the flesh is in the blood; and I have given it to you for making atonement for your lives on the altar; for, as life, it is the blood which makes atonement. (Lev 17:11)

> And anyone of the people of Israel, or of the aliens who reside among them, who hunts down any animal or bird that may be eaten shall pour out its blood and cover it with earth. (Lev 17:13)

This passage does not know profane slaughtering. Each spilling of blood must be atoned for.

The verb *sh-ḥ-t* (שחט) means "to kill" or "to slaughter." It may refer to the killing of people: the descendents of the Omri dynasty were slaughtered by Jehu's command (2 Kgs 10:7, 14). The sons of King Zedekiah were (ceremonially?) slaughtered by Nebuchadnezzar (2 Kgs 25:7). There is only one instant of "profane slaughter" mentioned in the Pentateuch: Abraham slaughtered a young goat (the term used is "to do it") to prepare a meal for his three guests. He also raised his hand to slaughter his son, but this

---

18. See Zevit, *Religions*, 280–81. Cultic control and chthonic sacrifice.

II: The Law (Torah) of Israel

would have been (and considered by his contemporaries to be) a sacrifice, not murder. Joseph's ten older brothers slaughtered a goat, not for food, but to use the blood for staining the garment of Joseph. Exodus talks about the "slaughter" of the Passover lamb. This too was a sacrificial act: "Take a bunch of hyssop, dip it in the blood which is in the basin, and touch the lintel and the two doorposts with the blood in the basin" (Exod 12:22). Nevertheless, later biblical references refrain from mentioning slaughter. They refer to the "Passover sacrifice" (*zevaḥ Pesaḥ*—זבח פסח, Exod 12:27) or talk about "doing the Passover" (Exod 12:48; Deut 16:1). The term "slaughter" is not used at all in Deuteronomy. It appears in 1 Samuel 14:32 and 34, when it refers to the killing of war booty. There the animals are treated as hunted animals, not as cattle. King Saul insists on spilling the blood in a formal ceremony. The slaughtering of war booty is also mentioned in 1 Samuel 15:9, though there the term "slaughter" is not used.

The term *sh-ḥ-t* (שחט) by itself refers to the act of killing, the shedding of blood. It only designates "sacrifice" when so specified: "He shall *slaughter* the bull *before YHWH*" (Lev 1:5; my translation and emphasis). The proper Hebrew term for "sacrifice" is *z-b-ḥ* (זבח). It does not require the specification "before the deity." Though the verb originally means "to slaughter," it generally designates a religious act (there are two possible exceptions, to be discussed in a moment). The victim may be human—Josiah is reported to have "sacrificed" the priests of Bethel (2 Kgs 23:20), fulfilling an earlier prophecy (1 Kgs 13:2).[19] Table 6.1 shows the occurrence of the term in the Pentateuch and the EP.

The Targum was the Aramaic explanation of the biblical text.[20] Later on it was codified as Targum Onkelos (Pentateuch) and Targum Jonathan (Prophets). These translations are interpretations and reflect the understanding of the text during the time of the Second Temple. The Aramaic term for *z-b-ḥ* (זבח—"to sacrifice") is *d-b-ḥ* (דבח), while *sh-ḥ-t* (שחט—"kill," "slaughter") translates as *n-k-s* (נכס).

Two nouns are derived from the root *z-b-ḥ*: *zebhaḥ*, or sacrifice (דבחא in Aramaic) and *mizbeaḥ* (מדבח, or מדבחא in Aramaic). There is no equivalent biblical Hebrew noun derived from the root *sh-ḥ-t*.[21] However, an Aramaic noun, *nikhsu* or *nikhsata* ("slaughter") is derived from the Aramaic

---

19. This is a reference to Ezekiel.
20. Sperber, *Bible in Aramaic*.
21. The terms would be *sheḥet*, following the *qetel* mode, or *mishḥat*, following the *miktan* mode.

root *n-k-s*. The Hebrew "sacrifice" is translated as "holy slaughter," or *nikhsat qudsha*. Both verbs appear in Leviticus 17:3–7 (see earlier reference). The Aramaic translation of the Rashi/Onkelos edition translates correctly: the Hebrew "slaughter" is translated *n-k-s*, while "sacrifice" translates as *d-b-ḥ*.[22] However the authoritative Onkelos translation of 17:5b translates the Hebrew "sacrifice" as "slaughter them as a holy slaughter unto YHWH" (Lev 17:5).[23]

The following tables shows the incidence of *z-b-ḥ* (in the *qal* stem) in the Pentateuch and the EP with their Aramaic translations.

Table 6:1.I. *z-b-ḥ* translated as sacrifice—*d-b-ḥ* (דבח)

Reference (*Statement of law in italics*)	Occasion
Gen 46:1	Jacob celebrates his arrival in Beersheba
Exod 5:3 (several repetitions)	Negotiations with Pharaoh
Exod 13:15	Father explains law of firstborn animals
Exod 20:24	Burnt offerings to other gods
Exod 22:19	Worship of other deities
Exod 32:8	Worship of golden calf
Exod 34:15	Worship of other deities and eating their sacrifice
Lev 9:4	Sacrifice of *shelamim* before YHWH
Lev 17:5	Sacrifices on the field
Lev 17:7	Sacrifices to goat-demons (*ze'irim*)
Deut 32:17	Sacrifices to demons
Judg 16:23	Philistine sacrificed to Dagon
1 Sam 1:3,4,21; 2:19	Elkanah offering sacrifices at Shiloh
1 Sam 15:15,21	Saul explains that he and the people sacrificed (war booty)
1 Sam 16:2,5	Samuel comes to Beersheba "to sacrifice to YHWH"
2 Sam 15:12	Absalom sacrifices (not specified)
1 Kgs 3:4	Solomon sacrifices on the Great Bamah in Gibeon

---

22. Rashi, *Leviticus*, 17:3–7.
23. Targum, Lev 17:5b.

II: The Law (Torah) of Israel

II. *z-b-ḥ* translated as slaughter—*n-k-s* (נכס)

Gen 31:54	Feast celebrating covenant with Laban
Exod 23:18	Offering blood of sacrifice on unleavened bread
Lev 17:5; Lev 19:5	*shelamim* sacrifices (eaten)
Lev 22:29	*todah* sacrifice (eaten)
Num 22:40	Sacrifice by Balak
Deut 12:15, 21	Eating meat
Deut 15:21	Eating of firstborn cattle
Deut 16:2-6	Passover sacrifice, eaten
Deut 17:1	Sacrificing animals with blemish
Deut 18:3	Portion due to the priest (*Cohen*)
Deut 27:7	*Shelamim*
Deut 33:19	Sacrifices of justice
Josh 8:31	Mount Gerizim, sacrificing burnt offering (*olah* and *shelamim*)
Judg 2:5	Sacrifice (not specified) to YHWH
1 Sam 2:13:15	Sons of Eli, taking more than their portion of the sacrifice
1 Sam 6:15	Men of Beth Shemesh offer *olah* and *shelamim*
1 Sam 10:8; 11:15	Samuel offers *olah* and *shelamim*
1 Sam 28:24	Witch of Endor slaughtering fattened calf
2 Sam 6:13	David brings ark to Jerusalem and sacrifices "an ox and a fat sheep"
1 Kgs 1:9; 19; 25	Adoniah offers sacrifices
1 Kgs 8:62, 63	*Shelamim* before YHWH (inauguration feast)
1 Kgs 13:2	Josiah will sacrifice the priests who had sacrificed on this altar
1 Kgs 19:21	Elisha sacrifices a yoke of oxen for a festive meal.
2 Kgs 17:35-36	HEP: "you shall not sacrifice to them [other gods]"
2 Kgs 23:20	Josiah sacrificing priests who had sacrificed in Bethel (1 Kgs 13:2)

In Table 6.1.I, *z-b-ḥ* is translated as "sacrifice" whenever the text talks about formal worship—whether rendered to YHWH or to other deities. When *shelamim* is part of a formal ceremony it is called "holy slaughter." For example, in Leviticus 9:4 the *shelamim* sacrifice follows the *hattat* and *olah* and concludes a solemn ceremony. The Hebrew text says: "and an ox and a ram to sacrifice as *shelamim* before YHWH." The Targum says: "and an ox and a ram to sacrifice as *holy slaughter* before YHWH"(my translation and emphasis). The Hebrew term "sacrifice of shelamim" requires the translation "holy slaughter." Exodus 34:15 refers to a formal pagan ritual, forbidding the eating of sacrifice to other deities. Here too *z-b-ḥ* translates as "to sacrifice a sacrifice." The "sacrifice" of the priests in Bethel is considered to be a legitimate execution.

All sacrifices involving eating are translated as "slaughter" (Table 6.1.II). The citations in Table 6.1.II generally refer to festive meals. The only exceptions are as follows: first, there are references to the slaughter (sacrificing) of priests by Josiah. Secondly, the witch of Endor sacrificed a "fatted calf," preparing a meal for Saul[24]—it is unlikely that this slaughter was profane. The author of the story would have taken it for granted that some religious ceremony was involved. Finally, Deuteronomy 12:15 incorrectly translates "תזבח" ("you shall sacrifice") as "תכוס" ("you shall slaughter"). I suggest that this is not an error, but a deliberate interpretation of the text, reflecting the practices of the Second Temple period when sacrifice outside the temple was strictly prohibited.[25] The original text explicitly permits *zebhah*. The scribes reasoned that sacrifices outside the sanctuary are forbidden; therefore the word must be interpreted as slaughter. However, although they permitted themselves to interpret the text, they did not dare to edit it.[26] This interpretation was not yet accepted in the Hellenistic era: LXX translates correctly, using the Greek term for "sacrifice," not the term for "killing/slaughter." The deliberate mistranslation of Deuteronomy 12:15 in the Targum ("slaughter" instead of "sacrifice") was accepted in the Latin Vulgate. Most Bible translations render the verb *z-v-ḥ* (זבח) incorrectly as "you may kill" or "you may slaughter." The only correct translation I found was in one Spanish Bible ("Pero puedes *sacrificar* [sacrifice] et comer en cualquier sitio").[27] *Thus the de Wette/Wellhausen theory is based on a mistranslation which reflects the cultic practices of the Second Temple period.*

Deuteronomy 12 includes a strange comment: "You shall not do as we do today: *every man [does] what is right in his eyes*" (12:8, my translation and emphasis).[28] This phrase only appears twice more in the Bible, when the

---

24. RSV translates: "she quickly killed it."

25. See below, chapter 11.

26. The Targum translates *"to do the Passover"* as *"to slaughter the Passover,"* and *"to sacrifice the Passover"'* as *"to slaughter"* (Deut 16:1,5).

27. *La Biblia*, Deut 12:15.

28. (Rashi, Deut 12:8, quoting Zebaḥ 117b, gives the following explanation: today, meaning at the time of Moses, all sacrifices are permitted in the tabernacle, including *asham* and *hattat*. After crossing the Jordan it was permitted to offer free-will sacrifices (every man does what is right in his eyes). This seems to me a forced explanation.

II: The Law (Torah) of Israel

author of the book of Judges deplores the anarchy at that time: (1) chapter 17 reports an incident directly relevant to Deut 12:8: "This man Micah had a shrine, and he made an ephod and teraphim, and installed one of his sons, who became his priest. "In those days there is no king in Israel; every man will do what is right in his eyes" (Jud 17:5-6, my translation). (2) The book ends on a pessimistic note: "In those days there is no king in Israel: every man will do what is right in his eyes" (21:25; my translation).[29] The author of Judges deplores the anarchy of his time and advocates the monarchy. It is possible that he quotes Deuteronomy 12:8. Alternatively, the passage is a later interpolation; not a part of the speech attributed to Moses, but an editorial comment inserted by the scribe who wrote the "first edition" of Judges[30]). I suggest that the book of Judges and the editorial comment in Deuteronomy 12:8 were written in the same period, possibly by the same scribe.

Deuteronomy 12, together with the laws concerning the tithe (14:22-27), the Passover laws concerning the three pilgrim festivals (16:1-17), and the ceremony of bringing the first fruit (26:1-11) envisage a society which offers sacrifices only at one major sanctuary, This utopia is totally unrealistic. The permission to sacrifice for meat consumption (12:15) does not solve the problem. It is ludicrous to assume a general pilgrimage to Jerusalem to offer the Passover sacrifice (Deut 16:5-6) or to bring there the "first of all fruit" in a basket. People needed accessible places all over Israel, where they could expiate their transgressions by bringing sin offerings or guilt offerings. The notion of "worship without sacrifice" was only introduced by the Babylonian exiles[31] who developed a liturgy which did not require a temple. The so-called "centralization edict" was not known during the time of the First Temple.

This raises another question of "how come?" Neither proscription of pagan rituals nor centralization of worship were observed in Israel during the time of the First Temple. Traditional rabbinical thinking simply states that Israel sinned. Classical scholarship has a different answer: Israel was monolatrous: neither true monotheism nor the centralization law had been formulated. The following chapters, based on the assumption that there was

---

29. In Exodus 15:26, God demands that Israel "shall do the right in his [God's] eyes."

30. I argued in the previous chapter that the Pentateuch was completed before the period of the second kingdom. This does not exclude earlier redactions. I assume that the HEP relied on earlier manuscripts. The author of the reports on Micah and on the "rape of the concubine" obviously favored the establishment of the monarchy and of a centralized sanctuary.

31. See chapter 11.

an exodus and a covenant in the desert, will propose a different sequence of the ethnogenesis of Israel.

Conclusion

1. The virtual identity of the Samarian and Masoretic Pentateuch shows that the Pentateuch existed before the establishment of the northern kingdom.
2. The Pentateuch is monotheistic, and includes the major ideas by which Israel was distinguished by other nations.
3. There is no theological/ideological difference between Deuteronomy and the Tetrateuch. Cult centralization is taken for granted, both in Leviticus and Deuteronomy. The use of any of the Canaanite holy places is strictly forbidden. A semi-profane sacrifice may be offered on earth-altars. The main topic of Deuteronomy is not the centralization of the cult, but the renewal of the covenant by Moses and the interdiction of the use of Canaanite cultic places.

III

The Ethnogenesis of Israel

7

From Wandering Aramean (ארמי אבד) to a Nation Bound by a Covenant

According to Faust, Israel did not yet exist as a nation when semi-nomads infiltrated the highlands of Canaan. The "ethnogenesis" of Israel was a protracted process: Israel's "self-identification" developed slowly, mainly through interaction with the Canaanites and Philistines.

> And as for Israel's actual origins, it seems as if ancient Israel was composed of peoples who came from various backgrounds: a semi-nomadic population who lived on the fringe of settlement, settled Canaanites who for various reasons changed their identity, tribes from Transjordan, and probably even a group who fled Egypt. In the end it is likely that many, if not most, Israelites had Canaanite origins.[1]

Faust misses the main attribute of Israel's identity: Israel is distinguished from the surrounding civilizations by the assertion that the deity created the world out of nothing (*ex nihilo* or by *fiat*), the claim of a public theophany, a covenant between God and the entire community, and the introduction of the Sabbath. The egalitarian ethos and the concern with ritual purity (and pork avoidance) are not the basis of Israel's ethnogenesis, but its result. The ethnogenesis of Israel started with the patriarchs and culminated in the acceptance of the covenant with YHWH.

---

1. Faust, *Israel's Ethnogenesis*, 186.

III: The Ethnogenesis of Israel

> This very day you have become the people of YHWH your God. Therefore obey YHWH your God, observing his commandments and his statutes that I am commanding you today. (Deut 27:9b–10)

In the following section I shall try to delineate the ethnogenesis of Israel starting with "the wandering Aramean," based on biblical sources, scrutinized with regard to their plausibility in the light of extrabiblical evidence.

Origins

There is abundant epigraphic evidence documenting life in the Middle East during the second millennium BCE.[2] Independent sources confirm that Semitic pastoral groups roamed between Mesopotamia and Canaan. Treaties between various populations were signed, following the procedures described in Genesis. They arranged long distance marriages. They were concerned about inheritance, and if the wife was barren they adopted the sons of one of her slaves. Firstborn rights were occasionally sold. Egyptian records document that during times of famine nomadic Canaanite/Semitic populations sought relief in the North Sinai/Nile Delta areas. Egyptian response varied. Generally they imposed restrictions, border control, and defensive walls in order to keep these "Asiatics" at bay. Sometimes they encouraged them. Some of these groups settled in the Delta, retaining their ethnic identity. Individuals were not restricted to the Delta area; many obtained important positions in Egyptian households and even dominant positions in government. Some also accepted Egyptian names/titles. But even after generations of sojourn in Egypt, these Semitic groups were not considered to be Egyptians. During the New Kingdom, these groups were conscripted to forced labor (Egyptian sources describe how they made bricks, fulfilling daily quotas). They were employed in building projects controlled by stick-wielding overseers.[3]

I assume that one of these Asiatic groups was called "B'nei Israel." Their existence cannot be proven. No record of a group of this name is found in Egyptian sources. Nevertheless, the basic framework of the biblical stories is plausible in view of their compatibility with the description of life in the Near East during the second millennium BCE. The term "slaves" evokes in us images of slavery in ancient Rome or in North America during the early

---

2. See Chavalas and Hostettler, "Epigraphic Light."

3. A detailed review of these data is given by Hoffmeier (*Israel in Egypt*, 52–76) and Kitchen (*Reliability*, 316–60).

From Wandering Aramean (ארמי אבד) to a Nation

nineteenth century: captives in wars, transported to a foreign country and sold individually to owners who could dispose of them at their will. The Israelites were not that kind of slaves. They had settled in a specific area in the Delta region. The original group had multiplied and prospered economically. They were organized into tribes and families, and were represented by their elders before the Egyptian government. They kept their language and identity even after a sojourn in Egypt lasting for several generations. They never claimed, nor were they accredited, to be Egyptians. They must have developed religious ceremonies as well as traditions about their history. These traditions may not be historically accurate, but they do reveal the ethnic identity of the group.

According to these traditions, the Israelites were a Semitic group whose origin was in Mesopotamia. They claimed an ethnic relationship with the Edomites, Moabites, Ammonites, and Arameans. They definitely did not see themselves as Canaanites, Amorites, or Egyptians. They were nomads wandering between Mesopotamia and Syria, but finally settled in Canaan. They immigrated to Egypt in time of famine, but their patrimony was the land of Canaan.

The Bible does not describe the religious practices of the Israelites. It tells us that the patriarchs built altars to offer simple sacrifices (*zevaḥ*—זבח) on special occasions. They did not offer burnt offerings (*olah*—עולה). The only exception is the story of Abraham sacrificing a ram as a burned offering (*olah*) to take the place of his son. There are no traditions of pagan rituals. The tradition refers to a deity with the appellation "El" (god), adding additional designations: El-olam, El-shaddai, Elohe-Israel.[4] Abraham refers to God as "the judge of all the earth" (Gen 18:25). The god of the patriarchs is never described as having a consort, and no pagan deity is identified in Genesis 12–50. The patriarchs communicated with the deity through visions. The tradition tells that they heard God—they never saw him. The patriarchs did not engage in magic practices. The story of Joseph implies the belief in a deity who rules the entire world. When Joseph interprets dreams, he explicitly denies having mantic powers: he merely communicates God's answers. Jacob has a vision of divine beings; he also wrestles with one, but he never sees God.

Israelite tradition stressed that the patriarchs owned a family burial ground in Hebron. Jacob insisted on being buried there. Each one of the

---

4. See Dever, *Recent Archaeological Discoveries*, 130–31. This does not prove that these terms identify the "god of Israel" with the "el of Canaan," as suggested by Dever.

three patriarchs had repeated visions in which their God promised them, under oath, that their descendents would be a great nation and inherit the land of Canaan. One of their family, Joseph, reached a prominent position in Egypt. He took an Egyptian name, title, and wife; he obtained an Egyptian burial. However, his coffin was kept in readiness to be returned to "his fathers' land," together with the rest of Israel. Theoretically it is possible that this tradition of the return to Canaan was invented after the exodus, to justify the conquest of Canaan. If so, where are the original traditions? Had they been wiped out?

The saga of the ethnogenesis of Israel differs remarkably from the saga of other nations. It is non-mythical. Heroes in Egyptian, Greek, German, and most other mythological sagas claim divine descent. The Pentateuch knows of the long-living heroes of antiquity (not as long living as some Mesopotamians, who lived thousands of years) who introduced mankind to agriculture, technology, and urban settlements:

> The sons of the gods saw that they (daughters of men) were fair; and they took wives for themselves of all that they chose ... The Nephilim (giants) were on the earth in those days—and also afterward—when the sons of the gods [my translation)]⁵ went in to the daughters of humans, who bore children to them. These were the heroes that were of old, warriors of renown. (Gen 6:2, 4)

These descendants of "the sons of elohim" were not the ancestors of Israel. Israel, as depicted in the biblical narrative, is a young nation. The patriarchs of Israel are neither divine nor heroic, but fallible humans, far from being ideal role models of decent behavior. Yet, they are distinguished from all other nations by their special relationship with an invisible God.

The stories of the lives of their ancestors may be embroidered. Nevertheless, the specific incidents narrated are realistic.⁶

Exodus

In contrast to the traditions concerning the patriarchs, the narratives about the exodus are highly embroidered and include reports of supernatural events. It is difficult to establish the actual conditions giving rise to the

---

5. NRSV translates "The sons of God." The Hebrew term (בני האלהים) should be translated "sons of the gods." NRSV translates "man of name" as "warriors of old."

6. The only exception is Jacob's wrestling with a divine being. The "cutting of the covenant" with Abraham (Gen 15) was a vision.

From Wandering Aramean (ארמי אבד) to a Nation

biblical narratives.[7] The basic natural events reported in the Pentateuch are as follows: the Israelites were one of the Asiatic groups conscripted to forced labor in the Delta by the Pharaohs of the New Kingdom. This service would mainly affect younger males. Working schedules would be negotiated with the authorities. It would not affect their food supply. They would groan, but could live with it. Later on the conditions became worse: "The Israelites groaned under their slavery, and cried out. Out of their slavery their cry for help rose up to ELOHIM" (Exod 2:23).

The exodus was a well-organized event under the guidance of a competent leader. Moses is described as a Hebrew who had been educated at the royal Egyptian court.[8] The Israelites left Egypt at a time when Egypt was stricken by a number of catastrophic events. They left with their cattle and portable possessions. In the Sinai desert they agreed to enter into a covenant with YHWH. Nevertheless, the law of the Sinai covenant was not accepted by Israel without struggle. Israel proved to be a "hard-necked people," refusing to accept the yoke of the covenant to which they had agreed, fearfully, in the presence of thunder and lightning, storms and earthquakes.[9] There were rebellions led by some of the previous leaders whose authority had been displaced by Moses. This led to a civil war in which Moses was victorious, with the help of the tribe of Levi. However, Israel was not yet ready for the conquest. There was an unsuccessful at-

---

7. There exists a large amount of research literature trying to establish which natural events might have given rise to the stories of exodus. For a discussion of the plagues, see Hoffmeier (*Israel in Egypt*, 146–55) and Kitchen (*Reliability*, 249–54); for the discussion of the route of the exodus, see Hoffmeier, *Israel in Egypt*, 164–222; see also Moshier and Hoffmeier, "Which Way Out."

8. See Hoffmeier, *Israel in Egypt*, 142–43.

9. Agus points out the following: "a) Even in the relations with the Almighty, only that to which a man, or a group, has agreed voluntarily, is binding on him, or on it. b) For such an agreement to be binding, it must be concluded under circumstances that would preclude any outside pressure whatever" (*Heroic Age*, 192). Therefore, medieval rabbis questioned the validity of the Sinai pact, because it was entered under stress: "The Lord arched the mountain over them like a tub and said to them: 'If you will accept the Torah, all will be well; but if not, you shall be buried [under this mountain]' . . . 'hence it is to be derived [the existence of] a cancelling declaration in regard to the acceptance of the Torah.'" Rashi explained, "If the Lord will summon the Israelites to court and will accuse them for not observing the Torah, they shall be in a position to say that [the acceptance at Sinai was not binding upon them since] they had accepted it under pressure" (*Shabbat*, 88a; quoted by Agus, *Heroic Age*, 262–63n29). The sages of the Mishnah considered the recitation of the *Shema* as a daily acceptance of the "yoke of the Kingdom of Heaven" (ibid., 197).

III: The Ethnogenesis of Israel

tempt to enter Canaan, and the Israelites had to spend about forty years in the desert, mainly in the area of Kadesh Barnea.[10] Then the old covenant was reaffirmed with a new generation of Israelites, born and raised in the desert. Israel conquered a part of the Transjordan, where some of the tribes settled. The leadership of the Israelites passed to Joshua, who was to lead the conquest of the promised land.

Exodus focuses on two major themes: the absolute sovereignty of YHWH over all nations and the establishment of the Sinai covenant. When Moses approaches Pharaoh in the name of YHWH, the answer is, "Who is YHWH, that I should heed him and let Israel go? I do not know YHWH, and I will not let Israel go" (Exod 5:2). The next ten chapters show the battle between YHWH and Pharaoh. Pharaoh insists that Israel must serve (עבד) him. YHWH's victory determines that, henceforth, Israel will worship (עבד) only him. The delays of the exodus are caused by YHWH, enabling him to demonstrate his power over the Egyptians: YHWH could have forced the exodus at any time, but Pharaoh's heart was hardened in order to unequivocally demonstrate YHWH's superiority over Pharaoh, Egypt, and Egyptian deities. There is never a doubt in the Bible about the final outcome. Pharaoh never had a chance, and YHWH forces him to act irrationally to court disaster. The exodus was a triumph noted by the entire world:

> The peoples heard, they trembled;
> pangs seized the inhabitants of Philistia.
> Then the chiefs of Edom were dismayed;
> trembling seized the leaders of Moab;
> all the inhabitants of Canaan melted away.
>
> (Exod 15:14–15)

---

10. How could the Israelites survive forty years in the desert? The translation of the term is misleading. Speaking of the desert, we think of the Sahara. The correct Hebrew term would be שממה. The term מדבר denotes semi-arid land on which sheep and goats can be supported. Nomads roamed in the *midbar jehudah* and the Negev until modern times. For thousands of years, nomadic groups traversed the northern Sinai peninsula with their flocks. Whatever route the Israelites may have chosen, it had been used previously. Of course, the census reported in Numbers chapters 1 and 26 are grossly exaggerated. It should be assumed that there were no more than a few thousand Israelites.

From Wandering Aramean (ארמי אבד) to a Nation

Moses is a reluctant prophet, a messenger of YHWH.[11] He is the main speaker, but not the hero of the last four books of the Pentateuch.[12] I suggest that the crucial moment in Moses' development is his vision of the burning bush (Exod 3:4).[13] In this vision, he realizes that "It is my task to organize the exodus." He shrinks from this task, but feels compelled to accept it as a mission from God. But who is this Deity who sends him on an impossible mission?

Moses does not dare to ask for his name directly. Instead he asks,

> If I come to the Israelites and say to them, "the God of your ancestors [fathers] has sent me to you," and they ask me, "What is his name?" what shall I say to them? (Exod 3:13)

The answer is this:

> *I am who I am* . . . Thus you shall say to the Israelites, '*I am* hath sent me to you' . . . This is my name forever, and this is my title for all generations. (Exod 3:14, 15b, my emphasis)

> *I am YHWH.* (Exod 6:2, my emphasis)

YHWH is not a "name," but an appellation. The absolutely monotheistic God of Moses cannot have a name. Who was there to name Him? The "Existing One" (I suggest the appellation *Existus*) was not created and was never named. Therefore, he is to be addressed by his title, "Lord." This insight is the beginning of mosaic monotheism—a radical new conception of the deity.

In his first meeting with the elders of Israel, Moses relays an unconditional promise by YHWH. The elders were familiar with the traditions of Genesis. When Aaron, in the name of Moses, told the elders of Israel "everything that YHWH had said to Moses," they understood the reference to the God of their fathers. "And the people trusted [the message]. And they heard that YHWH had given heed to the Israelites, and that he had seen their misery, they bowed down and worshipped" (Exod 4:31; my

---

11. For an interesting secular portrait of Moses, see Ahad Ha'Am, "Moses," in *Selected Essays by Ahad Ha'Am*, 306–29.

12. This is recognized in the Jewish Passover ritual. The *Haggadah* discusses the exodus, but refrains mentioning Moses, except in one biblical quote: "and Israel trusted in YHWH and Moses" (Exod 14:31). Moses is not a crafty politician. He rarely takes the initiative. Aaron speaks for him, and he does not direct battles; administrative reforms were suggested by his father-in-law. He does not make laws—he merely has "been prophetized" to report the word of God.

13. I call it a vision because of my prejudice.

III: The Ethnogenesis of Israel

translation). However, on this occasion Moses only talked about God's promise. The obligations of the covenant—"If you will listen carefully to the voice of YHWH your God, and to what is right in his sight, and give heed to his commandments and keep all his statues" (Exod 15:26)—are first mentioned after the crossing of the Sea of Reeds.

The books of the Bible are not impartial: they have a message to deliver. Their bias is expressed in editorial comments and in the selection of the material included.[14] They do not invent new stories, but distort the picture by omitting important data. The positive picture of the exodus drawn by the biblical narrator is enthusiastic. The victories over Egypt are highlighted, the suffering in the desert is downplayed. Careful reading of the text reveals a different view of the exodus reality. The narratives of Exodus/Numbers systematically exaggerate the hardship suffered by Israel in Egypt, the elation about their miraculous delivery from slavery, and their enthusiasm for the covenant. At the same time, they systematically play down the roots which the Israelites had established in Egypt, as well as the hardships and disappointments after the exodus. They magnify the miracles of the exodus, underrate the difficulties of the conquest, and are perhaps overenthusiastic about the future. Egypt is always depicted in negative terms. It is a place of "diseases I brought upon the Egyptians" (Exod 15:26). Chapter 28 of Deuteronomy pronounces a terrifying list of curses—fifty-three verses. Twice a long list of curses is topped with reference to the "boils of Egypt" (28:27) and "all the diseases of Egypt" (28:60). This is not a land to which one would return.

Moses faced opposition from the beginning of his mission. God promised to bring Israel to a "land flowing with milk and honey" (Exod 3:8). In the eyes of the opposition, Moses has taken them out of it: "Is it too little that you have brought us up out of a land flowing with milk and honey to kill us in the wilderness, that you must also lord it over us?" (Num 16:13). According to the dissenters, the experience of the Israelites was as follows: an egyptianized Moses came and promised a miraculous escape from bondage to return them to the land of their ancestors. Many were doubtful about the whole enterprise. At the Sea of Reeds, they called out, "Is this not the very thing we told you in Egypt, 'let us alone and let us serve the Egyptians'?" (Exod 14:12a). When Pharaoh responded to Moses' demand by increasing the burden, the Israelite officers cursed Moses and Aaron: "[May] YHWH look upon you and judge! You have brought us

---

14. See chapter 1 of this book, "Basic Assumptions," pp. 14–15.

From Wandering Aramean (ארמי אבד) to a Nation

into bad odor with Pharaoh and his officials, and have put a sword in their hand to kill us" (Exod 5:21).

After repeated delays, the Israelites left Egypt at night and got stuck at the swamps of Yam Suf, the Sea of Reeds. A contingent of Egyptian chariots pursued them and they were in despair, responding with a typical Jewish joke: "Aren't there any graves in Egypt, that you took us to die in the desert?" (14:11a; my translation). Only after they had escaped through the swamps, which had been dried out by a hot wind, and saw their pursuers perish in those lakes, they became confident:

> And YHWH rescued Israel from the *hand* [power] of Egypt, and Israel saw Egypt dead at the shore of the sea. And Israel saw the great *hand* [power] which YHWH did against Egypt; and the people were *in awe* of YHWH and *trusted* his servant Moses. (Exod 14:30–31; my translation and emphasis)[15]

The crossing of the Sea of Reeds marks the exodus; the difficulties of living in the desert started immediately. They lacked water. They were attacked by Midianite marauders. In comparison, life in Egypt had been relatively good. Young males had suffered, but the people had their cattle and their vegetables. They were not ready to face the hardship of a nomadic existence in the desert, looking forward to an uncertain future in a land which had to be conquered. They had felt at home in Egypt, and the memories of their past were nostalgic.[16] "The Israelites also wept again, and said, 'If only we had meat to eat! We remember the fish we used to eat in Egypt for nothing, the cucumbers, the melons, the leeks, the onions, and the garlic.'" (Num 11:4b–5) The generation of the exodus was not ready to conquer Canaan. When faced with the task of fighting well-armed Canaanites, they panicked.

> All the Israelites complained against Moses and Aaron; the whole congregation said to them, "Would that we had died in the land of Egypt! Or would that we had died in this wilderness! ... Would it not to be better for us to go back to Egypt?" So they said to one another, "Let us choose a captain, and go back to Egypt." (Num 14:2–3)

---

15. The hand of YHWH prevailed over the hand of Egypt.

16. Greifenhagen (*Egypt*) analyses the ambivalent attitude toward Egypt found in the Pentateuch. We differ in our interpretation of the data. Greifenhagen argues that the ambivalence reflects reality problems of the Persian/Hellenistic era. I suggest that it reflects the reality at the time of the exodus and wandering in the desert.

III: The Ethnogenesis of Israel

The heroic nature of Moses is not so much shown in his confrontation with Pharaoh, but in his battle with a stiff-necked Israel.

The Covenant

The exodus is not the main task of Moses. It is the prelude to the second main event: the establishment of the covenant between Israel and YHWH.

The biblical tradition insists that the Israelites enter the covenant of their own free will:

> "If you obey my voice and keep my covenant, you shall be my treasured possession out of all the peoples. Indeed the whole earth is mine, but you shall be before me a priestly kingdom and a holy nation. These are the words that you shall speak to the Israelites." So Moses came, summoned the elders of the people and set before them all these words that YHWH had commanded him. The people all answered as one: "Everything that YHWH has spoken we will do." (Exod 19:5, 7–8a)

Then Israel encountered a public theophany: each person present heard the words (deeds)[17] of the Decalogue: "I am YHWH your God" (Exod 20:2). This declaration is unique. In many religions, individuals avowed a theophany. The claim for a public theophany is only found in Israel. The actual historical conditions of that event are not clear,[18] but it was a frightening experience—the people could not stand it—and subsequently all provisions of the covenant were communicated by Moses, who quotes YHWH. The main conditions of the covenant were written on stone tablets, while the detailed provisions (presumably the law codex of Exodus 21–23) were written down by Moses, probably on parchment. These conditions were read to the community and the official "cutting of the covenant" was concluded in a formal ceremony in Exodus 24:1–11: "Moses wrote down all the words of YHWH" (Exod 24:4a). The blood of a sacrifice was divided. One half was sprinkled upon the altar.

> Then he [Moses] took the book of the covenant (ספר הברית), and read it in the hearing of the people; and they said, "All that YHWH has spoken we will do, and we will be obedient [we will listen—ונשמע]." Moses took the blood and dashed it on the people, and

---

17. The Hebrew word *davar* (דבר) means both "word" and "deed."
18. See chapter 1 of this book, "Basic Assumptions."

From Wandering Aramean (ארמי אבד) to a Nation

said, "See the blood of the covenant that YHWH has made with you in accordance with all these words." (Exod 24:7–8)

The ceremony concluded with a festive meal with seventy of the elders of Israel.

The covenant demanded a total religious reorientation. The idea of a supreme deity may have been acceptable to the Israelites, but it was unheard of to worship a deity without an image. The rebellion against Moses is not merely directed against his authority; it is also manifested in the rejection of his religious mission. The Israelites needed a visual representation of the deity and persuaded (or forced?) Aaron to cast the golden calf. Aaron tried to save the situation by declaring that "Tomorrow shall be a festival to YHWH" (Exod 32:5b). However, the people defiantly chanted the following: "These are your gods, O Israel, who brought you up out of the land of Egypt" (Exod 32:4), using the grammatical plural and omitting the name of YHWH. This rebellion led to civil war. Moses asserted his authority with the help of his tribe of Levi. The rule of YHWH was no longer challenged.

YHWH is a zealous God. Monotheism introduced religious intolerance,[19] demanding the destruction of the heretic by the sword (Deut 13).[20] The command of genocide is repeated several times in Deuteronomy, which makes a correct prediction: if the Israelites would not destroy the Canaanites, if they intermarried with them, they would also worship their gods. Only the complete annihilation of the indigenous population would assure complete adherence to the terms of the covenant. Officially, all Israel accepted the covenant, yet the undercurrent of old religious traditions persisted. The Israelites were aware of ancient Canaanite mythology and rituals. Their beliefs and religious practices originated in old times, when their ancestors were among the Asiatics who settled in the Nile Delta. "The fact that the early Israelites were in almost every case culturally indistinct from the Canaanites is not surprising. The biblical traditions do not hide the fact that Israelite origins come out of the Semitic stock of the Levant."[21]

---

19. A pagan traveler would have no problem worshiping the local deity of another group: there are many divine beings in many places, and all like to be acknowledged.

20. The war with the Midianites (Num 31)—whether historical or not—is a good example. When Israel engages in a friendly relationship with a neighboring tribe, intermarriage will follow, combined with the acceptance of other deities. Moses could not tolerate this: the other group must be killed.

21. Younger, "Early Israel," 196.

III: The Ethnogenesis of Israel

A rarely discussed problem of monotheism is the absence of a female deity. YHWH always acts on his own. He has no consort. All cults of the Middle East had female deities. One must assume that the Israelites in Egypt had their household gods—teraphim—and a tradition of female deities which were called upon. The scriptures ignore these features of religious experience, but it is improbable that such popular rites disappeared after the exodus.[22]

Moses faced a formidable challenge in transforming old pagan traditions into a monotheistic ritual (see the discussion of the priestly code in chapter 5, "The Religion of the Pentateuch," p. 96). The first step was the erection of a dismountable sanctuary. This *mishkan* ("dwelling") did not include the image of a deity.[23] Kitchen shows that portable sanctuaries were in use in the Middle East in the second millennium BCE.[24] The biblical data match those of non-biblical sources, using the same technical terms. The detailed description of the tabernacle and its furnishings correspond to those found in Mari and Ugarith. The Israelite tabernacle was small in comparison to other similar structures, but resembles them in plan (forehall, smaller inner sanctum, outer court surrounded by a fence) and materials used (wooden poles, curtains made of special costly materials). Technical terms used in Mari and Ugarith are linguistically close to the Hebrew terms.[25] These data refute those theories which, following Wellhausen, conclude that the tabernacle was invented by post-exilic priests. On the contrary, the detailed description of the dimensions of the tabernacle and of the materials used in its construction, as well as the exact instructions concerning the sacrificial ritual show that (at the time of the sojourn in the desert) Israel was a well-organized, stratified society, capable of maintaining a priestly class. In view of the literacy of Syria-Canaan at this time, we must assume that these priests maintained records. Because they were

---

22. Dever argues that "in ancient Israel most women, excluded from public life ... necessarily occupied themselves with domestic concerns ... those connected specifically with reproduction—conception, childbirth, lactation—but also those connected with rites of passage, such as marriages, funerals ... 'the religion of hearth and home' fell mainly to women in Israel, as it did anywhere in the ancient world." (*Biblical Writers*, 193). I suggest that such rites were known to Israel even before the sojourn in Egypt.

23. The golden cherubim spread their wings over the golden cover (*kapporeth*) of the ark, but they were not divine.

24. Kitchen, *Reliability*, 275–83.

25. E.g. *qeresh* (Hebrew) and *qersu* (Mari) = wooden frame; *a-h-l* (Hebrew, Ugarith) = tent; *mishkan* (Hebrew, Ugarith) = tabernacle.

nomads, they only carried with them two stone tablets, placed in a portable ark. The rest would be written on parchment. I suggest that most of the Pentateuch was written during the forty years of wandering. "And Moses wrote this law, and gave it to the priests, the sons of Levi who carried the ark of the covenant of YHWH, and to all the elders of Israel" (Deut 31:9). He probably delegated the task to various groups who collected oral traditions and law codices. Some sections will have been dictated by Moses. The final editing will have been done during the time of Joshua or even later. The *terminus ad quem* of the writing of the "master copy" PT is before the divided monarchy.

The years of wandering in the desert were crucial for the ethnogenesis of Israel. When Moses formally renewed the covenant before his death, he addressed a nation with a clearly developed ethnic consciousness. They saw themselves as a "special possession" of YHWH, the sole creator and ruler of the universe, bound by a covenant to follow his Torah. The acceptance of the covenant by all members of the congregation (עֵדָה)—men and women, young and old, rich and poor—made Israel a nation. This nation, though small and insignificant, is distinguished by having a law based on the principles of equality—the same law for the rich and the poor, the carrier of water and the king—a law which is based on the principles of justice and leads towards a good life. The nation had a written constitution, the Law of Moses (תורת משה), the Torah. In contrast to modern usage, this constitution is not expressed in terms of rights, but duties. The right of the individual is to enjoy the benefits of living in a just society. The duties are to be just, to be holy, and to serve only one invisible Deity. "From the moment the Israelites began to see themselves as distinct they became so, and should be treated accordingly by modern scholarship."[26]

---

26. Faust, *Israel's Ethnogenesis*, 28. Of course, Faust denies the exodus and sojourn. My analysis assumes that the identity of the Samarian Pentateuch and the Masoretic text show that the Pentateuch was known in Israel before the divided kingdom (see chapter four, "The Composition of the Pentateuch") and that the basic story of the sojourn in Egypt is compatible with archaeological data (see chapter three, "The Origin of Israel: Archaeological Interpretations," pp. 51–56).

8

From Conquest to Monarchy

Conquest and settlement

JOSHUA OBTAINED A SERIES of decisive victories over the Canaanite coalitions in open battle.[1] This was a time of euphoria, a victory of YHWH. If there were any pagan undercurrents, they were successfully suppressed. The Bible reports a formal renewal of the covenant under Joshua (Josh 24).[2] There is nothing remarkable about this—such was the common practice in the Middle East at those times. Though Joshua was successful in battle, the Canaanite population was not annihilated and remained in the lowlands, secure in their walled settlements. The HEP reports that the invasion under Joshua was undertaken by all Israel, but the actual "taking of possession" was done separately by different tribes.[3] Under these circumstances, it is remarkable that there are no reports about intertribal territorial wars. Judges reports intertribal conflicts, even warfare, but none of these are about possession of territory. When the tribe of Dan could not withstand the assault of the Philistines and migrated to the north, displacing the Canaanite population, they did not attempt to encroach upon the territory of any of the tribes of Israel (Judg 18).

---

1. See chapter three, "The Origin of Israel: Archaeological Interpretations," pp. 37–44.
2. See chapter four, "The Composition of the Pentateuch," p. 179.
3. The invading Israelites were a tribal nation. Each individual was identified by his tribal membership. Even at present times, a Samarian identifies himself as an Israelite of the tribe of Ephraim, Manasseh or Levi.

> The Israelites did what was evil in the eyes of YHWH, forgetting YHWH their God, and worshipping the Baals and the Asherahs. Therefore the anger of YHWH was kindled against Israel, and he sold them into the hand of King Cushan-rishataim of Aram-naharaim; and the Israelites served Cushan-rishataim for eight years. But when the Israelites cried out to YHWH, YHWH raised up a deliverer for the Israelites ... Othniel son of Kenaz ... The spirit of YHWH came upon him and he judged Israel; he went out to war, and YHWH gave King Cushan-rishataim into his hand ... So the land had rest for forty years. Then Othniel son of Kenaz died. The Israelites again did what was evil in the sight of YHWH. (Judg 3:7–12a)[9]

This was the first cycle. The book of Judges reports four additional major military confrontations with Israel's neighbors as such cycles, proceeding from breach of the covenant to remorse, victory, and relapse.[10] (a) The Canaanites were decisively defeated under the leadership of Deborah/Barak (Judg 4–5). After this battle, Israel ruled Canaan. (b) There were three defensive battles against invaders from Transjordan. Ehud fought the Moabites, who had subjugated Israel with the help of the Amalekites and Ammonites (Judg 3). Gideon defeated Midianite marauders (Judg 6–8) and Jephtah fought against the Ammonites in Transjordan (Judg 11–12). None of these invaders threatened Israel's possession of Canaan.

Abimelech was the son of Gideon and a Canaanite concubine. With the help of his Canaanite relatives in Shechem, he killed the legitimate sons of Gideon and was crowned king (Judg 9:5–6). The text then notes, "Abimelech ruled [*vayasar*—וישׂר] over Israel for three years" (Judg 9:22). He is not styled "king of Canaan" (though he was crowned in Shechem) but "ruler of Israel." At that time, there is no doubt about which nation possessed the land.

The Philistines had invaded Canaan from the sea and established secure cities in the coastal region. This constituted a serious threat to Israel. Two judges fought the Philistines: Shamgar ben Anath and Samson. The stories about Samson are elaborate; he killed many Philistines in a private guerilla war, but did not lead Israel in open battle. It should be noted that the other tribes did not gather to defend the Danites, and that the men of Judah delivered Samson to the Philistines. At the end of the period

---

9. The historicity of this event has been questioned. Cf. Kitchen, *Reliability*, 211–12.

10. These narratives are dramatic. (As I have suggested previously, they should not be read silently but recited aloud.)

described in Judges, the Israelites were securely established in Canaan, but vulnerable to a Philistine invasion.

In Those Days There Was No King in Israel; A Man Did What Was Right in His Eyes

There was no central government. Each tribe was ruled by a judge and a council of elders. Unfortunately, the text does not describe the principles on which their judgments were based, but it implies that all followed the law of the covenant. Some judges were self-appointed, following a religious vision (Gideon, Samson through his parents). Jephtah was approached by the elders of Gilead—he was a successful brigand—and negotiated conditions of employment (Judg 11). It is not known how Deborah was appointed judge.

There are narratives about cooperation between several tribes. Some judges ruled several tribes or even "all Israel." There are also reports of intertribal conflicts. Ephraim tried to assert its hegemony over Israel; this led to a civil war between the Transjordan tribes and Ephraim.

The last chapters of Judges (17–21) deplore the lack of a firm government. The verse "In those days there was no king in Israel. A man did what was right in his eyes" (Judg 17:6; my translation) is repeated four times. The main example of anarchy is the story about the concubine of a Levite traveler who was raped and murdered by the men of Gibeah in Benjamin. This narrative is highly embroidered and may be a late insertion. It is not referred to in other biblical sources.[11]

Lawlessness is also illustrated in chapters 17–18 of Judges: "There was a man in the hill country of Ephraim whose name was Micah ... This man Micah had a shrine, and he made an *ephod* and *teraphim*, and installed one of his sons, who became his priest" (Judg 17:1, 5). It seems that Micah wanted a "real" (Levitical) priest. The narrative continues to

---

11. The narrative of the war between Benjamin and the rest of Israel (chapters 19–21) ends the book of Judges, but it occurred (if at all) at the beginning of this period, while Phinehas was yet alive. The historical basis of this war is doubtful. The EP reports that some men of Gibeah raped the concubine of a travelling Levite. There was a public outcry in Israel, leading to a punitive expedition against the tribe of Benjamin and to civil war (Judg 19–21). The Benjaminites were initially victorious, but in the end they were almost annihilated. Yet Benjamin is a strong tribe at the time of Samuel. This story explains the special relationship between Saul and the Transjordan town of Jabesh Gilead. See Szpek, "Levite's Concubine," 1–10.

describe a wandering Levite, looking for employment. Micah hired him to be his priest. At this time the Danites, under pressure from the Philistines, had decided to emigrate and sent five men "to spy out the land." They passed the place of Micah and said to the Levite, "Inquire of God that we may know whether the mission we are undertaking will succeed." The priest replied, "Go in peace. The mission you are on is under the eye of YHWH" (Judg 18:5–6).[12]

The mission was successful. The Danites found a good land in the north, inhabited by a weak population and open to assault. Six hundred men of Dan set out from Zor'ah and Eshthaol (where Samson had lived) to migrate to the north. They passed by Micah's place, seized the ephod and teraphim, and persuaded the priest to come with them. The Danites conquered the area of Laish, killed the inhabitants, and built a new city called Dan. There they built a sanctuary in which the ephod and teraphim were installed. The priest is identified as Jonathan ben Gershom ben Moses, and may have been the descendant of Moses.[13] His descendants served as priests until 720 BCE (Judg 18:30).

When the historian comments that "A man did what was right in his eyes" (Judg 17:6; my translation), he refers to the behavior of Micah, to the robbery committed by the Danites, and to the installation of the ephod, teraphim, and priest. There is no condemnation of the ethnic cleansing of Laish.

Summary

By the end of the time of the judges, the Israelites had dispossessed the Canaanites. They were vulnerable to attacks by the Philistines who succeeded in displacing the Danites. The Israelites saw themselves as one nation bound by a covenant to serve YHWH, but they also practiced Canaanite rites. The tribes were autonomous, ruled by judges. The authority of some judges was sometimes recognized by several tribes. There was a central sanctuary which contained the ark. There was no central civil or religious authority.

---

12. The NRSV, REB, NAB, and NJB give different translations.

13. The MT reading is doubtful. The name is either Moshe or Manasseh. The *nun* of Menashe is "hanging," i.e., probably incorrect.

III: The Ethnogenesis of Israel

From Judges to Monarchy

The book of Judges ends by lamenting the anarchy and insecurity of Israel. Yet the first chapter of 1 Samuel describes a peaceful Israel. Eli presides as high priest of the sanctuary ("house of God") and as a judge for forty years. The holy ark is in Shiloh, a center for pilgrimages. There is a strange hiatus between the end of Judges and the opening of Samuel: At the beginning of the time of the judges, Phinehas was the high priest, and the ark (which had been in Shiloh at the time of Joshua) was with him in Bethel (Judg 20:27–28). Who was this Eli? His father's name is not given in the Bible. How did he become high priest? How was the ark returned to Shiloh and when was the "House of YHWH" erected? It appears that Eli displaced a high priest from the family of Phinehas. Biblical sources maintain silence concerning this event. The only reference available comes from the Samarian tradition. The Samaritan Joshua reports the following:

> Discord had arisen between the descendant of Phinehas [Uzi] and his cousin Eli, whose name being interpreted means "The Insidious" ... This man ... had obtained for himself the lordship over the treasure house of the children of Israel; and he had obtained through the knowledge of magic ... riches, proud rank, and wealth. And there was collected to him a multitude in Shiloh, and he built himself a shrine there.[14]

There were two attempts to establish a theocracy: the High Priest Eli and his successor, Samuel the prophet, judged "all Israel." In both cases their sons and deputies proved to be corrupt judges. The people demanded a king: "Then all the elders of Israel gathered together and came to Samuel at Ramah, and said to him ... 'Appoint for us, then, a king to govern [judge] us, like other nations'" (1 Sam 8:4–5).

Some biblical passages reject the monarchy as sinful, while others support it. This is a realistic description of the political situation at the time of Samuel. The EP offers three arguments against establishing a monarchy.

---

14. *Samaritan Chronicle*, 127–28, quoted in Anderson and Giles, *Tradition Kept*, 127. Aaron's two surviving sons—Eleazar and Ithamar—were the ancestors of two priestly families. The position of high priest was conferred on the family of Phinehas ben Eleazar and his descendants (Num 25:11–13). Eli belonged to the family of Ithamar, Aaron's youngest son. He and his descendants functioned as high priests for several generations, until Abiathar became the priest of King David. When David was old, Abiathar supported the unsuccessful claimant Adonijah (1 Kgs 1:7). When Solomon became king, he transferred the high priesthood to Zadok of the Pinehas-Eleazar branch. Abiathar was transferred to Anatoth (1 Kgs 2:26–27).

The first concerns the quality of the king. In a beautiful parable, Jotham tells about the trees who went out to anoint a king. (Judg 9:8–15). Neither the olive tree, nor the fig tree, nor the vine accepted the offer of kingship. They all are happy with their success, benefiting the world. Only the useless bramble is ready to become king.

The second objection is the fear of the power of kings. This is forcefully expressed in the bleak realistic picture of royal despotism drawn by Samuel:

> This will be the ways [law] of the king who reigns over you: he will take your sons . . . your daughters . . . the best of your servants, men and women, of your oxen and your donkeys, and make them work for him. He will tithe your flocks, and you shall be his slaves. And in that day you will cry out because of your king, whom you have chosen for yourselves; but YHWH will not answer you in that day. (1 Sam 8:11–18)

The main argument against monarchy is expressed by Gideon when he is offered the kingship: "The Israelites said to Gideon, 'rule over us, you and your son and your grandson also; for you have delivered us out of the hand of Midian.' Gideon said to them, 'I will not rule over you, and my son will not rule over you; YHWH will rule over you'" (Jud 8:22–23).[15] In the same vein, God comforts Samuel: "They have not rejected you, but they have rejected me from being king over them" (1 Sam 8:7b). Nevertheless, the people (העם) insisted: "No! but we are determined to have a king over us, so that we also may be like other nations, and that our king may govern [judge] us, and go out before us and fight our battles" (1 Sam 8: 19b–20).

In the end, there was a compromise: Israel will have a king, but he will not be like the kings of other nations. The king is not divine, but absolutely bound by the law of the Torah. He is not chosen by the people, but given to them by God through a prophet. The king's behavior is scrutinized by prophets, who may criticize him with impunity.

Prophets—male and female—were well-known in the Ancient Near East.[16] They predicted the future and pronounced blessings. Their utterances were written down, deposited in royal archives, and later tested for accuracy. The books of Samuel attest to the presence of prophets in Israel, and one might justifiably assume that they were also active in the period

---

15. The Hebrew verb *m-l-kh*, meaning "to be king," is avoided.
16. Kitchen, *Reliability*, 383–92.

III: The Ethnogenesis of Israel

of the judges, though the term is only used once in the book, referring to "Deborah, the prophetess" (Judg 4).[17]

The prophet in Israel is not considered to be speaking for himself. There is no Hebrew verb that means "to prophecy": the spirit of YHWH takes possession of the prophet. The verb is used in the passive stem: they have been prophesized. It is not clear how one became a prophet. The status is neither inherited nor bestowed by authority. Anyone may become a prophet without regard to social background. Prophets may contradict each other, each one speaking in the name of YHWH. The only way to distinguish between them is to wait and find out who turns out to be right (Deut 18:21-22). According to the HEP there were companies of prophets, but an individual might declare that he speaks in the name of YHWH. These prophets predicted the future for fees, performed as a group, went into states of ecstasy, danced and performed music (see 1 Sam 9/10). The performance of these bands of prophets was considered to be divinely inspired: "And the spirit of YHWH will come down upon you and you shall be prophetized with them" (1 Sam 10:6; my translation).[18] Some prophets achieved eminence and had considerable influence. They are referred to with the title *the* prophet[19]; their pronouncements had divine authority and are given in the *niphal* (נִבָּא). They had considerable political power. Samuel was recognized as chief judge, and Gad and Nathan were royal prophets. They admonished kings with impunity. They appointed kings (Saul, David, Jeroboam, Jehu) and toppled dynasties (Saul, Jeroboam, Omri). Zevit cites fifty-eight prophetic predictions from the EP.[20] Many of these are blessings or sentences of punishment for previous transgression. Such passages are not editorial comments of the historian, but reports based on his sources. This shows that, at the time of the EP, the experience of the immanence of YHWH was genuine. People expected mantic pronouncements. The

---

17. There are three references to "messengers to YHWH" (Judg 2:1; 6:11; 13:3; the terms is generally translated as "angel of YHWH"). The first is an admonition of Israel; the other two announce that Gideon and Samson will deliver Israel from the hand of the Midianites/Philistines.

18. The grammatical form (stem) in these instances is in the *hitpael* (התנבא).

19. See Fleming ("Etymological Origins") for a discussion of the term

20. Zevit, *Religions*, 482–86. His list includes predictions by Joshua, by Jotham (Judg 9:16-21) and by divine messengers (מלאך); none of them are styled "prophet." The stem (נבא) does not appear at all in Joshua, and only twice in Judges ("YHWH sent a prophet" [Jud 6:8] and "Deborah, a prophetess" [Jud 4:4]).

legends of the lives and deeds of some of the early prophets were accepted as possible/believable.

The royalist victory was absolute: all later reports take the hereditary monarchy for granted. Samuel was forced to sponsor a king. After rejecting Saul, he did not consider the abolition of the monarchy, but anointed a new king. The opposition also was winning—the king is subject to the Torah. He is appointed by a prophet and accountable to his scrutiny.

There are two traditions concerning the election of Saul. In the first narrative, Samuel anointed Saul in a private ceremony (1 Sam 9—10:16). In the second narrative, Saul is "caught by lot" (which was arranged by Samuel), and then Samuel introduced him: "'Do you see the one whom YHWH has chosen? There is no one like him among all the people.' And all the people shouted, 'Long live the king!'" (1 Sam 10:24). According to both versions, Saul did not want to be king. When the lot "caught him," he hid among the baggage (1 Sam 10:22). When first told by Samuel that he will be the king, he said, "I am only a Benjaminite, from the least of the tribes of Israel, and my family is the humblest of all the families of the tribe of Benjamin. Why then have you spoken to me in this way?" (1 Sam 9:21). Samuel does not answer, but we may rephrase the question. What are the repercussions of Samuel's choice? If Samuel wanted a strong, effective king, he should have chosen a recognized elder from a strong tribe, probably from Ephraim. Instead, he appoints the unknown son of a humble family, and his second choice, David, was not much better. He chose a person from a peripheral tribe. The choice of a king from Judah laid the foundation for the future division of Israel. There is a fundamental flaw in Samuel's behavior. He used his authority as a prophet to sabotage systematically the rule of Saul. He assembled the people in Mizpah to elect a king, and then announced, "Today you have rejected your God . . . you have said, 'No! but set a king over us'" (1 Sam 10:19). That is not the way to choose a successful king! After the election of Saul, everyone went home—Saul returned to his homestead—and some people expressed their disappointment. Then something unexpected happened: the elected king showed initiative, authority, and military skill. The king of the Ammonites besieged the Transjordan city of Jabesh-Gilead, setting humiliating cruel conditions for their surrender. According to Judges 21, there were kinship relations between Benjamin and Jabesh.

> Now Saul was coming from the field behind the oxen; and Saul said, "What is the matter with the people, that they are weeping?"

III: The Ethnogenesis of Israel

> So they told him the message from the inhabitants of Jabesh. And the spirit of YHWH came upon Saul in power when he heard these words, and his anger was greatly kindled. He took a yoke of oxen, and cut them in pieces and sent them throughout all the territory of Israel by messengers, saying, "Whoever does not come out after Saul and Samuel, so it shall be done to his oxen!" Then the dread of YHWH fell upon the people, and they came out as one. (1 Sam 11:5–7)

Thus Saul asserted his authority as king. At the same time, he acknowledged the importance of Samuel. After this victory, Samuel called the people to Gilgal "to renew the kingship." His parting speech is a masterpiece of rhetoric. He begins by announcing his retirement and asks whether he is guilty of corruption. After the people acknowledge that he was a just judge, he continued to denounce the monarchy: "The wickedness you have done in the sight of YHWH is great in demanding a king for yourselves" (1 Sam 12:17b). He then added that he would continue to pray for Israel, "and I will instruct you in the good and in the right way" (12:23b). There are more instances of Samuel's working against the king. Finally, there was an open break, and Samuel anointed David as pretender. This was the last stand of the opposition against the monarchy. The long-term result was that prophets were recognized as having moral authority. They were able to criticize a king and, later in the northern kingdom, acted as "kingmakers."

The monarchy, as an institution, was consolidated by a decisive act of David: the establishment of Jerusalem as a royal city. Jerusalem was conquered by David's private army, the "heroes of David," and his foreign mercenaries. It was not considered a part of the heritage of Benjamin or Judah, but "the City of David."[21] Furthermore, David brought the Ark and its tent to his city and established it on a place which he had personally bought. The central sanctuary was to be a "king's sanctuary" (מקדש מלך).[22] This status later gave the king administrative control over the cult. He could appoint and dismiss officiating priests, he controlled the placement of cult places all over the kingdom, and he had some control over its finances. I suggest that this control secured the Davidic dynasty. The kings of Israel never succeeded in establishing a royal residence with a major sanctuary. Control of

---

21. "But the people of Judah could not drive out the Jebusites . . . so the Jebusites live with the people of Judah in Jerusalem to this day" (Josh 15:63). Jerusalem is also assigned to Benjamin in Josh 18:28.

22. Amos 7:13.

the temple conferred responsibility for the cult. From this point on, the HEP judges each king: did he do what was right in the eyes of YHWH?

David's work culminated in the building of a temple by Solomon, to be the "dwelling place" (*mishkan*) of the "name of YHWH." The temple was formally inaugurated by the king—not by the officiating priest (1 Kgs 8). In the manner of Moses, Solomon addressed the people and then, "stretching his hands to heaven," asked for the protection of YHWH (1 Kgs 8:22–53). Biblical scholarship assigns this chapter to the Persian era or later. This is, of course, based on the Wellhausen fallacy. Solomon's prayer totally reflects the theology of the Pentateuch, which was known at this time (see chapter 4, "The Composition of the Pentateuch"): by the time of Solomon's reign, Israel had a written monotheistic law (PT). There existed a central sanctuary in which the required worship for YHWH was performed. We return therefore to the previous "how come" question. Why did the kings tolerate the unmistakable overt breeches of the (known) covenant?

9

The Religion of Israel During the Monarchic Period

I HAVE ARGUED IN previous chapters that monotheism does not deny the existence of divine beings, but deems them to be powerless in the face of YHWH. The Sinai covenant forbids any worship or physical representation of other gods. The idea of a supreme deity might have been acceptable to the Israelites, but it was unheard of to worship a deity without an image. We must assume that the religious traditions of the people of the exodus were influenced by ancient Canaanite rituals. All cults of the Middle East had female deities. The Israelites in Egypt probably had their household gods, or teraphim, and the women probably called upon female deities. These old rituals, augmented by Canaanite rituals encountered after the conquest, persisted in Israel until the destruction of the first temple.

During the time of the monarchy, YHWH was the supreme God of Israel and Judah. Oaths were sworn and contracts signed in his name. The prophets anointed kings in the name of YHWH, and kings were bound by the laws of the covenant. No king ever claimed divine status. No steles were erected in their honor. Thus the Siloam tunnel inscription proves that the technique of writing on monuments was available.[1] But the inscription does not mention the king, merely the workers in the tunnel. Prophets of YHWH could reprimand kings with impunity (David, Ahab), and were asked for political advice (1 Kgs 22). If one removes all editorial comments

1. The Siloam tunnel is an aqueduct, built at the time of King Hezekiah or earlier. The Siloam inscription was found underground in the tunnel, and describes how the workers, who had started at different ends of the tunnel, reached each other.

or historical explanations from the books of Kings and Chronicles, one sees that YHWH was worshiped both in Israel and Judah.

Between 930 BCE (the divided kingdom) and 722 BCE (the destruction of Samaria), three major sanctuaries devoted to the worship of YHWH existed: Jerusalem, Bethel, and Dan. After Jeroboam became king of Israel, he decided to found the two sanctuaries of Bethel and Dan in order to enable his subjects to worship YHWH in his kingdom. In these sanctuaries, there was a golden calf—in Jerusalem there were golden seraphim.[2] The redactor of Kings condemned the Israelite sanctuaries of Bethel and Dan as idolatrous, and refers to them as "The sins of Jeroboam, which he sinned and he caused Israel to commit" (1 Kgs 14:16). There are two reports of condemnation of the sanctuaries in Bethel and Dan by contemporary prophets: Ahijah and Jehu predicted the overthrow of the dynasties of Jeroboam because "you have done evil above all those that were before you . . . and made for yourself other gods, and cast images" (1 Kgs 14:9), and Ba'asha because "you walked in the way of Jeroboam" (1 Kgs 16:2). All later condemnations of the "sins of Jeroboam" are editorial comments by the HEP. There are no reports denouncing these sanctuaries since the beginning of the dynasty of Omri (885/886 BCE). The prophets Elijah and Elisha, though opposing the introduction of the cult of Baal during the Omrite dynasty, did not object to Bethel. Neither Amos nor Isaiah denounced the Bethel sanctuary. These prophets did not reject the sacrificial cult, but denied that it would wipe out the guilt of oppressing the poor. Their speeches show that the Israelites believed that the worship in these sanctuaries was legitimate and effective.

The terms *miqdash* (sanctuary) or *hekhal* (temple) are only used in reference to one of the central sanctuaries dedicated to YHWH or to the tabernacle where the ark is kept.[3] The term "house of" may refer to YHWH, to *bamoth*, or to other deities.[4] The sanctuary is distinguished from other cult places by its "holiness" (*miqdash*). Only priests may officiate. Access to the central part of the temple is only allowed to the high priest. The ritual is controlled by strict rules of ritual purity: only priests of unblemished language and free from bodily blemish or handicap may officiate. Laypeople may only attend in a state of ritual purity, which is defined in

---

2. See Kaufmann (*Religion of Israel*) for a discussion of the golden calf in Bethel.

3. The term *hechal* also may refer to a royal palace (Ahab, the king of Babel; 2 Kings, Chronicles, and Daniel).

4. Dagon (1 Sam 5:2) and Rimon (2 Kgs 5:18).

III: The Ethnogenesis of Israel

detail. Sacrificial rites (*zebhah*) outside the sanctuary may be performed by laypeople and attended by persons in a state of ritual impurity.

Israel had only three sanctuaries.[5] As Faust observes,

> In the Late Bronze Age ... temples were found at almost every site, with some sites having more than one. Conversely ... real temples are practically absent from most sites that can be labeled as Israelite ... The difference is very obvious in the Iron Age II [i.e. divided kingdom], when any site that can be safely labeled as Israelite shows no sign of an organized public cult.[6]

I suggest that the ritual of Shiloh and the three major sanctuaries followed the procedures described in Leviticus. The requirements of *avodah*—sacrifices at appointed times and expiatory sacrifices—were deemed to be met by the service in the official sanctuaries. According to Deuteronomy 12, these sacrifices, as well as "gifts, vows and freewill offerings" (Lev 23:38), are only acceptable if offered at a major sanctuary. This proscription was manifestly ignored. YHWH was worshiped as well on the "high places" (*bamoth*—בָּמוֹת)[7] (and probably at private shrines and homes). Furthermore, Canaanite rites were also practiced, specifically to Baal, Asherah, and the "host of heaven."

The three major sanctuaries were the only official temples. The book of Kings describes four additional forms of cult practices.

> 1. *Tolerance of worship on bamoth* (בָּמוֹת). Hezekiah and Josiah destroyed these places, but they were reinstalled by their successors.[8] The biblical formula describing the ritual of the *bamoth* is: "But the *bamoth* were not removed and the people still sacrificed and offered incense (מְזַבְּחִים וּמְקַטְּרִים) on the *bamoth*" (1 Kgs 22:44,[9] repeated regularly).

5. The HEP condemns every ritual performed outside the Jerusalem temple.

6. Faust, *Israel's Ethnogenesis*, 93–94. This statement illustrates one of the problems of the interpretation of archaeological data. Zevit (*Religions*, 123) lists a number of Israelite temples, based on a different definition of the term. A cult center is a large cult place comprised of more than one structure, which does contain a dedicated building for which the term "temple" seems inappropriate. A temple is a (large) single-roomed or multi roomed structure with adjacent or internal open spaces and courts used for cultic purposes. Such temples are not equivalent to a *hechal* (temple) or *mikdash* (sanctuary). Zevit's definition of the word "temple" includes places like the "house of *bamoth*" (1 Kgs 12:31).

7. Bamah, e.g.; *bamoth* is the plural; see Glossary.

8. See chapter 10, "Cultic Reforms," pp. 166–71

9. See also 1 Kgs 22:43b (NRSV).

This standard formula does not specify to whom these *bamoth* were dedicated. Several references indicate these Israelite cult sites were used before the establishment of the Jerusalem temple. When Saul asks for Samuel in an unnamed city (probably Ramathaim-Zophim) in the land of Zuph, he is told, "The people have a sacrifice today on the *bamah* ... He must bless the sacrifice" (1 Sam 9:12b–13). Another *bamah* was in Gibeon: "The king went to Gibeon to sacrifice there, for that was the great *bamah*" (1 Kgs 3:4; my translation). The book of Kings implies that there were many such *bamoth*, presumably dedicated to YHWH. Chronicles states explicitly that formal sacrifices were legitimately offered on the *bamoth*. "The people, however, still sacrificed at the *bamoth*, but only to YHWH their God" (2 Chr 33:17). These high places differed from the *bamoth* which had been introduced by Rehoboam and dedicated to local deities (1 Kings 14:23–24; also 1 Kings 15:12).

The discussion of the *bamoth* is another example of biblical scholarship ignoring the subtlety of the Hebrew language. The root of a Hebrew verb generally has three letters; i.e., *z-q-r*. A root may be expressed in several formations, called "stems" (*binyanim*).[10] A change of stem implies a change of meaning. For example, the root *z-k-r* means "to remember" in the stem *qal*, but in the stem *hiphil* it means "to remind." By such grammatical devices, the language of the Bible differentiates between solemn rituals performed at a major sanctuary and other religious ceremonies.

The verb *q-t-r* (קטר—"smoke, burn incense") appears in the Bible both in *piel* (קִטֵּר—*qitter*) and in *hiphil* (הִקְטִיר—*hiqtir*).

> (i) The *hiphil* of *q-t-r* always refers to a formal service in a sanctuary. The term refers either to the burning of the sacrifice on the altar or to the burning of incense, which can only be performed by a priest at an official sanctuary dedicated to YHWH. It is used in the reports on Jeroboam I (1 Kgs 12:33:) and Uzziah (2 Chr 26:16),[11] who usurped priestly functions and offered incense in the sanctuary. The offering of incense by Ahaz (2 Chr 28:3) occurred during a formal ceremony in the valley of Hinnom. When Hezekiah talks about the neglect of the obligatory service during the reign of Ahaz (2 Chr 29:7), he uses the *hiphil*: "They have not offered incense to the God of Israel."

---

10. See Glossary.

11. The offering of incense by Uzziah is only mentioned in Chronicles. Whether the report is historically reliable is irrelevant for the present discussion; *q-t-r* is rendered in *hiphil*.

III: The Ethnogenesis of Israel

(ii) The *piel* (*mqatter*—מְקַטֵּר—burning of incense) refers to less formal rituals. It may occur at any place—at a *bamah*, "under any green tree," on the roof, in front of the copper snake *Nehushtan*. It may be conducted by any person: "the people burned incense." The incense may be dedicated to various *elohim* (Seir, Queen of Heaven, Baal, and Ashera). All biblical references to the cult on the *bamoth* use the *piel* stem.[12] The burning of incense for the host of heavens (*tsvah hashamayim*) (e.g. 2 Kgs 23:5) refers to ceremonies which took place on roofs, at homes, in sacred groves or on altars erected by various kings.

The other verb of the standard formula describing the service on the *bamoth* is זבח—z-b-ḥ, or "sacrifice". This root also appears in two grammatical stems: *qal* (זוֹבֵחַ—*zoveaḥ*) or *piel* (מְזַבֵּחַ—*mezabbeaḥ*). The *qal* denotes a formal sacrifice at a sanctuary. The text generally refers to sacrifices to YHWH, but also uses the *qal* when referring to formal sacrifices to other deities (e.g., to Dagon, as in Judah 16:23). The *piel* of z-b-ḥ always refers to informal ceremonies and appears together with the *piel* of q-t-r.[13]

The Piel forms of q-t-r and z-b-ḥ (קַטֵּר, זַבֵּח) only appear in the Prophets and Writings (the Ketuvim). They do not occur in the Pentateuch. This difference cannot be ascribed to linguistic development, because in the EP, both grammatical constructions are used side by side: I suggest that the EP introduced new technical terms, designed to distinguish formal worship—*avodah*—from rituals outside the temple: "Solomon loved the Lord, walking in the statues of his father David; only, he sacrificed and offered incense in high places" (1 Kings 3:3; sacrifice in *piel*). In this instance, the reference is to the general practice of sacrifices outside a main sanctuary, not involving formal *avodah*: "The king went to Gibeon to sacrifice there" (1 Kgs 3:4a; sacrifice in *qal*); here the reference is to a major ceremony at the great *bamah*.

Second Kings reports that king Ahaz, like other kings before him, sacrificed on the *bamoth*: "he sacrificed and burned incense on the *bamoth*" (2 Kgs 16:4; my translation; both verbs use the *piel* stem). Here the text refers to the semi-profane rites performed all over the country, using the *piel*. But, in the same chapter, when king Ahaz usurped the function of the high priest and officiated at the ceremony in the temple, the text uses the *hiphil*: "and he offered his burnt offering and his grain offering, poured his drink offering, and dashed the blood of his offerings of well-being against the altar" (2 Kgs 16:13, in *hiphil*).

Solomon celebrated the transfer of the ark to the temple by an informal feast. The language indicates this: "King Solomon, and all the congregation of Israel, who had

---

12. Many of these *bamoth* may have been Canaanite cult places before the invasion, and therefore prohibited in Deuteronomy.

13. The only exceptions are in 1 Kgs (3:3 and 11:8), which uses *piel* for "sacrifice" together with *hiphil* for "offering incense."

assembled before him, were with him before the ark, *sacrificing* (*piel*) so many sheep and oxen that could not be counted or numbered" (1 Kgs 8:5).

Summary: During the time of the monarchy, YHWH was venerated at three sanctuaries and at the high places (*bamoth*). The ritual was based on the procedures described in Leviticus. The biblical language differentiates between two ceremonial levels:

a. The "offering of incense" to YHWH (*hiphil*, מַקְטִיר) and "sacrificing" (*qal*, זָבַח) is a solemn ceremony.

b. The *piel* sacrifice and *hiphil* burning (מְזַבֵּחַ, מְקַטֵּר) of incense was an informal event, open to anyone, and it differs from the formal service in the sanctuary.

c. The "burning of incense" (מְקַטֵּר) may occur at any place—at a "high place," "under any green tree," or "on the roof," and may be conducted by any person: the incense may be dedicated to various *elohim* (Seir, Queen of Heaven, Baal, and Ashera). Possibly this was not a solemn act of worship, but rather an act of obeisance, of respect to the spirits (*elohim*) of the supernatural world.

The systematic use of different stems clearly refers to two different rituals.[14] The use of *hiphil* always refers to a formal ceremony. The *piel* sacrifice (מְזַבֵּחַ) and *hiphil* burning (מְקַטֵּר) of incense was an informal event open to anyone, and differs from the formal service in the sanctuary.

2. *Several kings tolerated non-Israelite forms of worship.* Solomon contracted diplomatic marriages. He permitted his foreign wives to follow their traditions and even built *bamoth* for some of them (1 Kgs 11:1–8). It seems that, in Solomon's times, these cults were not practiced all over Israel, but they spread over Judah during the reigns of Rehoboam and Abiam. These cult places were abolished by Asa.[15]

3. *Attempts of synchronism/henotheism.* The first occurred in Israel/Judah during the reign of Ahab/Jezebel who attempted to introduce an official cult of Baal beside the cult of YHWH. During the reign of Ahab, an official Baal cult was maintained. "He served Baal [עבד] and worshiped him. He erected an altar for Baal in the house of Baal, which he built in Samaria" (1 Kgs 16:31b–32). The Baal cult was

---

14. Most translations ignore the differences, translating both form of *z-v-ḥ* as sacrifice and both forms of *q-t-r* as burnt offerings. The only correct translation I found is in the aforementioned Spanish Bible, which translates the *piel* of *q-t-r* as *quemar incensio* ("to burn incense") and the *hiphil* as *offrecer incensio* ("to offer incense").

15. A comprehensive discussion of the rituals at this time is found in Zevit, *Religions*, 457–65.

III: The Ethnogenesis of Israel

represented by the prophets of Baal. This was a form of henotheism: YHWH remained the God of Israel. Ahab submitted to the law of the Pentateuch and accepted the rebukes of Elijah. When preparing for war against Moab, the prophets of YHWH were consulted. At the same time, the official worship of Baal was also promoted. There was no attempt of syncretism (combining both traditions in one single religious system).[16] The worship of Baal continued under his son Ahaziah (1 Kgs 22:53). His successor Jehoram removed the sacred pillar (מצבה) of Baal, but the "house of Baal" remained. Jehoram of Judah, who had married Athaliah, daughter of Ahab, as well as his son Ahaziah, "walked in the ways of the king of Israel." But the text does not state explicitly that the worship of Baal was also introduced in Judah. (2 Kgs 8). After a bloody revolution, "Jehu wiped out Baal from Israel" (2 Kgs 10:28).

The second official introduction of a foreign cult took place during the reign of Ahaz (735–715 BCE), and the third under Manasseh (687–642 BCE). The data about Ahaz are contradictory. He is accused of "walking in the ways of the kings of Israel" and sacrificing and offering incense (*piel*) on the *bamoth*, on the hills, and under every green tree (2 Kgs 16:2–4; 2 Chr 28:2). According to 2 Kings, he introduced a new altar into the temple and officiated as priest: he burned the *olah* sacrifice (*hiphil*), sprinkling the blood on the altar (2 Kgs 16:12–13). According to Chronicles, he sacrificed (*qal*) to the gods of Damascus (2 Chr 28:23).

The most radical introduction of foreign cults was done by Manasseh (2 Kgs 21), who not only worshiped (עבד) the Baal and all the host of heaven, but also introduced altars dedicated to various deities into the temple district, including a statue of Ashera. These cults continued during the short reign of his son Amon.

4. *Canaanite rituals were also practiced at private homes*: houses, gardens, hills, and sacred groves. These were unofficial ceremonies, involving the burning of incense and offering of libations, dedicated to other gods: Baal, Ashera, the "host of heaven," or the Queen of Heaven. The term "sacrifice" is never used in connection with these private ceremonies. Jeremiah refers to "all the houses upon whose roofs offerings [incense?] have been made ["burned," in *piel*] to the whole

---

16. There is a hint of syncretism in some of the archaeological findings, cf. the following discussion.

host of heaven, and libations have been poured out to other gods" (Jer 19:13b).

It appears that these cults were officially ignored. Direct references to private ceremonies, we find only in the LP, mainly in Jeremiah. References to these cults in the EP are editorial comments. The main reference in the EP comes in the sweeping indictment by the HEP:

> And the people of Israel ... set for themselves pillars and sacred poles [*asherim*] on every high hill and under every green tree; there they made offerings [burned incense, *piel*] on all the *bamoth*, as the nations did whom YHWH carried away before them. (2 Kgs 17:10–11)

We therefore have the following data. The official worship in the three sanctuaries continued without interruption both in Israel and in Judah (though occasionally curtailed). There were four brief periods of unofficial introduction of foreign cults: cult places for foreign queens (Judah; 930–908 BCE); worship of Baal (Israel, perhaps Judah; 873–842 BCE); Ahaz (Judah; 743–747 BCE) and Manasseh/Amon (Judah; 698–640 BCE).[17] These rituals were abolished by the reforms of Asa, Jehu, Joash, Hezekiah, and Josiah. The HEP condemns every king of Israel for maintaining the sanctuaries of Bethel and Dan, and every king of Judah except Hezekiah and Josiah for allowing the service on the *bamoth*. Thus Kings and Chronicles read like a listing of sinful kings. In fact, Israel maintained the official service of YHWH in two sanctuaries for 208 years. The additional official worship of Baal during the Omrite dynasty only lasted for thirty-two years. Judah maintained the Jerusalem temple service for 344 years, and allowed additional Canaanite services during 106 years.

Was this service "monotheistic"? The Pentateuch gives clear criteria determining whether a rite is monotheistic. The sacrificial ritual must absolutely refrain from any imagery or material representation of the deity. It should have no magical function—it is not performed to control the cosmos or to sustain the deity. The liturgy must be directed to a deity who is absolutely unique, and the sole creator and ruler of the universe and should be free of mythological references. This is manifested repeatedly in the psalms which formed the basis of the Jerusalem service.[18]

---

17. Chronology based on Cogan, *Racing Torrent*, 236.

18. This may be ambiguous. For example, Psalm 29 has been interpreted as describing the war between YHWH and Yam, the sea). If this hymn was sung in the temple, did

III: The Ethnogenesis of Israel

How were these services conducted? How were the Sabbath, the New Moon, or the agricultural festivals celebrated? The HEP does not describe these rites because his audience knew what he was talking about. Josiah, for example, commanded a great Passover celebration, but the ceremony itself is not described (2 Kings 23:21–23).

When Amos (5:21–23) and Isaiah (1:11–14) denounce the sacrificial cult, they refer to it in the language of the Pentateuch: they list the prescribed sacrificial animal species: ram, buffalo, bull, sheep, and he-goats. They also use the Pentateuch terms for various sacrifices and festivals: *hag, atzereth, hodesh, shabbath, moed, olah, minhah*, and *zebah*.[19] They refer to the lifting hands in prayer. These speeches indicate clearly that the people in Israel, as well as in Judah, were familiar with the ritual described in Leviticus. A detailed description of a temple ritual is given in 2 Chronicles 29:20–30. Preliminary to the festival is the purification of the temple and its vessels. The sacrificial animals were brought in, and the king commanded the priest "to offer them on the altar of YHWH." Seven bulls, rams, and lambs were slaughtered, and their blood was sprinkled upon the altar. Then the he-goats were brought to the king and the assembly for a sin offering. They (the king and who else?) laid their hands upon them. The sin offerings were made "for the kingdom and the sanctuary and Judah" and by special command of the king "for all Israel;" Musical instruments were played and hymns were sung. The sacrificial ritual follows the rules set out in Leviticus. The songs and music refer to the Psalms. From all these data we may conclude that the sanctuary cult was "yahwistic."

Archeological data confirm the biblical reports and illustrate their meaning. They show an abundance of Israelite cult sites, including small horned altars in domestic shrines, limestone household altars, ceramic cult stands. Some of the altars and cult objects are plain without any imagery or inscriptions. Others are clearly dedicated to Baal or Ashera. Two inscriptions (Khirbet el-Qom and Kuntilled 'Ajrud) refer to YHWH and to Asheratah.[20] Thousands of terra-cotta human figurines have been found,

---

the audience imagine a fight between independent forces in which (a pagan) YHWH finally emerged as victor? Or did they express their joy of serving an almighty, superior deity (monotheistic)? Even if this hymn was called out at the temple, I doubt that any of the participants thought about its theological ramifications. Nowadays, when the psalm is recited at the synagogue during the Sabbath services, most of the participants do not understand what it says; they simply enjoy singing.

19. See Glossary.

20. Dever *Recent Archaeological discoveries*, translates *wl'šrth* as "his Ashera." Zevit

The Religion of Israel During the Monarchic Period

and "virtually all of these figurines are females,"[21] indicating widespread fertility cults. These findings are generally interpreted as proving that true monotheism only developed in the post-exilic period.[22] Dever, accepting the Wellhausen fallacy, states,

> Indeed, the overwhelming archaeological evidence today of largely indigenous origins for early Israel leaves no room for an exodus from Egypt or a 40-year pilgrimage through the Sinai wilderness ... As for Leviticus and Numbers, these are clearly additions to the "pre-history" by very late Priestly editorial hands, preoccupied with notions of ritual purity, themes of the "promised land," and other literary motifs.
>
> Most biblical scholars now agree that true monotheism (i.e. not merely "henotheism") arose only in the period of the Exile and beyond.[23]

The acceptance of the Wellhausen fallacy leads to a distorted picture of the religion of Israel during the monarchic period. Dever tends to ignore the continuous existence of the worship of YHWH at the three official royal sanctuaries in Jerusalem, Bethel, and Dan. The presence of cult sites and cult objects is evidence of religious rituals. They do not show anything about the theology underlying the cult. Dever asserts,

> The early Israelite cult was monolatrous, but certainly not monotheistic in the philosophical sense.
>
> The archaeological discoveries we have surveyed make it indisputably clear that local shrines and even rival temples continued in use after Solomon, and that Ba'al and Asherah were *commonly* worshipped down to the very end of the Monarchy. *Monotheistic*

(*Religions*, 360, 390) translates it as "Asherata."

21. Ibid., 157.

22. For a comprehensive discussion of monolatry and monotheism, see Heiser, "Monotheism."

23. Dever, *Biblical Writers*, 99, 197. See chapter 3, "The Origin of Israel: Archaeological Interpretations," [x-ref]. Essentially, Dever's argument is as follows: The first "proto-Israelites" were semi-nomadic groups, one of which may have been called Israel, which infiltrated the highlands of Canaan during the thirteenth/twelfth century BCE. There was no exodus, no sojourn in the desert, no invasion of Canaan under Joshua. There was no nation of "Israel" avowing monotheism. Therefore, monotheism must be a late development.

III: The Ethnogenesis of Israel

Judaism was a product of the Exile, not earlier... Until then, the ancient fertility cults of Canaan held powerful sway. (my emphasis)[24]

The first part of this quote is factual. The passages emphasized by me are interpretations not derived from the data, which by themselves neither show how "common" these practices were, nor that monotheism was not known. Cult places or artifacts which contain imagery are not monotheistic. For this reason, there can be no archaeological evidence of a monotheistic cult. Monotheism requires image-free cult places/objects. There is abundant archaeological evidence that YHWH was worshiped in Israel, but most are profane: seals, contracts, petitions, and prayers. Many archaeological findings—cult places, altars, and incense holders—are compatible with a monotheistic ritual. Dever describes cult places and artifacts with pagan imagery. There the deity can be identified. There are also many cult places without inscriptions, pagan imagery, or female figurines. These are the monotheistic sites of monotheistic worship. Dever argues that archaeological findings prove the existence of a popular private syncretistic religion, with heavy emphasis on the adoration of a female deity:

> The Bible almost totally ignores private and family religion, women's cults and "folk religion," and indeed the religious practices of the *majority* in ancient Israel and Judah ... Thus, if "religion" is what the majority of people actually do in the name of the deity or deities ... then archaeology can give us a more realistic picture of Israelite religion.[25]

This is equivalent to arguing that Catholic Europe was a pagan society. Anthropologists from outer space would find countless images of the deity and of semi-divine beings, angels, and saints, who were clearly worshiped. They might also find evidence for "reform movements." Cromwell's puritans considered the cult of Rome to be pagan and systematically destroyed what they called shrines of idolatry. But the adulation of saints does not invalidate Christian monotheism. Saints are asked for intervention, but do not have divine power: the credo is monotheistic. Jews in nineteenth-century Poland feared evil spirits and developed rituals to protect themselves against them. Contemporary Jews may wear amulets to protect themselves from the evil eye. They also write petitions which are inserted in the cracks of Western Wall in Jerusalem. This does not constitute pagan worship.

---

24. Dever, *Recent Archaeological Discoveries*, 165–66.
25. Dever, *Biblical Writers*, 173–74; author's emphasis.

The Religion of Israel During the Monarchic Period

The Israelites, the "people of the land" were not biblical scholars. They were not debating fine points of monotheistic theology. They were in awe of the old "holy places" and of the possible powers of the old gods (*elohim*— אלהים). They accepted—without reflection—stories about God which are not appropriate for an image of an all-powerful deity.[26] Minor divinities (*elohim*) are subordinate to YHWH, but they may be able to help or to harm. The monotheistic cosmos includes malevolent spirits. You surely do not want to offend them. Perhaps it would have been prudent for Job to pacify Satan before he would talk God into a malicious contract.

Let us imagine a group of women burning incense and offering libations to the Queen of Heaven in order to support a woman during delivery. Such rites are "pagan" if they think that the Queen of Heaven exists independently of YHWH (or even existed before him) and that she has special powers which are beyond what YHWH can do. They are "monotheistic" if it is understood that YHWH is the sole creator of the world, including the Queen of Heaven, who derives her powers from him. Burning incense to honor her images in their household shrines was considered to be an act of obeisance, not an act of worship. This may be sophistry and was rejected by the latter prophets. My point is that monolatrous behavior of the population does not invalidate the strict monotheism of the Pentateuch. Biblical scholarship tends to oversimplify. Dever's bias is shown by the following examples.

> This syncretistic cult can now be illustrated directly *by archaeological finds that antedate most of the biblical texts,* and therefore constitute primary evidence [my emphasis].[27]

This statement is based on the assumption that most of the Pentateuch, especially the text of the P source, was only composed in the postexilic period.

> The primary features of the pre-monarchic Israelite cult were as follows: (1) Worship was a localized affair, with open air sanctuaries or even simple household shrines serving most ordinary folk in ordinary practice. There were few, if any actual temples and no centralized worship.[28]

---

26. Maimonides interprets all such passages as symbolic. References to the Deity describe merely human experience, not the qualities of God.

27. Dever, *Recent Archaeological Discoveries,* 165

28. Ibid., 165.

III: The Ethnogenesis of Israel

Dever forgets to mention that centralized worship existed in Shiloh until its destruction, and perhaps also in Gilgal. He neglects to address that the central cult, and many local shrines, were dedicated to the service of YHWH and probably monotheistic (see earlier discussion for the relevant criteria).

> (2) In the rarity of elaborate clerical or priestly institutions, any Israelites (males at least) could officiate in worship. Anyone could build an altar, plant a sacred tree, erect a stela, or offer sacrifices.[29]

This observation is based on texts from Joshua, Judges, and 1 Samuel. Dever neglects to point out that there were different levels of ritual, and that the formal *avodah* was the prerogative of a priest.

> (3) The most prominent rituals were simply the frequent presentation of food and drink offerings—grains, cereals, olive oil, wine, and sacrifices of sheep or goats—the principal agricultural products of Canaan centuries before the appearance of the Israelites.[30]

That is certainly correct. However, these rituals were part of Israel's heritage from before the invasion of Canaan. Though they are formally defined in the Mosaic legislation, we should assume that they reflect older traditions. As pointed out earlier, it is to be expected that the Israelites in Egypt would have ritual traditions which included sacrifices and were ultimately related to the religious customs of their Canaanite/Middle East background. This also goes for the following point.

> (4) There *may have been* more periodic public festivals; the ones we know of were also borrowed from Canaan and followed the Canaanite agricultural year [my emphasis].[31]

What does he expect? These agricultural festivals were not borrowed by Israelite invaders from the local population. They had been practiced for thousands of years, since agriculture was developed. The distinguishing mark of the Israelite rituals is not the offerings of an agricultural society, but their transformation into monotheistic ceremonies. They neither have a magic function, nor are they needed by the deity; they are expressions of devotion and gratitude, celebrating the exodus. The *avodah* ("worship") of YHWH replaces the *avodah* ("servitude") for Pharaoh.

29. Ibid., 165.
30. Ibid., 165.
31. Ibid., 165.

Therefore the biblical festivals are memorials of Israel's history as well as expressions of devotion and gratitude. But they are never conceived as needed by the deity.

Dever claims the following:

> We know that there never was a single monolithic religion of all Israel. Rather, here existed, often side by side, various strands, such as the partly Canaanite cult of the period of the judges; the "official" religion of the Jerusalem temple; a "popular" religion in the countryside; the "ethical monotheism" of the classical prophets; the "Mosaic reform" of the Deuteronomistic school; the post-Exilic priestly school with its religion of' "ritual purity" (the foundation of later Judaism). Yet these various stages of religious development all tend to be combined in the final, idealized version that we have in the Hebrew Bible—*almost as though the Israelite religion had been handed down to Moses as a finished creation and did not undergo any subsequent change* [my emphasis].[32]

The last sentence of the preceding of quotation shows that Dever is aware of the theological cohesiveness of the monotheistic Pentateuch. Implicitly, he recognizes that the Pentateuch is a coherent religious/theological statement, a consistent monotheistic document. By denying its early roots, he must assign it to later times. Here Dever clearly confuses "religion" with "religious practice." The various "strands" of religion cited above illustrate to what degree the laws of the Pentateuch were implemented. Dever recognizes that "the eloquent prophetic protest against the ever-present threat of idolatry ... the prophets knew what they were talking about" (ibid., 165). Exactly! Classical prophecy was not a "strand" of Israelite religion. The prophets knew and interpreted the Pentateuch. They emphasized what they considered to be its essential message. The "priestly school" was not a "stage of religious development"—after all, they aimed to implement the laws of the Pentateuch—but did not compose it.

> The Hebrew Bible is a "minority report" ... written by priests, prophets and scribes who were intellectuals, above all religious reformers.[33]

---

32. Ibid., 123.
33. Dever, *Biblical Writers*, 173.

III: The Ethnogenesis of Israel

> The Hebrew Bible is a highly sophisticated literary creation which was written by and for the intelligentsia ... Such a document may reveal very little about the actual religion of the masses.[34]

Deuteronomy 31 assigns the recording and preservation of the "law of Moses" to the priests, but it was written "for the masses." The texts explicitly state that the law was read (called out) before all the people and that the covenant was accepted in a public ceremony by the entire congregation. They may not have contemplated its theological implications (this may have been done by the "intelligentsia," whatever that means). Most prophets were neither priests nor aristocrats. Amos was a cowboy. The epigraphic evidence (letters, contracts) show that commercial transactions were performed by ordinary people in the name of YHWH.[35] This shows that the worship of YHWH was not an elitist cult.

> Thus it is clear that in ancient Israel, until the Exile, Asherah and Ba'al were not shadowy numina, dead and discredited gods of old Canaan. Rather, the pair were potent rivals of Yahweh himself, and for the masses their cult ... remained an attractive alternative to the more austere religion and ethical demand of Yahwism ... The conflict between Ba'al and Yahweh was no sham battle, with the triumph of the God of Israel assured, but a crisis that threatened Israel's faith and indeed her existence for centuries.[36]

This interpretation is not corroborated by historical data: after the destruction of Samaria in 722 BCE, the remaining population of the northern kingdom of Israel continued to worship YHWH and succeeded in assimilating the new Cuthean population. This clearly shows that yahwistic monotheism was entrenched in Israel. It could not have happened if the Pentateuch was only composed three hundred years later. Dever downplays the yahwistic cult.

I have suggested (see p. 6) that a critical evaluation of the biblical text must distinguish between reports of events and of their interpretation. This principle should also be applied to the scrutiny of biblical scholarship. Dever declares:

---

34. Dever, *Recent Archaeological Discoveries*, 123.

35. Hess (*Israelite Religions*, 78) discussing Zevit, notes that "his conclusions about the widespread worship of multiple deities remain one-sided because the inscriptional data representing a unique emphasis on Yahweh is not fully considered."

36. Dever, *Recent Archaeological Discoveries*, 123, 127, 164.

The Religion of Israel During the Monarchic Period

> Yahwism was not "handed down from heaven" to Moses, an immutable spiritual ideal; it was worked out in bitter experience on the soil of Canaan, in constant tension and dialogue with Israel's pagan neighbors.[37]

Dever is in error: the presence of syncretistic rituals does not imply the absence of monotheism. Monotheism was not "worked out"; it did not arise slowly, but was a "sudden revelation," a paradigm shift in religious thinking. Dever's conclusions are not derived from his data, but from his basic assumptions: the denial of mosaic monotheism and the assumption of a postexilic redaction of the Bible. Hence he renders a distorted picture of the religious life of Israel in the monarchic period.

---

37. Ibid., 79.

10

Prophecy and Reform

BY THE MIDDLE OF the ninth century BCE, both Judah and Israel had accepted the Pentateuch—the "Law of Moses," though its implementation was flawed. About the middle of the eighth century BCE, two religious movements began which changed the religious consciousness of the nation. a) The Latter Prophets stressed the universality of YHWH's rule as well as the primacy of his demand for social justice. b) From the beginning of the seventh century, a group of reformers (mistakenly called "the Deuteronomistic school") insisted on abolishing every vestige of Canaanite cults.

The Latter Prophets

About the middle of the eight century BCE there arose a number of prophets whose speeches were recorded in writing. These latter prophets (LP, נביאים אחרונים), Jonah, Hosea, Amos, Isaiah, Jeremiah, and Ezekiel, emphasized the following ideas which, though present in the Pentateuch, are not stressed in the books of the EP.

1) The latter prophets are explicit and consistent monotheists:

> I am a Hebrew...and I am in awe of YHWH, the God of heaven, who made the sea and the dry land. (Jonah 1:9; my translation)[1]

---

1. The dating of Jonah is controversial. Main biblical scholarship, accepting the Wellhausen fallacy, ascribes it to the Persian period. Kaufmann comments: "The critical opinion ... that the universalism of classical prophecy reached its highest peak here in repudiation of Jonah's narrow outlook—supposedly a reflex of Jewish national sentiment in postexilic times—is a tissue of errors" (*Religion of Israel*, 282). I include him because

Prophecy and Reform

The one who made the Pleiades and Orion, and turns deep darkness into the morning, and darkens the day into night; who calls for the waters of the sea, and pours them out on the surface of the earth, YHWH is his name. (Amos 5:8)

2) God is concerned with all the nations of the earth, not only with Israel. Though the Pentateuch asserts that God is the ruler of every nation, its story (from Genesis 11:10 on) is about Israel. Other nations and places are mentioned only when encountering Israel. Monotheism implies a cosmopolitan God: he can be approached all over the world, not merely in the promised land: Jonah is sent to Nineveh and cannot escape YHWH by going to Tarshish.[2] The latter prophets address various other nations, who will be judged for moral transgressions. For example, the prophesies against neighboring nation (Amos 1–2) accuse them of cruelty—crimes against humanity.

3) Israel is judged by a severe moral standard:

Are not you not like the Cushites to me, O People of Israel? says YHWH.
Did I not bring Israel up from the land of Egypt,
And the Philistines from Caphtor and the Arameans from Kir?
The eyes of the Lord YHWH are upon the sinful kingdom.
(Amos 9:7–8)

You alone have I known of all the families of the earth;
therefore I will punish you for all your iniquities. (Amos 3:2)

Israel's major sin is social injustice, the flouncing of the moral commandments of the covenant:

There is no faithfulness or loyalty,
and no knowledge of God in the land.
Swearing, lying, and murder,
and stealing and adultery break out; bloodshed follows bloodshed.
Therefore the land mourns,
and all who live in it languish. (Hos 4:1b–3a)

---

his story is an appropriate expression of the view that the deity is to be found anywhere and is concerned with all humanity.

2. Compare that with the attitude of the Israelites at the time of Joshua 22: will God be manifested only in the land of Canaan?

III: The Ethnogenesis of Israel

> I will grant them no reprieve,
> because they sell the innocent for silver
> and the destitute for a pair of shoes.
> (Amos 2:6; my translation)

> Alas for those who devise wickedness
> and evil deeds on their beds!
> When the morning dawns, they perform it,
> because it is in their power.
> They covet fields, and seize them;
> houses, and take them away;
> they oppress householder and house,
> people and their inheritance. (Mic 2:1–2)

> Your princes are rebels and companions of thieves.
> Everyone loves a bribe and runs after gifts.
> They do not defend the orphan,
> and the widow's cause does not come before them. (Isa 1:23)

4) The formal worship at the three sanctuaries was thought to satisfy the requirements of Leviticus. The latter prophets reject this complacency. Sacrifices do not expiate moral transgressions. God needs no sacrifice.

> Your countless sacrifices, what are they to me? Says YHWH
> I am fed up with burnt offerings . . . I have no desire for the blood of bulls . . .
> When you come to appear before me—who asked you to trample my courts?
> Do not continue to offer useless gifts. (Isa 1:11–13, my translation)

> For I desire steadfast love and not sacrifice,
> the knowledge of God rather than burnt offerings. (Hos 6:6)

> I hate, I despise your festivals,
> and I take no delight in your solemn assemblies.
> Even though you offer me your burnt offerings and grain offerings,
> I will not accept them
> I will not listen to the melodies of your harps.
> But let justice run down like waters,
> and righteousness like an ever-flowing stream. (Amos 5:21–24)

Israel will not be saved by religious ceremonies, but by the establishment of a just society:

> Even though you make many prayers, I will not listen;
> your hands are full of blood.
> Wash yourselves; make yourselves clean
> remove the evil of your doings from before my eyes
> cease to do evil, learn to do good;
> seek justice, rescue the oppressed,
> defend the orphan, plead for the widow. (Isa 1:15b–17)

The picture of Israel drawn by the prophets is biased: Israel was not a lawless society. The Yabneh-Yam Ostracon, from the end of the seventh century BCE, is a petition sent by a farmhand to the local governor. He complains that his garment had been unjustly confiscated and he asks for a remedy. This letter shows that the writer of the letter had access to a professional scribe (unless he was literate) and that he anticipated redress. That is not the picture of a lawless society.[3] There is no evidence of social unrest. The prophetic speeches are powerful, but did not lead to rebellion. The impact of the prophesies was not immediate.

Summary

The prophetic message, though foreshadowed in the Pentateuch, constitutes a new development in the ethnogenesis of Israel.

a. God, the creator of the universe, is concerned with all the nations of the world. In the future, all the world will recognize God's sovereignty.

b. God manifests himself and can be approached all over the world, not merely in the promised land.

c. The prime demand of the covenant is the establishment of a just society. Israel's major sin is social injustice, the flouting of the moral commandments of the covenant.

d. God needs no sacrifices.

This prophetic message enabled the Babylonian exiles to maintain their ethnic identity. It had not yet been absorbed by the Samarian exiles. The importance of these ideals only becomes evident after the destruction of the temple.

---

3. See p. 135, n. 4 on biased reporting of the sins of Israel

III: The Ethnogenesis of Israel

Cultic Reform

Hezekiah

Apparently kings as well as priests ignored the burning of incense to the Queen of Heaven or other rituals conducted on "every hill and under every leafy tree." This tolerance may reflect a realistic policy: these practices were entrenched in Israelite traditions. It may have been rationalized: they were not "*avodah*." Probably there existed a group of scribes who rejected the service on the *bamoth* as idolatrous. The HEP reports that "YHWH warned Israel and Judah by every prophet and every seer, saying, 'turn from your evil ways and keep my commandments and my statutes'" (2 Kgs 17:13a). An example of such prophetic appeal is found in Judges 2:1-5. However, there is no biblical record of a prophet denouncing the *bamoth* after the time of Baasha.

Only two kings of Judah removed the ancient "high places" (*bamoth*): Hezekiah and Josiah. Their "reforms" occurred while these kings attempted to regain part of the destroyed kingdom of Israel and wanted to establish Jerusalem as the only legitimate sanctuary.

During the second half of the eighth century BCE, the prophecies of doom (Amos, Isaiah) seemed to become fulfilled. Judah was attacked by Pekah, king of Israel, and Rezin, king of Damascus. Ahaz asked for help from Assyria (2 Kgs 16:5-8). Assyrian sources confirm that Ahaz paid tribute to Tiglath-Pileser. From 734 BCE on, Assyria dominated the region for about one hundred years.[4] There were several Israelite rebellions against Assyria, resulting in the destruction of Samaria (722 BCE). The upper class of the northern kingdom was deported. Samaria became an Assyrian province.[5]

Ahaz, king of Judah, had introduced foreign cults at the end of his reign. His son Hezekiah witnessed the destruction of Samaria. Judah had not rebelled, was not invaded by Assyria, and prospered during the first fourteen years of Hezekiah's reign. Hezekiah was able to fortify many cities. Lachish became a formidable fortress. The building of the Siloam tunnel in Jerusalem was an engineering feat, celebrated in the famous inscription (which does not mention the king). Nevertheless, in spite of these successes, Judah must have been in deep shock: Israel had sinned and YHWH had permitted

---

4. See Cogan, *Racing Torrent*, for Assyrian and Babylonian inscriptions relating to ancient Israel.

5. For a thorough review see Knoppers, *Jews and Samaritans*, 18-44.

Prophecy and Reform

the destruction of the northern kingdom! The country was ready to return (*t'shuvah*/repentance) to YHWH and to renew the old covenant.

The book of Kings describes Hezekiah's reform in one sentence.

> He removed the high places [*bamoth*], and broke the pillars [*mazevoth*], and cut down the sacred pole [Asherah]. He broke in pieces the bronze serpent that Moses had made, for until this day the people of Israel had burned incense to it [מְקַטְּרִים, *piel*]; it was called Nehushtan. (2 Kg 18:4)

Chronicles, on the other hand, spends three chapters (2 Chr 29–31) on Hezekiah's reform.[6] According to Chronicles, Hezekiah's first act was the purification of the temple. Chronicles cites the list of the officials involved as well as a detailed description of their activities: which objects were removed and destroyed, and which were purified (2 Chr 29:3–19). This is followed by a detailed description of the ceremonies celebrating the reopening of the purified sanctuary (2 Chr 29:20–36).[7] The ritual began with a sin offering: "And the priests slaughtered them and made a sin offering with their blood on the altar, to make atonement of all Israel. For the king demanded that *the burnt offering and the sin offering should be made for all Israel*" (2 Chr 29:24; my emphasis). The rededication of the temple was the preamble of an attempt by Hezekiah to regain control over all Israel. A proclamation was sent:

> O people of Israel, return to YHWH ... Do not be like your ancestors and your kindred who were faithless to YHWH, the God of their ancestors, so that he made them a desolation, as you see ... Come to this sanctuary which he has sanctified forever. (2 Chr 30:6b–8)

---

6. The book of Kings differs consistently from Chronicles in its reports of the relationship between Judah and the northern kingdom of Israel. Chronicles omits the story of the selection of Jeroboam by Ahijah the Shiloni (1 Kgs 11). 2 Chronicles 9:29 and 10:15 merely mentions the prophecy but do not report any details. Chronicles does not deal with the history of the northern kingdom, unless it concerns reports on the relations with Judah. It also relates incidents of collaboration between the two kingdoms which are omitted in Kings. In the view of the book of Kings the secession of Israel was ordained by God, a punishment for the sins of Solomon. The "sin of Jeroboam" led to the destruction of Israel, the exile of the ten tribes, and the settlement of a strange nation. Only Judah remains as the legitimate remainder of Israel. This reflects the view of the Babylonian exiles, leading to the policies of Ezra and Nehemiah and the break between Jews and Samarians. Chronicles stresses that the northern kingdom remains a part of Israel, bound by the covenant, even after the destruction of Samaria. See ibid., 82–101.

7. See earlier discussion, pp. 110–113.

III: The Ethnogenesis of Israel

The message was clear, but the response was mixed. The Passover was celebrated in the presence of people from Judah and some Israelite immigrants who had settled in Judah, as well as visitors from Asher, Manasseh, and Zebulon. This was a new ritual: traditionally, the Passover was a family feast.

> Now when all this was finished, all Israel who were present went out to the cities of Judah and broke down the pillars, hewed down the sacred poles (*asherim*) and pulled down the high places (*bamoth*) and the altars throughout all Judah and Benjamin, and in Ephraim and Manasseh, until they had destroyed them all. (2 Chr 31:1)

Hezekiah's reform was more radical than the previous ones by Asa and Joash. Asa had destroyed all Canaanite cult places. Hezekiah also destroyed the ancient venerable N'ḥushtan, to which the people offered incense (*piel*), and the *bamoth*, which were the ancient pre-monarchic cult places of Israel.[8] All the kings of Judah, excepting Hezekiah and Josiah, accepted these *bamoth*: "But the *bamoth* were not taken away [סָרוּ]" (1 Kgs 15:14).

The abolishing of the *bamoth* was a political act which proclaimed that the full *avodah* service can only be performed in Jerusalem.[9] Hezekiah, and later Josiah, attempted to revoke the secession of Israel. The authors of Kings/Chronicles praise Hezekiah, but do not offer any explanation as to why the *bamoth* should be removed. Deuteronomy 12 forbids the use of any Canaanite cult place. Purists may have rejected the *bamoth* on these grounds. But it would have been difficult for the invading Israelites to find any suitable location which had not been dedicated previously to some Canaanite deity. There seem to be only three places which were free from such contamination. The altar of Gilgal was erected on neutral ground, Bethel had been dedicated by Jacob, and the Jerusalem temple was erected on the threshing ground of Arauna the Jebusite, purchased by David (2 Sam 24:18–25). Hezekiah/Josiah interpreted Deuteronomy chapter 12 as demanding the total centralization of the cult, to the exclusion of any other place. They decreed that Jerusalem was the only place where "God's name will dwell."

Hezekiah's encroachment on the territory of Israel constituted a rebellion against Assyria. The result was a catastrophic invasion of Judah. The important city of Lachish was destroyed after a long siege but Jerusalem was not conquered. This is celebrated in 2 Kings, 2 Chronicles, and Isaiah

---

8. See chapter 9, pp. 148–51.

9. This does not eliminate religious slaughter "within your gates." I suggest that the notion of secular slaughter was inconceivable at this time.

as a victory, and gave rise to the belief that YHWH will never allow the destruction of the house where his name dwells. It was of little consolation to the inhabitants of Judah outside of Jerusalem. Judah was laid to waste. Hezekiah's reform was abolished by his son Manasseh, whose task was to rebuild a devastated country. Manasseh became a loyal vassal of the Assyrian king, and during his long reign of fifty-five years Judah was peaceful and prosperous. He attempted to introduce a syncretistic ritual: he is the only king who is reputed to have introduced the Asherah into the temple itself. His son Amon was assassinated, and the cults introduced by Manasseh were abolished by the new young king Josiah.

Josiah

The biblical report of the Josianic reform has been called a "historic romance." Römer calls the report on the reign of Josiah (2 Kings 22–23) "the foundation myth of the Deuteronomistic school."[10]

There are two reports on Josiah: 2 Kings 22–23 and 2 Chronicles 34–35. Both agree that during the reigns of the two previous kings, Manasseh and Amon, foreign cults were encouraged and practiced in the temple. After the assassination of Amon (the aims of the assassins are not reported), the eight-year-old Josiah became king by popular support. During his reign, the cults introduced by Manasseh were abandoned, and at a later stage all Canaanite places of worship were destroyed. At the age of twenty-six, in the eighteenth year of Josiah's reign, the temple was renovated and a scroll of the Torah was found. The king was extremely distressed, assumedly after reading the curses of Deuteronomy, and there was a formal renewal of the covenant followed by the destruction of all the *bamoth*. According to Chronicles, Josiah already "began to seek after the God of his ancestor David" (2 Chr 34:3) at the age of sixteen years and started his reforms at the age of twenty years by destroying all the cult places introduced by Manasseh. Because Chronicles is the later book, scholars tend to dismiss this chronology as a late addition. Actually, the Chronicle version appears to be more realistic. It is inconceivable that the expensive renovation of the temple could have been started without a prior commitment to reinstate the cultic practices from the time of Hezekiah. The guardians of the eight-year-old king would not have continued the practices of Manasseh/Amon. They educated the king and shaped his mind. When the king was sixteen,

10. Römer, *So-Called*, 49.

III: The Ethnogenesis of Israel

he reached maturity and officially supported the abolition of the Manasseh temple cult; however, he could not be decisive until he was twenty years old and his rule was consolidated. At that time, the king started to destroy Canaanite places of worship, as well as the *bamoth*. I suggest that this follows the finding of the Torah of Moses. The last stage of the reform came during the eighteenth year of his reign.

This story is problematic. The text reports that the king commanded "to bring out of the temple of YHWH all the vessels made for Baal, for Asherah, and for all the host of heaven; he burned them outside Jerusalem in the fields of the Kidron, and carried their ashes to Bethel" (2 Kgs 23:4b). This could not have happened at the eighteenth year of his reign: the removal of Canaanite cult artifacts would have been the first stage of the temple renovation. The conquest of Bethel, in the former kingdom of Israel, only occurred at the last stage of the reform.

What was found in the temple archives? It certainly was not any ordinary copy of the Pentateuch.

The High Priest Hilkiah stated to Shaphan, "I found the book of the Torah—(את ספר התורה)" (2 Kgs 22:8), not merely a book; this is even clearer in 2 Chronicles 34:14, which specifies "the book of the torah of YHWH, by the hand of Moses [את ספר תורת יהוה ביד משה]."[11] Both Kings and Chronicles later refer to "the book of the covenant [ספר הברית]."[12] The latter term appears only in these two places, and in Exodus 24:7. There is no other biblical report of what happened to the "book of the covenant." It surely was well-guarded. The most likely place for keeping this and other important documents was in the ark and later in the temple. I suggest that Hilkiah found the original, either of Deuteronomy or, possibly, the "book of the covenant" mentioned in Exodus.

Why was the king so upset? The traditional interpretation is that he reacted to the Deuteronomy curses (Deut 28:15–68). However, the king and his advisers must have known the provisions of the covenant and the consequences of breaking it. He may not have known the Hezekiah interpretation of Deuteronomy proscribing the sacrifices on the *bamoth*. Manasseh had reigned for fifty-five years, reinstated the *bamoth*, and may have persecuted people who wanted to ban them (2 Kgs 21:16). Deuteronomy may

---

11. The translation "a book" is incorrect, in view of the accusative את.

12. See 2 Kgs 23:21; 2 Chr 34:3; however, the citation in 2 Kings does not refer to the book of the covenant mentioned in Exodus, because the Passover rules mentioned in that verse refer to Deuteronomy. The Passover of Exodus was a family affair.

have been suppressed, only to be remembered by older people. It is probable that the king's guardians were aware of Hezekiah's interpretation of Deuteronomy. The youthful king may have thought that he was following the ways of Asa and David. He now faced a new interpretation which called the service at the *bamoth* an abomination.

It is also possible that the extreme emotional reaction to the reading of the newly discovered scroll was a publicity exercise. The reaction of the king was a preamble to the official renewal of the covenant, which allowed the king to resort to extreme measures of destroying all the Canaanite cultic places. The king assembled the people and "made a covenant before YHWH, to follow YHWH . . . and all the people *stood* (2 Kgs 23:3; my translation; NRSV translates "joined"). This differs from the reports of other covenants which were accepted by the congregation with enthusiastic exclamations. The people stood silently and listened to the king. The Josianic "reform" must have appeared to be sacrilegious in the eyes of many. The historical reports, as well as the prophesies of Jeremiah, confirm that the population continued to offer incense to the Queen of Heaven.

The destruction of the *bamoth* in Judah was the preamble to an attempt to annex parts of the former kingdom of Israel. The important event is the destruction of the altar in Bethel. Bethel was not a *bamah*, but had been the official sanctuary of Israel, dedicated to YHWH. Josiah, like Hezekiah before him, declared that Jerusalem is the only legitimate place to serve YHWH, thereby ignoring the Israelite community in Samaria. In the eighteenth year of his reign, the king celebrated his success in Bethel with a huge Passover celebration in Jerusalem. The HEP is enthusiastic about this event: "No such Passover had been kept since the days of the judges who judged Israel, or during all the days of the kings of Israel or of the kings of Judah" (2 Kgs 23:22). This does not indicate that the Passover was not known. Passover was a family festival. The sacrifice was offered by the head of the house, not by Levitical priests. The public Passover of Josiah was an innovation (previously introduced by Hezekiah) intended to reinforce the centralization of the cult.

Josiah's reform was a failure. His reign ended with a political/military disaster, and his reforms were abolished after his death.

11

Worship Without Sacrifice

JOSIAH'S REFORM WAS A failure. He was killed at Megiddo (609 BCE) and Judah ceased to be an independent state. The last kings of Judah were removed or installed by foreign monarchs. The abolition of the venerated *bamoth* must have appeared sacrilegious in the eyes of most people, and they were immediately reinstated after the death of the Josiah. At the time of Zedekiah, both political parties argued in the name of YHWH. This shows clearly that the *bamoth* were considered to be legitimate places of worship to YHWH. Nevertheless, the popular worship of the Queen of Heaven was tolerated (see Jeremiah 44).[1]

It appears that Israel was not merely a stiff-necked people in the face of YHWH. They were also stiff-necked warriors in the face of mighty empires.[2] There had been several rebellions against Assyria, and it took the Assyrians three years to conquer Samaria, even after the king had been taken prisoner. Jehoiakim rebelled against Babylon. Jerusalem was put under siege. After the king died, his son Jehoiachin surrendered and was exiled together with "all the officials, all the warriors, ten thousand captives, all the artisans and the smiths" (2 Kings 24:14). This was an exaggeration. There remained enough warriors and artisans to mount another rebellion

---

1. Kings and Chronicles report that each of the last four kings of Judah "did what was evil in the eyes of YHWH," but does not specify what they did. It is generally assumed that these passages refer to the restoration of the *bamoth*. They do not mention the worship of the Queen of Heaven (see Jeremiah 44).

2. After the destruction of Jerusalem, many exiles became mercenaries, establishing military colonies.

Worship Without Sacrifice

At this time, there existed two political groups in Judah. Both talked "in the name of YHWH." The first group assumed that YHWH would never allow the destruction of the temple—after all, the Assyrians did not succeed in conquering Jerusalem. They expected that the rebellion against Babylon would be successful, and that the exiles (as well as the temple vessels, which had been captured by Nebuchadnezzar) would be returned. They demanded that Judah rebel against the Babylonians. Jeremiah reports,

> The prophet Hananiah son of Azzur, from Gibeon, spoke to me in the house of YHWH, in the presence of the priests and all the people, saying, "Thus says YHWH Zebaoth, the God of Israel: I have broken the yoke of the king of Babylon. Within two years I will bring back to this place all the vessels of the House of YHWH, which King Nebuchadnezzar of Babylon took away from this place and carried to Babylon. I will also bring back to this place king Jeconiah son of Jehoiakim of Judah, and all the exiles from Judah who went to Babylon, says YHWH, for I will break the yoke of the king of Babylon." (Jer 28:1b-4)[3]

The other group, led by Jeremiah, predicted that rebellion against Babylon would fail and that the temple would be destroyed. This was considered to be a blasphemy, and Jeremiah was imprisoned. About the same time, Jeremiah and Ezekiel (among the exiles in Babylon) introduced two new ideas:

a. God rewards or punishes each individual according to his deserving. The new generation is not to be punished for the sins of their forefathers, but judged on its own merit (Jer 31:29; Ezek 18:2).

b. The Diaspora will be a reality; it is possible to live a good (and just) life in the Diaspora (Jer 29:1–7).

The war party carried the day; Judah rebelled, and the unthinkable happened. The temple was destroyed, and the nation collapsed.

Once you assume that divine intervention determines the course of history, there are three possible logical interpretation of these events:

1) The destruction of the temple was a victory of Marduk over YHWH. Such interpretation was accepted by most of the nations vanquished by the Assyrians and Babylonians. They assimilated to the victorious culture and lost their identity. This attitude is acknowledged implicitly in the following report on King Ahaz: "He sacrificed to the gods

---

3. It is immaterial that Jeremiah and later commentators considered Hananiah Ben Azur to be a false prophet.

III: THE ETHNOGENESIS OF ISRAEL

of Damascus, which had defeated him, and said, 'Because the gods of the kings of Aram help them, therefore I will sacrifice [*piel*] to them, so that they may help me'" (2 Ch 28:23).

2) Judah prospered during the reign of Manasseh, and declined when Josiah desecrated the local shrines of "the Host of Heaven." This interpretation was not beyond the thinking of the time, as is clearly stated by the exiles in Egypt, talking to Jeremiah:

> As for the word that you have spoken to us in the name of YHWH, we are not going to listen to you. Instead, we will do everything that we have vowed, making offerings to the queen of heaven and pour out libations to her, just as we and our ancestors, our ancestors, our kings and our officials, used to do in the towns of Judah and in the streets of Jerusalem. We used to have plenty of food, and prospered, and saw no misfortune. But from the time we stopped making offerings to the queen of heaven and pouring out libations to her, we have lacked everything and have perished by the sword and by famine. (Jer 44:16–18)

3) The destruction of the temple was not a victory of Marduk, but demonstrated the power of YHWH. It was the deserved punishment for the sins of Israel. The sins of Manasseh were so horrendous that even the repentance of Josiah could not avert the punishment. Yet it is not the end of Israel. God's covenant with Abraham guarantees that there will be a "remnant of Israel" who will return to YHWH. Then there will be an end to the exile.

Other exiled populations had accepted the verdict of the gods. They worshiped the deities of the victors and of the places to which they were sent. Not so the exiles of Judah. They decided to "return to God" (*t'shuvah*), to abolish all vestiges of idolatry, and to follow strictly the provisions of the Pentateuch. This led to a codification of the law. The deportees to Babylon (the "Golah") were equal to this task. The first group included King Jehoiachin and his family, officers and fighting men, craftsmen and smiths (2 Kgs 24:14–16). They were literate and included many priests, Levites, and a major prophet, Ezekiel. Anyone above the age of thirty would remember the reforms of Josiah. Furthermore, the Assyrian/Babylonian policy of deportation was aimed at resettling the captive population in another country.[4] One need not assume that they were put in chains and dragged to

---

4. The chief officer of the Assyrians tried to persuade the men of Judah—insisting on addressing them in Hebrew—to accept exile as a positive solution. "Rabshakeh stood and called out in a loud voice in the language of Judah [יהודית], 'Hear the word of the great king, the king of Assyria ... do not listen to Hezekiah ... come out to me; then

Worship Without Sacrifice

their new settlements. They would move in caravans, carrying baggage with them. They would be able to take with them written material—historical records, descriptions of ritual, prophetic announcements, legal codes, and records of oral traditions. The scribes of the exiles collected the legal material available. They also reviewed the oral traditions and written annals at their disposal. One should point out that the collection (and editing) of the old writings, as well as the interpretation of the law, was not controlled by the priests, but by the scribes. Ezra is called "the scribe," and his authority stemmed from his knowledge, not from his priestly status. Priests had no legislative power. I assume that those who earned the title of *sofer* (scribe) would collect available manuscripts and order them, according to specific topics (history, law, ritual, etc.).

The scribes accepted their sources as authoritative, divine revelations, and copied them, even when they were aware of contradictions between various sources. The very fact that they did not change the original texts demonstrates their respect for their sources. The editorial activity of the scribes consisted mainly in choosing which sources to include in their books, and in comments about their historical significance. They might correct what they considered to be mistakes of earlier writers and update their spelling, but would not introduce idiosyncratic ideas. The perspective of the Golah was summarized, but not invented, in the two collections of history books—the EP and Chronicles. They are propaganda in the sense that they want to educate their audience, but they are not new books; they report on the past and interpret it.[5] They are the testimony of a nation that would not accept defeat.

The exiles decided to follow the law of the Torah strictly. They were aware of contradictions and unclear passages within the Torah. Furthermore, by this time the Torah was out of date. Therefore, the "men of the

---

every one of you will eat from your own vine and your own fig tree, and drink water from your own cistern, until I come and take you away to a land like your own land, a land of grain and wine . . . that you may live and not die'" (2 Kgs 18, 28–32). This is a propaganda speech, but Assyrian documents confirm that the Assyrians promoted the resettlement of deported populations.

5. Neither collection intends to give a comprehensive history of Israel. Because they have different aims, they report different events. The EP concentrates on the history of all Israel. Its main question is, did they keep the covenant? They did not. The writer of the Chronicles hopes for the reestablishment of the Davidic dynasty and the temple service in Jerusalem. He is interested in genealogical tables, which were important to the exiles returning to Judah in the Persian period, and concentrates on the history of Judah, starting with the history of David. He expects the restoration of a united kingdom of Israel.

III: The Ethnogenesis of Israel

great synod" (scribes/rabbis) relied on oral traditions and rules of interpretation to render the laws of the ancient Torah suitable for the living conditions of their time. It was asserted that this "oral Torah" was communicated to Joshua and the elders by Moses, transmitted orally throughout generations, and carried the authority of the Torah.

The exiles concluded that *t'shuvah* required the unconditional avoidance of any "service to other gods." This eliminated sacrifice outside the temple, because any sacrifices outside the temple may be tainted by idolatry. By the time of Ezra, it was accepted by the Babylonian community that sacrifices may only be offered at the central sanctuary of Jerusalem. They concluded that the verb *z-b-ḥ* in Deuteronomy 12:15 and 21 could not possibly refer to "sacrifice." The rabbis did not dare to change the text of the Torah. However, the Aramaic translation expressed their interpretation: it incorrectly translates *z-b-ḥ* as slaughter. The Vulgate accepted this interpretation. It is not found in the Septuagint.[6] Thus the Wellhausen fallacy is based on a mistaken translation, deliberately introduced by rabbinical sources.[7] It is not clear when this mistranslation was introduced but we see that at the time of Ezra the majority of the congregation spoke Aramaic and did not understand the original. Officials "read from the book, from the law of God, with interpretation" (Neh 8:8); Rashi states that "they read the Targum."[8]

The logical inference from the prophetic writings is: YHWH can be worshiped anywhere in the world. He does not need sacrifices. Israel can fulfill its covenant obligations by refraining from idolatry and fetishism, and by following the moral/social mandates of the Pentateuch: "Justice, justice you shall pursue" and "Love your neighbor as yourself." This was a totally new religious concept. At that time, people could not conceive of worship without sacrifices or designated cult places.[9] The religious revolution by

---

6. Sacrifices were offered in Elephantine and, later, in Leontopolis, the temple of Onias. LXX translates *z-b-ḥ* as "sacrifice."

7. The difference of the logical train of thought is as follows. Rabbis: Moses says, no sacrifice outside the temple, therefore *z-b-h* does not mean sacrifice. Wellhausen: Deuteronomy says until the time of Josiah sacrifices were offered outside the temple. Therefore Deuteronomy was not written by Moses.

8. Rashi, *MGK*, Neh 8:8. The biblical text does not explain how the animals (which are suitable as sacrificial offerings) are to be killed. The oral Torah, i.e., the rabbinical rules of profane slaughter—*shechitah*—filled this gap.

9. It would have been perfectly acceptable, according to the understanding of the time, to shift to the worship of the local deities of the lands of the exile. Non-Jewish writers of the time noted disapprovingly that Jews refused to participate in any form of

Worship Without Sacrifice

the Babylonian Golah was not the development of monotheism, which had already been clearly articulated in the Pentateuch, but the acceptance of the idea that YHWH might be worshiped at any place on earth, without sanctuary and without sacrifices. This was a true paradigm shift, crucial for the sustenance of all monotheistic religions.

This prophetic message had not yet been absorbed when the northern kingdom was destroyed. Amos and Isaiah had been active only twenty-five years previously. The exiles from Samaria were not able to worship YHWH without a temple and without sacrifices, and lost their ethnic identity. Only because the prophetic message was well-understood in Judah 150 years later, the exiles were able to give a positive answer to the question, "How could we sing YHWH's songs in a foreign land?" (Ps 137:4). You certainly can do so! Jonah found God everywhere: he talked with him even in Nineveh.

Thus, quietly, without fanfare and without formal religious statements, the Babylonian exiles revolutionized religious worship. They introduced alternative rituals, without a holy sanctuary and without sacrifices. This was a slow and ongoing process, beginning with the exile and leading to the ritual codified in the Mishnah. This new form of worship may be offered at any place, even at home. Römer points out that sanctuaries were distinguished by inscriptions on the face of the building.[10] Jews, by fixing the *mezuzah*, made every home a sanctuary. The religious rites of Judaism are mainly expressions of thanksgiving; there are appropriate formulas for every occasion. Strictly speaking, there is no "profane slaughter" in Judaism. The act of slaughtering is itself a religious ritual.[11]

There will have been doubts in the mind of the exiles: would God punish them, the third generation, for the sins of Manasseh? "The parents [fathers] have eaten sour grapes and the children's teeth are set on edge" (Jer 31:29; Ezek 18:2).

The answer is clear. Both Jeremiah and Ezekiel reject the idea that people pay for the sins of their fathers.[12]

---

local worship.

10. Römer, *So-Called*, 176.

11. Contemporary orthodox slaughter—*shehitah* requires that some of the blood must be covered with earth or ashes) and the following benediction must be pronounced: "Blessed art Thou . . . who sanctified us with His commandments and commanded us to cover blood with earth." This too is, in my opinion, a sacrificial act.

12. This contradicts the Decalogue, which explicitly states that God will punish the breaker of the covenant for three generations,

III: The Ethnogenesis of Israel

The initial question of this study was, how come? Why did Israel/Judah not disappear? My proposed answer is that two new religious concepts were articulated by Judaism. Both constitute a quantum leap in religious thinking. The paradigm shift to monotheism is clearly manifested in the text of the Pentateuch. It was not easily accepted, but had been absorbed in Israel by the second half of the eighth century BCE. Judeans, as well as Samarians, rejected paganism and accepted the law of the Pentateuch as authoritative. The paradigm shift of the ritual was never formally expressed. The important theological "leap" was the *Emunah*, meaning the "trust" or "belief," that YHWH will accept the new non-sacrificial rituals: Israel will not be forgotten by God, even if its devotions are offered in a non-holy land at a non-holy location. Thus the Judeans were able to maintain their identity in foreign lands. This necessarily led toward the separation, which is regretted by Wellhausen. The absolute rejection of paganism prevented Jews from participating in the important festivities of the local population. Non-Jewish writers of the time noted disapprovingly that Jews refused to participate in any form of local worship. The absence of sacrifices was suspiciously irreligious, and Jews were accused of "atheism"—after all, they had no God in their temple.

Wellhausen quotes Spinoza:

> That the Jews maintained themselves so long in spite of their dispersed and disorganized condition is not at all to be wondered at, when it is considered how they separated themselves from all other nationalities in such a way as to bring upon themselves the hatred of all ... Experience shows that their conservation is due in great part to the hatred which they have incurred.[13]

Spinoza does not explain why the Jews separated themselves from the people among whom they lived. The hatred of their neighbors was the price they paid for being different. The traditions of the Pentateuch and the prophets enabled the exiles to maintain their identity and hope for the future. They did not need to invent them. This was their heritage. The exiles defied history: the destruction of the temple was not a victory of Marduk, but a manifestation of the power and justice of YHWH. There is an optimistic vision of the future. Israel will be redeemed. War will be abolished, and Jerusalem will be the seat of united nations (Isa 2:4):

---

13. Cited in Wellhausen (*Prolegomena*, 548). For Wellhausen's comments on Spinoza, see earlier discussion in chapter 2, "The Wellhausen Fallacy."

> He will judge between the nations
> and shall arbiter among many peoples;
> they shall beat their swords into mattocks
> and their spears into pruning hooks;
> nation shall not lift up sword against nation
> neither shall they learn war any more.

Mark well, this is not an imperialistic vision. Israel does not rule the world. Other nations will maintain their identity: "On that day Israel will be a triad with Egypt an Assyria, a blessing in the midst of the earth. YHWH Zebaoth will bless them. *Blessed be Egypt my people, Assyria the work of my hands, and Israel my possession*" (Isa 19:24–25; my emphasis). Thus the promise to Abraham will be fulfilled: his descendants will be a blessing to the nations.

Glossary

Aggadah	a legend, parable, or anecdote in rabbinical literature
apotropaic	magic rites to seek protection from evil supernatural forces
asham	"guilt-offering sacrifice"
atzereth	"solemn assembly"
avodah	"work," "service"; technical term for formal service in a sanctuary
bamah, bamoth (pl.)	"High place," sacred place of worship, generally an open space, probably on a hill; etymology not certain
bara	"create"; always refers to divine creation
binyan(im)	"stem" (construction): conjugation of verb, with each stem conveying a specific meaning
bulla (pl. *bullae*)	impression of a seal (mainly on clay in Israel)
corvée	labor owed by a vassal to his Lord, also forced labor
defective spelling	see *ḥaser* spelling
Deuteronomistic history	According to prevalent scholarship, the historical books of the Bible were composed by the author(s) of Deuteronomy
ephod	Sleaveless garment, mainly worn by a priest. However, the ephod of Gideon and Micah were probably idols. The *ephod* is also used when oracles are asked for
emunah	"trust," generally translated incorrectly as "belief"
eschatology	"vision," revelation about the "end of the days" of this world
ethnos	a population sharing distinctive culture and identity

Glossary

Gemara	see "oral" Torah; discussion of Mishna; see "Talmud"
golah	"exile"; also used as a collective designation of the Judean exiles in Babylon
ḥag	"festival," referring to the three pilgrim festivals of Pesah, Sh'vuoth, and Succoth
Hagiographa	"holy writings"; biblical books except Torah and Prophets
ḥaser spelling	only gives the root consonants, but omits *matres lectiones*
hattath	"sin offering"
Hebrew Bible	*Torah* (Pentateuch), *Nevi'im* (Prophets), *Qetubim* Hagiographa). This leads to the acronym *TeNaKH*
henotheism	worship of one god, without denying the existence of others
hieratic writing	cursive form of ancient Egyptian writing
hitpael	Stem assigning a reflexive meaning to the verb
ḥodesh	"New Moon"
Holiness Code	Leviticus 17–27: "you shall be holy, for I YHWH am holy" (19:2); "You shall love your neighbor as yourself" (19:17); the operational definition of how to live a holy life
immanence	The manifestation of the deity (or the supernatural world) in the physical world
isheh	"offerings by fire"
ketib	The written Masoretic text, cannot be changed, even if it is read (*qere*) or understood (*sebirin*) differently
Ketuvim	see Hagiographa
Male	see "*plene*"
matres lectiones	the Hebrew letters 'a, h, v, y, when designating vowels
Masoretic Text (MT)	the traditional text of the Hebrew Bible
mazkir	Secretary, official at the royal court
mezuzah	case affixed to the doorpost, including a parchment with biblical texts (such as "Hear, Israel . . .")
MG	The *Miqra'oth Gedoloth* is the classical rabbinical Bible, with Hebrew text, Aramaic translation, and rabbinical commentators
midrash	rabbinic commentary to the scriptures, includes *aggadah*

Glossary

minḥah	"present"; refers to grain offerings
Mishkan	Tabernacle; "place of dwelling," where "the name of God" dwells
Mishnah	see "oral Torah"
mnemohistory	the past as remembered by the people
moed	"appointed time"; refers to festivals of the lunar calendar
monolatry	worship of one god, recognizing the existence of other deities
Nevi'im	Prophets; subdivided into "Early Prophets" (EP) and "Latter Prophets" (LP). The EP includes the historical books of Joshua, Judges, Samuel, and Kings
Niphal	stem assigning a passive meaning to a verb
numina	spiritual, of divine power
ʿolah	"Burnt offering" (holocaust); totally burned, only to be offered by a priest
Oral Torah	Orally transmitted rabbinical interpretation of the Pentateuch, later codified in the Talmud. Traditionally based on oral instructions, including rules of interpretation, revealed by Moses
ostracon/ ostraca (pl.)	broken potsherds with inscriptions
paradigm shift	a (sudden, dramatic) fundamental change in basic assumptions
piel	stem which generally intensifies the meaning of a verb
plene (*malē*)	spelling which includes some *matres lectionis*
Prolegomena	critical introduction; generally refers to Wellhausen's *Prolegomena to the History of Ancient Israel*
pseudepigraph	a book falsely attributed to a known ancient author
qal	the simple form of a stem, designating the original meaning of the verb
qere	MT footnote: "the text should read"
redactor	editor who compiles various sources into one text
Samarian	Samaritans prefer to be called Samarians
Samaritan Pentateuch	The Samarian version of the Pentateuch

Glossary

Samaritan book of Joshua	Samarian Chronicle, mainly dealing with the period of Joshua
sebirin	correction footnote in MT: "This text means…"
shlamim	"Sacrifice"; the meaning of the term is not clear. It is generally translated as "peace offering" or "well-being" offering. The meat may be eaten.
shekel	"weight," monetary unit
sofer	"scribe," royal official
stele or stela	stone slab, generally with inscription
surface survey	general survey of archaeological sites; no digging
tenemos	enclosed sacred space
Talmud	The codified rabbinical discussions and decisions of the "oral Torah." Includes the Mishnah and Gemara.
Tannaim	rabbis of the Mishnah
Targum	Aramaic translation of (most of) the Hebrew Bible
teraphim	"household idols" (exact meaning of the term disputed)
tetragrammaton	the four-letter name of God (YHWH)
theophany	(Visible) manifestation of a deity. In the Pentateuch, the theophany is auditory
todah	optional thanksgiving sacrifice, to be eaten
Torah	"the Law"; the five books of the Pentateuch
transcendence	the deity is not a part of the universe
t'shuvah	"return" to God and to a right way of living; repentance
ts'vah hashamayim	"host of heaven"
Vulgate	Latin translation of the Bible, mainly by Saint Jerome
zebaḥ	"sacrifice"

Aramaic and Hebrew terms reference

דבח (Aramaic): "sacrifice"

זָבַח (Hebrew, qal): translated as "דבח" or "נכס"

זִבֵּחַ (*piel*)

נכס (Aramaic): "slaughter," "kill"

קטר: "burning Incense"; קִטֵּר: (*piel*); הִקְטִיר: (*hiphil*)

Partial Index of Additional Topics

Ai, 47–49

bamoth, 148–51
Bible as historical document, 5–10

centralization of cult, 106–110
covenants—Hittite, Assyrian and
    Pentateuch, 35–37
  Sinai covenant, 95–97, 130–31
  Fields-of-Moab covenant, 74–75
creation, 90–91
creative writing in biblical
    scholarship, 56–59
cultic reform, 167–81

Eli, 140

Gibeon, battle of, 7–8

female deities, 132, 154–56

Hezekiah, 11–12, 166–69

Israel, election of, 93–96
  origins of, 122–124

Jephtah, 136
Jericho, 45–47
Joshua account of conquest, 44–49
Josiah, 169–71

literacy in biblical times, 32–34

Merenptah stele, 45
Mesha stele, 10–11
monotheism, 88, 90–91
  creation story, 90
  Levitical ritual, 100–101
  era of judges, 135–36
  during monarchy, 146–49
Moses, 125–30
Mount Gerizim/Mount Ebal, 74–81

sacrifice, 97–100
Samuel, 140–144
sanctuaries, 147–148
Saul, 143–144
Siloam inscription, 146
surface surveys, 37–44

Bibliography

Agus, Irving A. *The Heroic Age of Franco-German Jewry: the Jews of Germany and France of the Tenth and Eleventh Centuries, the Pioneers and Builders of Town-Life, Town-Government, and Institutions.* New York: Yeshiva University Press, 1969.

Ahad Ha'Am. "Moses." In *Selected Essays by Ahad Ha'Am*, translated by Leon Simon, 306–29. Philadelphia: Jewish Publication Society, 1912.

Ahlström, Gösta W. "The Role of Archaeological and Literary Remains in Reconstructing Israel's History." In *The Fabric of History: Text, Artifact and Israel's Past*, edited by Diana Vikander Edelman, 116–41. JSOT Supplement Series 127. Sheffield, UK: JSOT, 1991.

Anderson, Robert T., and Terry Giles. *Tradition Kept: The Literature of the Samaritans.* Peabody, MA: Hendrickson, 2005.

Auld, A. Graeme. "The Former Prophets (Joshua, Judges, 1st & 2nd Samuel, 1st & 2nd Kings)." In *The Hebrew Bible Today*, edited by Steven L. McKenzie and Patrick Graham, 52–68. Louisville: Westminster John Knox Press, 1998.

Avishur, Yitzhak, and Michael Heltzer. *Studies on the Royal Administration in Ancient Israel in the Light of Epigraphic Sources.* Tel Aviv, Israel: Archaeological Center, 2000.

Bateson, Patrick. "Genes, Environment and the Development of Behaviour." In *Genes, Development and Learning*, edited by T. R. Halliday and P. J. B. Slater, 52–81. Vol. 3 of *Animal Behaviour*. New York: Freeman, 1983.

La Biblia: La Palabra de Dios Para Todos. Fort Worth: Centro Mundial de Traducción de la Biblia.

Bietak, Manfred. "On the Historicity of the Exodus: What Egyptology Today Can Contribute to Assessing the Biblical Account of the Sojourn in Egypt." In *Israel's Exodus in Transdisciplinary Perspective: Text, Archaeology, Culture and Geoscience*, edited by Thomas E. Levy et al., 17–37. New York: Springer, 2015.

Boman, Thorleif. *Hebrew Thought Compared with Greek.* Translated by Jules L. Moreau. New York: Norton, 1970.

Buber, Martin. *I and Thou.* New York: Scribner, 1958.

Callaway, Joseph A. "New Evidence on the Conquest of 'Ai." *JBL* 87.3 (September 1968) 312–20.

Cassuto, Umberto. *The Documentary Hypothesis and the Composition of the Pentateuch: Eight Lectures.* Jerusalem: Hebrew University Magnes Press, 1961.

Chavalas, Mark W., and Edwin C. Hostetter. "Epigraphic Light on the Old Testament." In *The Face of Old Testament Studies: A Survey of Contemporary Approaches*, edited by David W. Baker and Bill T. Arnold, 38–58. Grand Rapids: Baker, 1999.

Bibliography

Chavalas, Mark W., and Murray A. Adamthwaite. "Archaeological Light on the Old Testament." In *The Face of Old Testament Studies: A Survey of Contemporary Approaches*, edited by David W. Baker and Bill T. Arnold, 59–96. Grand Rapids: Baker, 1999.

———. "The Context of Early Israel Viewed Through the Archaeology of Northern Mesopotamia and Syria." In *Critical Issues in Early Israelite History*, edited by Richard S. Hess et al., 151–61. Winona Lake, IN: Eisenbrauns, 2008.

Clines, David J. A. *The Theme of the Pentateuch*. JSOT Supplement Series 10. Sheffield, UK: JSOT, 1978.

Cogan, Mordechai. "Into Exile: From the Assyrian Conquest of Israel to the Fall of Babylon." In *The Oxford History of the Biblical World*, edited by Michael D. Coogan, 321–65. New York: Oxford University Press, 1998.

———. *The Racing Torrent: Historical Inscriptions from Assyria and Babylonia Relating to Ancient Israel*. Jerusalem: Carta, 2008.

Collins, John Joseph. *Introduction to the Hebrew Bible*. Minneapolis: Fortress, 2004.

Coogan, Michael David. "Archaeology and Biblical Studies: 'The Book of Joshua.'" In *The Hebrew Bible and its Interpreters*, edited by William Henry Propp et al., 19–32. Winona Lake, IN: Eisenbrauns, 1990.

Craigie, Peter C. *The Book of Deuteronomy*. Grand Rapids: Eerdmans, 1976.

Crane, Oliver Turnbull. *The Samaritan Chronicle, Or the Book of Joshua, the Son of Nun*. New York: Alden, 1890.

Davies, Philip R. *The Origins of Biblical Israel*. New York: Clark, 2007.

Dever, William G. "Archaeology, Material Culture and the Early Monarchial Period in Israel." In *The Fabric of History: Text, Artifact and Israel's Past*, edited by Diana Vikander Edelman, 103–15. JSOT Supplement Series 127. Sheffield, UK: JSOT, 1991.

———. "The Exodus and the Bible: What Was Known; What Was Remembered; What Was Forgotten?" In *Israel's Exodus in Transdisciplinary Perspective: Text, Archaeology, Culture and Geoscience*, edited by Thomas E. Levy et al., 399–408. New York: Springer, 2015.

———. *Recent Archaeological Discoveries and Biblical Research*. Seattle: University of Washington Press, 1990.

———. "Syro-Palestinian and Biblical Archaeology." In *The Hebrew Bible and its Modern Interpreters*, edited by Douglas A. Knight and Gene M. Tucker, 31–74. Philadelphia: Fortress, 1985.

———. *What Did the Biblical Writers Know and When Did They Know It? What Archaeology Can Tell Us about the Reality of Ancient Israel*. Grand Rapids: Eerdmans, 2001.

Faust, Avraham. "The Emergence of Iron Age Israel: On Origin and Habitus." In *Israel's Exodus in Transdisciplinary Perspective: Text, Archaeology, Culture and Geoscience*, edited by Thomas E. Levy et al., 467–82. New York: Springer, 2015.

———. *Israel's Ethnogenesis: Settlement, Interaction, Expansion and Resistance*. London: Equinox, 2006.

Finkelstein, Israel. "The Rise of Early Israel: Archaeology and Long-Term History." In *The Origin of Early Israel—Current Debate: Biblical, Historical and Archaeological Perspectives*, edited by Shmuel Aḥituv and Eliezer D. Oren, 7–39. Beer-Sheva 12. Beersheba, Israel: Ben-Gurion University of the Negev Press, 1998

———. "Southern Samarian Hills Survey." In *NEAEHL* 4:1313–14.

Bibliography

———. "The Wilderness Narrative and Itineraries and the Evolution of the Exodus Tradition." In *Israel's Exodus in Transdisciplinary Perspective: Text, Archaeology, Culture and Geoscience*, edited by Thomas E. Levy et al., 39–53. New York: Springer, 2015.

Fleming, Daniel E. "The Etymological Origins of the Hebrew nābî': The One Who Invokes God." *CBQ* 55 (1993) 217–24.

Garbini, Giovanni. *Myth and History in the Bible*. JSOT Supplement Series 362. London: Sheffield Academic Press, 2003.

Ginzberg, Louis. *Legends of the Jews*. New York: Simon and Schuster, 1961.

Gottwald, Norman K. *The Hebrew Bible: A Socio-Literary Introduction*. Philadelphia: Fortress, 1985.

Grabbe, Lester L. *Yehud: A History of the Persian Province of Judah*. Vol. 1 of *A History of the Jews and Judaism in the Second Temple Period*, edited by Lester L. Grabbe and James H. Charlesworth. London: T. & T. Clark International, 2004.

Greenstein, Edward L. "The Role of Theory in Biblical Criticism." In *Proceedings of the Ninth World Congress of Jewish Studies: Jerusalem, August 4–12, 1985*, 167. Jerusalem: World Union of Jewish Studies, 1986.

Greifenhagen, F. V. *Egypt on the Pentateuch's Ideological Map: Constructing Biblical Israel's Identity*. JSOT Supplement Series 361. London: Sheffield Academic Press, 2002.

Halevi, Judah. "Kuzari." In *Three Jewish Philosophers*, edited by Isaak Heinemann, 1–146. New York: Atheneum, 1979.

Hasel, Michael G. "Merenptah's Reference to Israel: Critical Issues for the Origin of Israel." In *Critical Issues in Early Israelite History*, edited by Richard S. Hess et al., 47–60. Winona Lake, IN: Eisenbrauns, 2008.

Hawkins, Ralph K. "The Survey of Manasseh and the Origin of the Central Hill Country Settlers." In *Critical Issues in Early Israelite History*, edited by Richard S. Hess et al., 165–79. Winona Lake, IN: Eisenbrauns, 2008.

Heiser, Michael. "Monotheism, Polytheism, Monolatry or Henotheism? Toward an Assessment of Divine Plurality in the Hebrew Bible." *BBR* 18.1 (2008) 1–30.

Herring, Basil. *Joseph Ibn Kaspi's Gevia' Kesef: a Study in Medieval Jewish Philosophic Bible Commentary*. New York: KTAV, 1982.

Hess, Richard S. *Israelite Religions: An Archaeological and Biblical Survey*. Grand Rapids: Baker Academic, 2007.

———. "The Jericho and Ai of the Book of Joshua." In *Critical Issues in Early Israelite History*, edited by Richard S. Hess et al., 33–46. Winona Lake, IN: Eisenbrauns, 2008.

Hess, Richard S., et al. *Critical Issues in Early Israelite History*. Winona Lake, IN: Eisenbrauns, 2008.

Hoffmeier, James K. *Israel in Egypt*. Oxford: Oxford University Press, 1997.

Hofstadter, Douglas R. *Gödel, Escher, Bach: an Eternal Golden Braid*. New York: Basic, 1979.

Kaufmann, Yehezkel. *The Religion of Israel*. Translated and abridged by Moshe Greenberg. New York, Schocken, 1972.

Kitchen, Kenneth A. *On the Reliability of the Old Testament*. Grand Rapids: Eerdmans, 2003.

Klingbeil, Gerald A. "'Between North and South': The Archeology of Religion in Late Bronze Age Palestine and the Period of Settlement." In *Critical Issues in Early Israelite History*, edited by Richard S. Hess et al., 111–50. Winona Lake, IN: Eisenbrauns, 2008.

Bibliography

Knight, Douglas A. "The Pentateuch." In *The Hebrew Bible and its Modern Interpreters*, edited by Douglas A. Knight and Gene M. Tucker, 263–96. Philadelphia: Fortress, 1985.

Knoppers, Gary N. *Jews and Samaritans: the Origins and History of Their Early Relations*. Oxford: Oxford University Press, 2013.

Lemche, Nils Peter. "On the Problems of Reconstructing Pre-Hellenistic Israelite (Palestinian) History." In *Perspectives on Hebrew Scriptures: Comprising the Contents of Journal of Hebrew Scriptures, Volumes 1–4*, edited by Ehud ben Zvi, 215–33. Piscataway, NJ: Gorgias, 2006.

———. "Good and Bad in History: The Greek Connection." In *Rethinking the Foundations: Historiography in the Ancient World and in the Bible: Essays in Honour of John Van Seters*, edited by Steven L. McKenzie et al., 127–40. New York: Walter de Gruyter, 2000.

Levy, Thomas E., et al., eds. *Israel's Exodus in Transdisciplinary Perspective: Text, Archaeology, Culture and Geoscience*. New York: Springer, 2015.

Long, V. Philips. "Historiography of the Old Testament." In *The Face of Old Testament Studies: A Survey of Contemporary Approaches*, edited by David W. Baker and Bill T. Arnold, 145–75. Grand Rapids: Baker, 1999.

Mazani, Patrick. "The Appearance of Israel in Canaan in Recent Scholarship." In *Critical Issues in Early Israelite History*, edited by Richard S. Hess, et al., 95–109. Winona Lake, IN: Eisenbrauns, 2008.

Mazar, Amihai. *Archaeology of the Land of the Bible*. New York: Doubleday, 1992.

Merrill, Eugene H. "Deuteronomy and de Wette: A Fresh Look at a Fallacious Premise." *JESOT* 1.1 (2012) 25–42. http://jesot.org/wp-content/uploads/2012/04/JESOT-1.1-Merrill.pdf.

Miller, Patrick D. "Israelite Religion." In *The Hebrew Bible and its Modern Interpreters*, edited by Douglas A. Knight and Gene M. Tucker, 201–37. Philadelphia: Fortress, 1985.

Moshier, Stephen O., and James K. Hoffmeier. "Which Way Out of Egypt? Physical Geography Related to the Exodus Itinerary." In *Israel's Exodus in Transdisciplinary Perspective: Text, Archaeology, Culture and Geoscience*, edited by Thomas E. Levy et al., 101–8. New York: Springer, 2015.

Na'aman, Nadav. "The Exodus Story: Between Historical Memory and Historiographical Composition." *JANER* 11.1 (2011) 39–69.

———. "Out of Egypt or Out of Canaan? The Exodus Story Between Memory and Historical Reality." In *Israel's Exodus in Transdisciplinary Perspective: Text, Archaeology, Culture and Geoscience*, edited by Thomas E. Levy et al., 527–33. New York: Springer, 2015.

Niditch, Susan. *Oral World and Written Word: Ancient Israelite Literature*. Louisville: Westminster John Knox Press, 1996.

Ortiz, Steven M. "Deconstructing and Reconstructing the United Monarchy: House of David or Tent of David (Current Trends in Iron Age Chronology)." In *The Future of Biblical Archaeology: Reassessing Methodologies and Assumptions*, edited by James K. Hoffmeier and Alan Millard, 121–47. Grand Rapids: Eerdmans, 2004.

Parpola, Simo, and Kazuko Watanabe, eds. *Neo-Assyrian Treaties and Loyalty Oaths*. State Archives of Assyria 2. Helsinki, Finland: Helsinki University Press, 1988.

Bibliography

Percy, Walker. *The Message in the Bottle: How Queer Man Is, How Queer Language Is, and What One Has to Do with the Other.* 8th ed. New York: Farrar, Straus and Giroux, 1982.

Pitard, Wayne T. "Before Israel: Syria-Palestine in the Bronze Age." In *The Oxford History of the Biblical World*, edited by Michael D. Coogan, 33–77. New York: Oxford University Press, 1998.

Polzin, Robert. *Moses and the Deutoronomist: a Literary Study of the Deuteronomic History, Part One: Deuteronomy, Joshua, Judges.* Bloomington, IN: Indiana University Press, 1993.

Propp, William H. C. "The Exodus and History." In *Israel's Exodus in Transdisciplinary Perspective: Text, Archaeology, Culture, and Geoscience*, edited by Thomas E. Levy et al., 429–36. New York: Springer, 2015.

Purvis, James D. *The Samaritan Pentateuch and the Origin of the Samaritan Sect.* Cambridge, MA: Harvard University Press, 1968.

Rad, Gerhard von. *Deuteronomy: A Commentary.* Translated by Dorothea Barton. Philadelphia: Westminster John Knox Press, 1966.

———. *Das fünfte Buch Mose: Deuteronomium.* Göttingen, Germany: Vandenhoeck & Ruprecht, 1964.

Rashi. *Pentateuch with Targum Onkelos, Haphtaroth and Rashi's Commentary.* Edited by M. Rosenbaum and A. M. Silbermann. 5 vols. Jerusalem: Silbermann, 1934.

Ray, Paul J., Jr. "Classical Models for the Appearance of Israel in Palestine." In *Critical Issues in Early Israelite History*, edited by Richard S. Hess et al., 79–93. Winona Lake, IN: Eisenbrauns, 2008.

Redmount, Carol A. "Bitter Lives: Israel In and Out of Egypt." In *The Oxford History of the Biblical World*, edited by Michael D. Coogan, 79–121. New York: Oxford University Press, 1998.

Römer, Thomas C. *The So-Called Deuteronomistic History: A Sociological, Historical, and Literary Introduction.* New York: T. & T. Clark, 2005.

Segal, M. H. "The Book of Deuteronomy." *JQR* 48 (1958) 315–51.

Schneider, Thomas. "Modern Scholarship Versus the Demon of Passover: An Outlook on Exodus Research and Egyptology through the Lens of Exodus 12." In *Israel's Exodus in Transdisciplinary Perspective: Text, Archaeology, Culture, and Geoscience*, edited by Thomas E. Levy et al., 537–53. New York: Springer, 2015.

Shen, Peidong, et al. "Reconstruction of Patrilineages and Matrilineages of Samaritans and other Israeli Populations From Y-Chromosome and Mitochondrial DNA Sequence Variation." *Human Mutation* 24 (2004) 248–60.

Sperber, Alexander. *The Bible in Aramaic.* Vols. 1–3. Leiden, Netherlands: Brill, 2004.

Stager, Lawrence E. "Forging an Identity: The Emergence of Ancient Israel." In *The Oxford History of the Biblical World*, edited by Michael D. Coogan, 123–75. New York: Oxford University Press, 1998.

Stanford, Michael. *The Nature of Historical Knowledge.* New York: Blackwell, 1986.

Sweeney, Marvin A. "The Latter Prophets (Isaiah, Jeremiah, Ezekiel)." In *The Hebrew Bible Today: An Introduction to Critical Issues*, edited by Steven L. McKenzie and M. Patrick Graham, 69–94. Louisville: Westminster John Knox Press, 1998.

Szpek, Heidi M. "The Levite's Concubine: The Story That Never Was." *Women in Judaism* 5:1 (2007) 1–10.

BIBLIOGRAPHY

Thompson, Thomas L. "Text, Context and Referents in Israelite Historiography." In *The Fabric of History: Text, Artifact, and Israel's Past*, edited by Diana Vikander Edelman, 65–92. JSOT Supplement Series 127. Sheffield, UK: JSOT, 1991.

Tov, Emanuel. *Textual Criticism of the Hebrew Bible*. Minneapolis: Fortress, 1992.

Van Seters, John. *Abraham in History and Tradition*. New Haven: Yale University Press, 1975.

———. *Prologue to History: The Yahwist as Historian in Genesis*. Louisville: Westminster John Knox Press, 1992.

Walton, John H. "Interpreting the Bible as an Ancient Near Eastern Document." Paper presented at Southern Seminary, 2004.

Weinstein, James. "Exodus and Archaeological Reality." In *Exodus: The Egyptian Evidence*, edited by Ernest S. Frerichs and Leonard H. Lesco, 87–103. Winona Lake, IN: Eisenbrauns, 1997.

Wellhausen, Julius. *Prolegomena to the History of Israel: With a Reprint of the Article "Israel" from the Encyclopaedia Britannica*. Meridian Books Library Edition. Gloucester, MA: Peter Smith, 1973.

Wenham, Gordon J. "Pondering the Pentateuch: The Search for a New Paradigm." In *The Face of Old Testament Studies: a Survey of Contemporary Approaches*, edited by David W. Baker and Bill T. Arnold, 116–44. Grand Rapids: Baker, 1999.

Whybray, R. N. *The Making of the Pentateuch: a Methodological Study*. JSOT Supplement Series 53. Sheffield, UK: JSOT, 1987.

Williamson, H. G. M. *Studies in Persian Period History and Historiography*. Tübingen, Germany: Mohr Siebeck, 2004.

Wood, Bryant G. "The Search for Joshua's Ai." In *Critical Issues in Early Israelite History*, edited by Richard S. Hess et al., 205–40. Winona Lake, IN: Eisenbrauns, 2008.

Younger, K. Lawson, Jr. "Early Israel in Recent Biblical Scholarship." In *The Face of Old Testament Studies: a Survey of Contemporary Approaches*, edited by David W. Baker and Bill T. Arnold, 176–206. Grand Rapids: Baker, 1999.

———. "The Rhetorical Structuring of the Joshua Conquest Narratives." In *Critical Issues in Early Israelite History*, edited by Richard S. Hess et al., 3–32. Winona Lake, IN: Eisenbrauns, 2008.

Younker, Randall W. "Integrating Faith, the Bible, and Archaeology: A Review of the 'Andrews University Way' of Doing Archaeology." In *The Future of Biblical Archaeology: Reassessing Methodologies and Assumptions*, edited by James K. Hoffmeier and Alan Millard, 43–52. Grand Rapids: Eerdmans, 2004.

Zertal, Adam, and Nivi Mirkam. "Mount Manasseh (Northern Samarian Hills) Survey." *NEAEHL* 4:1311–12.

Zevit, Ziony. "The Biblical Archaeology versus Syro-Palestinian Archaeology Debate in Its American Institutional and Intellectual Contexts." In *The Future of Biblical Archaeology: Reassessing Methodologies and Assumptions*, edited by James K. Hoffmeier and Alan Millard, 3–19. Grand Rapids: Eerdmans, 2004.

———. *The Religions of Ancient Israel: A Synthesis of Parallactic Approaches*. London: Continuum, 2001.